Professional Writing

Palgrave Study Skills

Business Degree Success
Career Skills
Cite Them Right (9th edn)
Critical Thinking Skills (2nd edn)
e-Learning Skills (2nd edn)
The Exam Skills Handbook (2nd edn)
The Graduate Career Guidebook
Great Ways to Learn Anatomy and Physiology
How to Begin Studying English Literature
   (3rd edn)
How to Study Foreign Languages
How to Study Linguistics (2nd edn)
How to Use Your Reading in Your Essays
   (2nd edn)
How to Write Better Essays (3rd edn)
How to Write Your Undergraduate Dissertation
Improve Your Grammar
Information Skills
The International Student Handbook
The Mature Student's Guide to Writing (3rd edn)
The Mature Student's Handbook
The Palgrave Student Planner
Practical Criticism
Presentation Skills for Students (2nd edn)
The Principles of Writing in Psychology
Professional Writing (3rd edn)
Researching Online
Skills for Success (2nd edn)
The Student's Guide to Writing (3rd edn)
The Student Phrase Book
Study Skills Connected
Study Skills for International Postgraduates
Study Skills for Speakers of English as a Second
   Language
The Study Skills Handbook (4th edn)
Studying History (3rd edn)
Studying Law (3rd edn)
Studying Modern Drama (2nd edn)
Studying Psychology (2nd edn)
Success in Academic Writing
Teaching Study Skills and Supporting Learning

The Undergraduate Research Handbook
The Work-Based Learning Student Handbook
Work Placements – A Survival Guide for
   Students
Write it Right (2nd edn)
Writing for Engineers (3rd edn)
Writing for Law
Writing for Nursing and Midwifery Students
   (2nd edn)
You2Uni: Decide. Prepare. Apply

Pocket Study Skills

14 Days to Exam Success
Blogs, Wikis, Podcasts and More
Brilliant Writing Tips for Students
Completing Your PhD
Doing Research
Getting Critical
Planning your Dissertation
Planning Your Essay
Planning Your PhD
Reading and Making Notes
Referencing and Understanding Plagiarism
Reflective Writing
Report Writing
Science Study Skills
Studying with Dyslexia
Success in Groupwork
Time Management
Writing for University

Palgrave Research Skills

Authoring a PhD
Getting to Grips with Doctoral Research
The Foundations of Research (2nd edn)
The Good Supervisor (2nd edn)
The Postgraduate Research Handbook (2nd edn)
The Professional Doctorate
Structuring Your Research Thesis

Professional Writing

Third edition

Sky Marsen

palgrave
macmillan

KH

First published 2003
Second edition published 2007
Third edition published 2013 by
PALGRAVE MACMILLAN

Palgrave Macmillan in the UK is an imprint of Macmillan Publishers Limited,
registered in England, company number 785998, of Houndmills,
Basingstoke,
Hampshire RG21 6XS.

Palgrave Macmillan in the US is a division of St Martin's Press LLC,
175 Fifth Avenue, New York, NY 10010.

Palgrave Macmillan is the global academic imprint of the above companies
and has companies and representatives throughout the world.

Palgrave® and Macmillan® are registered trademarks in the United States,
the United Kingdom, Europe and other countries

ISBN: 978-1-137-30901-3

This book is printed on paper suitable for recycling and made from fully
managed and sustained forest sources. Logging, pulping and manufacturing
processes are expected to conform to the environmental regulations of the
country of origin.

A catalogue record for this book is available from the British Library.

A catalog record for this book is available from the Library of Congress.

10/6/14

Contents

Figures, Tables and Analysed Examples   vi
Dedication   vii
Acknowledgements   viii
Preface   ix

1   The Writing Process   1
2   Style and Effect   24
3   Short Business Documents   50
4   Research Methods   76
5   Business and Technology Journalism   98
6   Writing for the Public   135
7   Reports and Proposals   163
8   Critical Thinking for Management   202
9   Working in Teams   218
10 Revising and Editing   235

Appendix: Job Applications   267
References and Bibliography   283
Index   289

Figures, Tables and Analysed Examples

Figures
Figure 1: Mind map   16
Figure 2: Storyboard   18
Figure 3: Inverted pyramid   138

Tables
Table 1: Nightmare instructions   14
Table 2: Writing actions   19
Table 3: Common wordy clichés   37
Table 4: Linkers and their functions   42
Table 5: General business writing principles   51
Table 6: Survey questions   80
Table 7: Checklist for evaluating Internet sources   91
Table 8: Specialist and journalistic style   116
Table 9: Checklist for evaluating websites   150
Table 10: Guidelines for press conferences   161
Table 11: Layout of business proposal   178
Table 12: Layout of business plan   180
Table 13: Layout of investigative report   190
Table 14: Criteria for evaluating team member contributions 228
Table 15: Revision chart   263

Analysed Examples
Example 1: Paragraph transitions   46
Example 2: Letter format   58
Example 3: Memo format   60
Example 4: Revised email   64
Example 5: Bad news email A   70
Example 6: Bad news email B   71
Example 7: Botox article   105
Example 8: Academic style   112
Example 9: Journalistic style   114
Example 10: Mars article – content   126
Example 11: Mars article – layout   132
Example 12: Press release   140
Example 13: Investigative report   193
Example 14: Structure of concession   212
Example 15: Article on gun control   213

To my business writing students – present, past and future

Acknowledgements and Thanks

Various people have supported, in different ways, the writing and rewriting of this book since its first edition. Thanks to you all.

For this third edition, I would like to thank Genevieve Hilton, Katerina Tsetsura and Anne Peirson-Smith for invaluable insights into the public relations industry internationally. My gratitude also goes to people who have discussed various issues of writing with me in the last year, notably Sudesh Mishra and Justin Hill for their insights on creativity, and Charles Bazerman, for his advice on pedagogical aspects. Thank you too to Janet Attrill, who has given me enthusiastic feedback on drafts, as a model reader.

For all their support throughout the writing and rewriting of the book in different editions, I would like to thank Robert Biddle, at the Human-Oriented Laboratory, Carleton University, for his invaluable suggestions on Internet communications and digital writing. Also, many thanks to colleagues and students at the California Institute of Technology, who have given me valuable feedback on teaching activities and the framing of communication tasks – especially Steven Youra, for our insightful exchanges on communicating technical concepts to non-specialists, and Ken Pickar and his engineering teams for their input on teamwork and project management. Thank you, too, to my colleague Derek Wallace, for our conversations on writing, and for his willingness to take on extra administration and teaching to give me time to work on the book.

Last but not least, I extend thanks to all those who have used the book in their classes and given me feedback. Thanks especially to Donna Banicevich Gera for discussing the book with me on many occasions and giving me useful tips, and to Simone Celine Marshall at Otago University for detailed suggestions.

Preface

Under current trends, the twenty-first century will be characterised by an increasing diversification of the consumer market, global communications, and the collapse of traditional professional boundaries. In this climate, competence in transferring skills, addressing diverse audiences and understanding emerging needs becomes paramount for professional success. To a very large extent this competence is enhanced by the ability to understand, construct and manipulate written information in order to use it effectively in a variety of situations. Good business means good writing!

This book is a brief but comprehensive introduction to major aspects of professional writing for different media. Its content is interdisciplinary, offering a rare opportunity to synthesise methods and ideas developed in text analysis, journalism and management. By combining conceptual aspects of written communication with practical applications, the goal of this book is to assist readers to express ideas effectively in different written formats, in a variety of professional contexts internationally.

Distinctive features

The main features of the book, in its third edition, are:
- An eclectic theoretical foundation, informed by genre theory, rhetoric, discourse analysis and narrative theory. In addition to its theoretical background, the third edition is based on information on business practice collected through communication with professionals in the United States, Australia, New Zealand and Hong Kong, from both corporate and entrepreneurial fields. The aim was to gather and then disseminate information that is relevant for professionals communicating in international business today.
- As in its previous two editions, a direct, concise and student-oriented approach. The book has expressly avoided the density of many other books on writing, opting instead for a more hands-on approach, which student-writers should find very accessible. The aim was to design an easily consultable text that includes clear instructions on selected areas of interest, gives analysed examples that place the instructions into perspective, and provides the opportunity for practice.

Audience

The book is written primarily as a university text for one-semester undergraduate courses in professional writing or business communication. However, it is by no means limited to this audience. Because it gives useful tips and conceptual resources to overcome the most common troublespots in professional writing, it will serve as a practical guide to anyone who wants to become more confident in choosing an appropriate style and layout to suit the occasion. Those who will benefit most from the guidelines offered here include:

- students in professional writing and business communication courses
- new professionals, who may be thrust into a professional situation that requires the production of formal written documents (such as consulting reports, newsletter articles, or copy for a website) without prior training
- entrepreneurs, business people and scientists who want to inform management or the public of a new development, product or invention in their field, but lack the linguistic and/or communicative expertise to produce an effectively constructed written text.

Skills

By working through the book, readers will gain the skills to:

- understand and use essential terminology and key concepts in describing writing within the context of business communication
- understand and use the requirements of writing problem-solving reports for clients and management, journalistic articles for the wider public, and digital texts
- adapt written communication for a specific audience and purpose, and understand the role of different media in communication
- perceive writing as a process involving planning, drafting, revising and editing, and become aware of their own procedures of writing
- understand the uses of writing in collaborative projects and in project management
- develop awareness of critical thinking issues in relation to management and business contexts

Trajectory

In its third edition, the book consists of ten main chapters and one reference chapter:

Chapter 1: The writing process

This chapter looks at the planning and thinking aspects of writing. Using an approach informed by genre, rhetoric and narrative, it discusses ways to analyse a brief, understand audiences and plan a writing project.

Chapter 2: Style and effect

This chapter looks at elements of style and tone, and their effects on audience perception. It outlines a new typology of style going from specialised to public, and discusses such aspects of writing as appropriate length of sentences for different effects, word choice and sentence variety as a technique to maintain reader interest.

Chapter 3: Short business documents

This chapter overviews and analyses the major short documents produced in business contexts. These include everyday communication texts, such as agendas and minutes of meetings, letters, memos and email. It also discusses the nature of 'bad news' messages and gives some guidelines on writing these effectively.

Chapter 4: Research methods

This chapter looks at the role and methods of researching in the preparation of professional documents. It provides guidelines on research skills, preparing questionnaires for interviews and using the Internet to obtain data. It also discusses copyright and plagiarism issues as they relate to business.

Chapter 5: Business and technology journalism

This chapter discusses genres used to inform the public of recent developments in technology, science and business. It overviews journalistic techniques of writing and magazine layout matters, and focuses on feature articles, which can be written for magazines or newsletters.

Chapter 6: Writing for the public

This chapter looks at public relations genres, such as press releases, web content and public speeches. It considers the differences between print, broadcast and digital media in communicating with the public, and explores the increasing importance of online social networks (social media) for businesses.

Chapter 7: Reports and proposals

This chapter looks at two major professional documents: problem-solving reports and proposals. It puts these into perspective by examining the differences between essays, articles and reports (the main kinds of documents professionals produce), and explains their structure and components.

Chapter 8: Critical thinking for management

This chapter looks at aspects of reasoning and persuading in professional documents and mass media texts. It examines issues of faulty or manipulative reasoning, and overviews the uses and abuses of statistics in the popular media.

Chapter 9: Working in teams

This chapter overviews the role of teamwork and collaboration in projects. It describes different role allocating models for team projects, and explains the stages of project management and the terms used to describe its elements.

Chapter 10: Revising and editing

This chapter focuses on sentence structure and grammatical aspects of writing. It provides guidelines on the revising and editing process, and explains some common troublespots at the sentence level. The chapter is a reference tool for all aspects of writing and can be used at any stage in a particular writing task, or be revisited at different times in the duration of a course.

Appendix: Job applications

This chapter looks at some important considerations in the job-hunting process. These include ideological and personal factors, such as assessing values and professional aspirations, as well as practical techniques, such as writing a CV.

For those of you who have used the book in its previous editions, you will find that the third edition is updated, extensively revised and re-organised, in light of feedback from lecturers who have adopted the book in their courses, and students who have learned from it.

For those of you who are coming to the book for the first time (and possibly to the world of business communication for the first time too), I hope you find the material given here useful and interesting.

Sky Marsen
January 2013

The Writing Process

Focus:

- Writing as a process that involves planning, drafting and revising
- Rhetorical and genre analysis
- Writing in business contexts
- Planning a writing project

The skill of writing is acquired through conscious and persistent effort: unlike our ability to speak, it is not an innate skill. There are several reasons that writing is more complex than speaking. One is that it is separate from any form of physical interaction: writing can take place at a totally different time and place from reading. This leaves the written text more open to misunderstanding than the spoken text. Since they are not likely to be present when their readers read their document, writers must try to perceive their text from the readers' point of view and write in a way that is clear and relevant to their audience. Another reason is that writing is thought-active. The simple fact that you want to write about a topic triggers thought processes that give this topic a particular shape out of a range of alternatives. To paraphrase Flannery O'Connor, we don't know what we think until we read what we write. The changes that take place from thinking to writing explain why many novice writers complain that their final result is not what they initially wanted to express, or that what they mean comes out differently on the written page.

Because of the complexity of written communication, a successful written text does not emerge spontaneously, but requires considerable preparation and revision. Even a brief e-mail requires some revision to ensure it's clear and accurate. And although much business and technical writing follows standard conventions of style and organisation, each task presents a new problem to solve with its own audience and situation. This chapter looks at some major, tested, techniques for creating effective written documents, from concept to delivery copy.

The techniques discussed here are not the only way to write; there are almost as many variations of the writing process as there are writers.

Professional writers of all varieties, business, academic, journalistic and creative, gradually develop their own technique of writing. If it works, then stick with it – if not, consider different techniques.

In fact, writers could be classified into two major categories, *top-down* and *bottom-up* writers. Top-down writers begin by brainstorming an outline of their document, and then filling it in with content. They work better when they see the structure of their text, and like to have a 'map' or 'big picture' of the whole document before writing the details. Bottom-up writers, on the other hand, prefer to free-write their ideas without attention to structure. They are more data-driven, and end up with many points, facts and examples before they consider how to give form and coherence to their draft.

Regardless of what category of writer you are, effective writing is the result of a process consisting of three interconnected stages: the planning or conceptualising stage, the drafting stage and the revising/editing stage. In contrast to what is commonly believed, it is the first and third stages that require the most time and attention. You will find that by having a clear vision of what you want to accomplish (stage 1), and giving yourself adequate time to rephrase, delete, rearrange and add information to sections (stage 3), you are creating your work. In fact, many professionals who make their living from writing state that planning and revising take about 85 per cent of the time assigned to a task. The drafting stage is just a bridge between careful planning and structuring information. All well-prepared professional documents require this process of writing, although how long each stage takes varies depending on the length and significance of the document, and on whether you are a top-down or bottom-up writer.

Rhetoric and genre

US President Theodore Roosevelt once said that 'the most important single ingredient in the formula of success is knowing how to get along with people' (Maxwell 2007: 41). Also, research in business communication has repeatedly shown that successful business professionals are those who actively participate in the culture of their organisation, that is, those who fit in the organisational environment – the team players. Understanding that the writing you do as business professionals creates and sustains relationships with managers, peers, stakeholders, clients and the public (or, negatively, breaks these relationships) is the first step in conceptualising business writing as a social activity. The guidelines proposed here are informed by rhetorical and genre theory, which takes into account audience, purpose and context (Swales 1990; Bazerman and Prior 2004; Bhatia 2004; Cockcroft and Cockcroft 2005).

Rhetoric proposes that all texts aim to have a particular effect on their readers or listeners, for example, to persuade, motivate, inform, warn. If this desired effect is not achieved, it most likely means that the writer or speaker did not accurately assess the reader's dispositions or the situation in which the communication took place. It could also mean that the way the information was presented conflicted with, or did not meet, reader expectations. Like film and fiction, writing, too, has different genres. Genre theory proposes that document formats, such as report, article, essay, email, etc., exhibit certain standard features that capture the requirements of particular rhetorical situations, and are therefore appropriate for these situations. For example, a magazine feature article is shorter than a scientific article and therefore cannot contain as much detail as the latter; a report is divided into sections with headings for easy skimming and 'chunking' information into categories, etc. Although genres change over time, and indeed need to be revised to reflect changing circumstances and emerging media, the conventional structure of a type of text is shared knowledge between writers and readers, and forms a recognised and accepted way to exchange information. As we will see in subsequent chapters, genre considerations include such elements as degrees of formality and document length.

Keeping these factors in mind, when planning a piece of writing consider:

- Who is the *audience?* What do they already know about the topic? What do they *not* know? What do they not *want* to know? In what areas are they likely to be specialised (so that you may form analogies between your topic and those areas)? How much detail do they need? How much of the big picture do they need?
- What is the *purpose* of the document? For example, does the document inform? Analyse? Clarify? Persuade? Will it be used as the basis for a decision? How do you want to change or affect the readers through your document?
- What is the most appropriate *genre*? What is the best format in which to present your information related to the situation? Would an email do the job, or do you need to produce a full investigative report?
- What is the most appropriate *medium* for the audience, purpose and genre? Would your message be clearer if transmitted electronically, or in print, or maybe orally on the phone or in person? If you're sending a report to a client, would a PDF attachment to an email be the best way, or should you send a printed copy through the post? Or both?
- What is the most appropriate *style* of writing? Different genres are conventionally written in a particular style; for example, a report is

expected to be written in more formal style than an email, and a newsletter article is expected to have a lighter tone than a contract. How do you want to appear through your writing? Knowledgeable? Considerate? Strict? Friendly? Your style, formed through sentence structure and word choice, will help you to achieve your desired writing persona.

The professional world abounds with examples where making the wrong decision on the above factors led to costly and serious misunderstandings. For instance, a famous case occurred during the *Columbia* Space Shuttle Incident in 2003 (*Columbia Investigation Board Report* 2003; Gurak and Lannon 2007). *Columbia* disintegrated upon re-entry into the Earth's atmosphere, which led to an investigation board being formed to find out what went wrong. Among other matters, such as technical damage done to the shuttle during the launch, the board found several serious communication factors that contributed to the accident.

In one of these, the engineers responsible for evaluating the condition of the shuttle during and after the launch suspected that the wing had been damaged by a piece of foam that was dislodged during the launch, and they presented their suspicions to management during a briefing session. However, they made a tactical error by choosing a PowerPoint presentation to convey their findings. In fact, they put the most important information in one crammed slide. The management, who were expecting serious scientific results to be presented in a technical report, did not place as much significance on the presentation as was needed because, for them, information on PowerPoint slides did not carry enough urgency. In this example, engineers and management did not share the same genre expectations, and so important technical findings were lost in communication fog.

Such considerations make it desirable for organisations to take measures to ensure consistency in the uses of language by all employees. Large organisations have what is known as *house style* to maintain a consistent style among all documents, and to induct employees in the uses of language favoured by the organisation. This usually comes in the form of a manual or guide that describes the company's templates and conventions for using such techniques as abbreviations, spelling, numbers and fonts. When joining a new company find out about the house style. If starting a new company make house style a priority in your communication plan, to support clarity and uniformity in document design.

More on house style is given in the last chapter. More information on genre, medium and style is given in Chapters 2 and 3. The next section looks at audience considerations.

Audience analysis

Every act of writing takes place in a new context, with a unique time, place or reader. *Audience adaptation* (or *accommodation* as it is sometimes called) refers to the skill of arranging words, organising thoughts, and formatting a document to best achieve your desired effect on the target audience. *Audience dynamics* refers to the relationship that writers form with their readers through their style, and through the amount and structure of information that they provide. The audience dynamics are effective when the readers get a sense of satisfaction that the questions raised in the text were relevant to their interests, and the answers or solutions provided were convincing. In contrast, audience dynamics are ineffective when the readers feel frustrated or offended because the writer's tone is condescending, the answers or solutions provided are simplistic in relation to the complexity of the questions, or the argument is emotive and based on generalisation. To maximise your ability for effective audience dynamics, assess the reader's needs, knowledge and interest by conducting an audience analysis before writing.

In all, for a text to be successful, there must be *writer–reader complicity*. In other words, the readers must feel that the writer is on their side, supporting their interests and respecting their needs. If readers feel that a writer treats them as an example of a general category, rather than as specific individuals, they are more likely to resist accepting the information given.

For an example of bad audience dynamics and lack of writer–reader complicity, consider the following text, which comes from a government information leaflet telling employers about laws governing sexual and racial discrimination. It is tactless because, by grouping all employers into one category, it implies that the readers may be practising gender discrimination. Also, it fails to bring in the main topic (the Equal Opportunity Act) till the very end, when there is actually no space to give any information about it.

> Sexual and racial discrimination is practised by various employers, in retail, small business, industry and corporate environments in a number of parts of the country; it is an important community problem and a direct cause of considerable personal distress.
>
> As an employer, as a Human Resources Officer, or as a business owner, it is important for you to know about the Equal Opportunity Act.

Here is a revised version which creates more complicity between the issuing authority and the readers by addressing the readers directly and showing them that the information given is for their benefit. Also, this version has improved presentation and appearance by including a title and bullet points, and by introducing the main topic earlier.

Employers and the Equal Opportunity Act

You can play an important part in preventing discrimination if you are responsible for employing staff in

- retail
- small business
- industry
- corporations

The Equal Opportunity Act has been legally enforced since it was passed by Parliament in 1975. This Act makes it illegal for anyone to discriminate – to treat people unfairly because of their gender, race, colour, descent, or ethnic origin.

If you know of anyone in your business environment that rejects a suitable candidate for a position because of their gender, or ethnic group tell them about the Equal Opportunity Act. You can also ask the Commissioner for Community Relations for more information.

Marketing executives and consumer researchers, who have a strong interest in understanding market responses, and who, therefore, conduct extensive research in mass perceptions, take into account five factors of audience analysis:

- Education
- Status
- Attitude
- Demographics
- Psychographics

Education refers to the readers' knowledge (or lack of knowledge) in the topic that you are writing about. What would be the likely interest of the readers in your topic, and what aspects of your topic are most likely to interest them? Should you begin with the big picture to put the readers into perspective, or go straight to the details that you want to focus on? Are you writing to people of the same educational background as yours (i.e. peers), or to those of different training?

Status refers to the writer's degree of authority and/or power relative to the readers. Are you writing to your boss, to a group of peers, or to someone who is junior to you? Is your reader a client with whom you intend to continue doing business, or the general public that you can only see from a bird's eye view? Are you an expert presenting information to a non-specialist audience, or a novice showing to an authority how much you know about a subject?

Attitude refers to the state of mind you expect the readers to be in when they read your document. Will your message find them hostile, neutral or positive? How motivated are they to read your document? Are you proposing revolutionary changes to a situation you think your readers will resist changing? Are you informing them of a breakthrough that will undoubtedly improve the quality of their lifestyle, and that they will be happy to know about? Are you giving them good or bad news?

Demographic analysis works on the principle that the population can be grouped, and that each group shows a tendency to think or behave in broadly similar ways. Demographic characteristics include gender, occupation, social class (i.e. income level), age, location/nationality (i.e. international or local audience).

From a person's demographic profile, certain inferences can be made about their degree of knowledge, expectations and aspirations, though they are not always foolproof. For example, in most Western societies a middle-class white woman is probably educated to upper secondary school or tertiary level but not necessarily. Also, teenagers are not likely to be classical music fans, but, again, this may not be so. Demographic research is based on the lowest common denominator of prevailing social trends, and, therefore, operates mostly on stereotype.

Psychographics refers to the lifestyle, values, leisure activities and social self-image that the readers are likely to have. Marketing research shows that people react favourably towards products and services that they see as representative of themselves. Similarly, readers will respond differently to your message according to their values. What are their interests, opinions and hobbies? In the rapidly changing and diversifying contemporary world, interests and values are less and less tied to demographic issues. For example, when computer games first started to develop, they were associated with a target market of young males in the 15–25 age group. As this form of entertainment evolved, the target market changed, and there are now computer games that attract females, older males, and other demographic groups. An analysis of the computer game market, therefore, is more likely to benefit from a psychographic examination that would see the computer game market as a special interest group, rather than a demographic.

Demographic and psychographic analyses are especially relevant in journalistic, marketing and public relations writing where you address a wider public.

In addition to these categories, consider whether you have only *primary* readers or also *secondary* and *immediate* readers. In many cases, the person who will first read the document is not the primary audience. It could be a manager or editor, an intermediary between the writer and the primary audience – this is the immediate audience. The immediate reader often acts as a form of filter or quality-control agent of the information before it reaches the primary reader. Additionally, you could have a secondary audience of readers who are likely to read the document even if they are not the target group.

Consider an example. If you submit an article for publication to a specialist magazine, you are writing for a public that is interested in the topic of your article; they are your primary audience. However, before the article reaches this audience, it will be read by the magazine's editor, who will make the final decision about whether to publish the article or not. The editor is, then, the immediate audience (and maybe the only audience, if s/he rejects the article!). If published, the article may also be read by readers who are not primarily interested in the topic: they could be journalism students, for example, studying the article as an example of writing. They would be the secondary audience.

Matters get complicated when a document has different levels of audience, primary, immediate and secondary, who have different interests and/or subject-knowledge. Such cases make it difficult to imagine whom you are writing to. A solution to this problem is to include a section that gives background and definitions of terminology for novices, or, in reports, to include an appendix with more technical details for experts. This way you would be distributing information in a clearly marked and accessible way to the different groups of readers. Returning to the example of the article to the editor, you could include a letter with your article explaining to the editor your goals in writing the article, and justifying your content and stylistic choices (indeed article submissions are generally accompanied by a proposal). This way you address the editor's concerns, and cater for your primary audience's anticipated questions.

As a final note to audience analysis, remember to include yourself in the analysis, since you are an interlocutor in the communicative exchange.

Analyse your role: as a professional you are always performing a role that is more or less detached from your personal concerns. Also, as part of your professional position you will be asked to play different roles for different situations. For example, if you are the CEO of a company you would have top management responsibilities, such as making executive decisions on major financial initiatives and making long-term plans on new product development. However, when addressing shareholders in situations such as public relations speeches, conferences and product exhibitions, you assume the sub-role of equal, sharing the same values and working towards the same interests. The language you use should reflect this equality, or your audience will be alienated and discouraged.

Writing in business

Writing in business contexts is pervasive. In fact, most tasks in the workplace are accompanied by some form of writing. Even face-to-face interactions, such as meetings, are preceded and followed by such documents as agendas and minutes. Business documents can be *internal, external* or both. Internal documents are circulated within the organisation, and include such genres as memoranda (memos), in-house templates and style guides. External documents are directed at clients, other companies, the media and the public, and include such genres as sales letters and disclosure statements. Many genres, such as certain kinds of reports and email, can be both internal and external. Also, some genres are associated with specific professions while others are general. For instance, most business people, no matter what their actual job, write proposals to request funding or approval for a project, while public relations officers write annual reports and press releases, and human resources officers write employment contracts and job descriptions.

Two terms are important when considering business writing: *project* and *brief*. Tasks in management most often take the form of projects. A project at management level brings together specialists from different fields in order to accomplish an aim, which could include developing a new product, creating an advertising campaign, solving a problem, or evaluating the company's strategic plan. Most of the work of managers takes place within the scope of defined projects. In all cases, a project takes place within specified time parameters (deadlines are important in business) and a budget framework. It also addresses particular questions or issues and has specific goals and objectives to achieve (more on project management in Chapter 9). All this information goes to project members through a *brief*.

Basically, a brief (also known as *terms of reference* in longer projects) is an instruction to perform a task. If it's internal, it may be a short and direct command: 'Investigate the ways in which the company could use cloud computing'. This task would then become your project, and you would need to decide how best to approach it. A brief could also involve detailed specifications spread over several pages. The latter is often the case in briefs to conduct lengthy investigations after a crisis. Problem-solving reports are based on a brief provided by the client or manager, which indicates what is required and how the commissioned specialists should structure their report. Similarly, advertising companies that organise competitions on campaign skills issue a brief which candidates must address to win funding and/or a position in the company.

However, a brief is not only a formal document that presents issues to be addressed in a project. It also sets the stage on which project members will perform. This is because writing itself is not, as is often assumed, a purely mental activity. Rather, it involves the whole sensory framework: think of the physical arousal produced by an action novel or a sexy story: words can cause perspiration, a racing heartbeat, laughter and tears. In fact, it could be said that understanding a text means having the sensation of being where the action takes place. This line of reasoning is informed by the narrative approach to business communication, which sees companies as being organised as stories. The narrative approach recognises that narrative, or storytelling, is a fundamental part of our cognitive framework and manifests in many human endeavours and creations. Narrative exists not only in the stories we tell or write, but also in our perception of the world (Taylor 1993; Taylor and Van Every 2000).

Adapting this approach for professional writing, we can see the brief as giving the information for the story of the project. It contains, explicitly or implicitly, information on stakeholders, issues, problems, strengths and limitations of a business situation. Therefore, a useful way to analyse a brief and establish a plan of action for a project is to read it in terms of three categories:

Scene: this includes big-picture matters, such as the scope and framework of the project, the audience(s) and its relation to you as project member, the stakeholders who may not be the audience of your writing but are involved in some way in the project, and the event or context that triggered the project. Generally, the scene involves the level of power and perspective your project involves. If your project is part of a top management strategy, it will have a larger scope and a more long-term planning orientation, involving more issues and anticipating changes and developments. If it is part of a middle management strategy, it will involve more immediate concerns and specific issues. A top management perspective requires more research and analysis and tends to produce more complicated and lengthier documents than a middle management perspective, which looks at issues concerned with a specific product or service.

Content: This includes the issues that you need to cover, or questions that you must answer. The content is determined to a significant extent by the raw materials, sources and limitations that you are given to handle the project, such as funding, deadlines, access to resources and equipment. For example, if you have one day to produce a one-page report, obviously what you write will not be as detailed or analytical as when you have two years and unlimited resources to investigate and solve a problem. Historical aspects are also part of the content. For example, if you are investigating the advantages of cloud computing (to continue the example begun above), in addition to analysing cloud computing itself, you would need to look at the use of computers and networking in your company and in your industry as a whole.

Treatment: This includes the tasks into which the project should be divided in order to be completed successfully. It is the plan of action and the steps to be taken. The treatment includes physical and interactive actions, such as organising meetings and conducting interviews and focus groups, and the type of documents that you decide to produce for a situation. For example, a simple email message may be sufficient in some situations. In other cases, you may need to follow-up your email message with a formal letter or maybe a memo, while a more serious situation would require the submission of a proposal leading to a full report. The treatment also includes the ways in which to present information according to audience needs. For example, if you decide that a PowerPoint presentation is enough to inform an audience of your progress on a project, what kinds of data will you use in the presentation? Would a verbal description suffice? Should you use tables, charts and graphs? Should you provide a full financial analysis of the situation?

The problems that can arise when the scene, content and treatment of a project are not properly interpreted can clearly be seen in disaster situations. The NASA space programme provides another example of this, in the famous and well-documented example of the *Challenger* space shuttle disaster in January 1986. It is now widely recognised that the explosion of the shuttle was largely due to misunderstandings that occurred in the exchange of written information between NASA officials before the launch. Although some officials had detected a functioning error in the shuttle and knew what had to be done to fix it, they did not communicate their finding in an appropriate way to the responsible parties (Herndl, Fennell and Miller 1991).

A brief can also productively be improvised to assist in the writing process even in cases when it is not handed out by others. For instance, if you find your progress in a project is hindered by some uncertain factor, or if you want to achieve an aim but have no idea how to go about it, you should find that conceptualising and writing down your situation in the form of a brief (i.e. a set of instructions or issue statement to yourself) may prove very productive.

A final point about professional projects: recording and detailing your projects is vital in corporate contexts, where mobility is high and staff are transferred or change position often. The person replacing you should be able to continue your work without interruption. This is known in IT contexts as working in 'drop dead' mode, which means that if a team member or manager were to drop dead, s/he should leave adequate documentation and specifications on their work so that projects are not disrupted because they were wholly dependent on their initiator's habits and methods. Keeping notes on a project is, therefore, essential. The 'Document Planning Template', based on the tripartite model described above, can be used or adapted to help you organise writing tasks in a project.

Document Planning Template

Scene

1 Scenario (situation that triggered the task)

2 Purpose (s) of document

3 Target date for delivery

4 Audience analysis

Content

1 Main message to convey

2 Key Issues

    a) _____

    b) _____

    c) _____

    d) _____

Treatment

1 Genre

2 Supplementary Documents

    a) _____

    b) _____

    c) _____

As an opportunity to reflect on these guidelines, consider what can go wrong in communication. One area that is notorious for miscommunication is the writing of technical instructions or user manuals. In many cases, these instructions are at best obscure, at worst dangerously misleading. Look at Table 1 for some real-life instructions from hell, and think about how each reflects unsolved problems at the planning stage. What should the writers do to improve these?

Table 1: Nightmare instructions

From a technical manual:
Since the user interface for analyzer calibration refers to calibration as 'calibration', this chapter will refer to the process of calibration as calibration.

From a manual for a database package:
An action is to be taken on the third non-consecutive day that an event occurs.

From a technical manual for the British military concerning the storage of nuclear weapons:
It is necessary for technical reasons that these warheads should be stored with the top at the bottom and the bottom at the top. In order that there may be no doubt as to which is the top and which is the bottom, for storage purposes it will be seen that the bottom of each warhead has been labelled with the word 'TOP.' (Cited in a book on computer science published by the Computer Science Department of the University of Virginia – www.cs.virginia.edu/cs/50/book/ch-programming.pdf).

From a software user manual:
When you first start the application, the options bar appears on the top left of your screen, and is where option settings are set for the options used with the currently selected tool.

WARNING: The options bar may not be located on the top left of your screen.

Generating content

Generating content is an analytical practice. This is where researching and thinking come in. Depending on the audience and purpose, different types of research would be relevant. For example, you may decide that interviewing would supply you with essential facts; or you may decide that doing a historical research on a topic would be more suitable; or perhaps a combination of methods would help. Collecting facts, however, is not sufficient. You need to think about the significance of these facts and to interpret them. This is where your skills of *analysing* ideas (tracing their constituent elements), and *synthesising* them (evaluating their significance in a given context) come in.

The process of generating ideas tests your capacity for critical and creative thinking: your ability to imagine all possible aspects or factors of a problem. Analytical thinkers do not simply arrive at the most obvious solution to a question; they test out a range of possible answers and keep an open mind. As happens with chaos theory, sometimes information that initially seemed irrelevant proves to be the key. To be able to trace analogies between seemingly disparate topics and to suggest innovative solutions are skills highly sought in professional and corporate environments. In fact, at the cutting edge of many industries and business endeavours are individuals who are not only highly motivated and organised, but also creative and versatile in their thinking.

The following are some ways to generate ideas. Try them and see which combination suits you.

Brainstorming

Brainstorming is a creative technique pioneered by Alex Osborn in the 1950s (Osborn 1963), and has since been very productive in generating new concepts in business contexts. Brainstorming lets you list all the ideas that come to your mind randomly about a particular topic. Brainstorm by writing single words, phrases or full sentences – whatever comes to mind. Many writers find that brainstorming in groups is particularly productive. In fact, brainstorming sessions are now routine practice in many corporations, used to solve problems and to design new products. For example, IBM holds such sessions regularly both within one department and across departments and sections. Also, many popular products were initially conceived during brainstorming sessions: for instance, the popular site Twitter was conceived as a Short Message Service(SMS)-based social networking site by Jack Dorsey, during a day-long brainstorming session.

Mind mapping

Mind mapping was devised by Tony Buzan and is similar to brainstorming but more visual and less linear. Mind maps are built up in a four-stage process:

- Start with a word or image central to your topic
- Place it in the middle of a big sheet of paper and draw a line radiating from it to a major subdivision of the topic
- Circle that subdivision, and draw a line radiating out from it to a more specific subdivision
- Continue the process until you run out of ideas

Mind-mapping is especially useful to those who find it easier to assimilate and understand schematic information than linear or sentence-based reasoning. See Figure 1 for an example of a mind map.

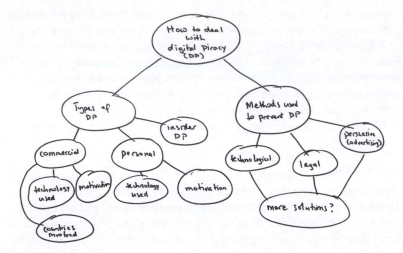

Figure 1   Mind Map

Asking journalist questions

Journalists' questions begin with what is known as the five Ws and one H interrogatives:

Who?
What?
Where?
Why?
When?
How?

You can approach your task by listing as many journalists' questions about your topic as you can. Questioning encourages you to look at a topic from many different perspectives, and may help you to narrow the issue that you are investigating. Journalists' questions are especially useful when your task involves much factual information, because they actually force you to answer them by providing specifics rather than open-ended or ambiguous statements. News reporters, who need to convey facts as quickly and objectively as possible, use these questions to craft their news stories.

Bouncing ideas

Bouncing ideas means talking about your project to someone. The aim here is to listen to yourself talk about your task, so it is not important if your interlocutor is versed in your topic or not. In fact, some writers find that talking about their topic to someone who is a total outsider helps them to clarify issues.

If you are having trouble solving a particular problem, talk about why you are having trouble. Variations on this method include talking to yourself or talking into a recording device, which has the advantage of capturing your thoughts exactly. Some people are most productive in generating and developing ideas when they can move around and create kinetic energy.

Writing scientific categories

If your topic involves interpreting a scientific development or process to a non-specialist audience, simplify and analyse the topic in your own mind by brainstorming as many statements as possible under these categories:

Existence: How can the existence of *X* be shown?
Quantity: How large/small is *X*/How fast?
Comparison: Is *X* greater/less than *Y*? In what ways is *X* different from *Y*?
Correlation: Does the speed of *X* vary with its weight?
Causality: If *X* occurs, will *Y* also occur? How do we know?

Outlining

When *outlining* you first come up with section topics, then a summary of the document, and then gradually expand your ideas to create the final document. After some brainstorming, extract the key themes that you have identified and give them headings. Under each heading, brainstorm some more points that are related to the heading's theme. Having 'filled' the headings, you will have chunks of information on each theme, which make up a summary of your final document. You can then decide what sequence would be most appropriate, and re-order your section headings in that sequence. Outlining is effective for top-down writers, those who begin with a big picture plan of the whole document, and then build up the details as they go. When writing a report, the outline acts as a first draft that can be submitted to a manager or client to show the progress of a project.

Storyboarding

This is a spatial type of outlining used in film and multimedia projects. Small screens are drawn on a page depicting the main visual elements of major scenes in a project. Under each screen is some script describing the main action and indicating any areas that need to be developed for the particular scene. In the case of writing, the screen can be replaced with a descriptive heading. Spatial experimentation can help you find a logical order in which to present your ideas; in other words, you can re-shuffle the screens till you find the most appropriate sequence. For both outlining and storyboarding, do not delete documents or files until the project is finished, because you may find that information you thought was redundant becomes relevant again at a later stage.

Figure 2 is a storyboard outline of the sections of a report on the causes and consequences of DVD piracy. The outline distributes section headings without, at this stage, considering the final sequence.

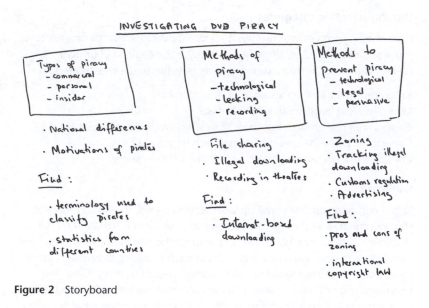

INVESTIGATING DVD PIRACY

Types of piracy
 - commercial
 - personal
 - insider

• National differences
• Motivations of pirates

Find :
 • terminology used to classify pirates
 • statistics from different countries

Methods of piracy
 – technological
 – leeching
 – recording

• File sharing
• Illegal downloading
• Recording in theatres

Find :
 • Internet-based downloading

Methods to prevent piracy
 – technological
 – legal
 – persuasive

• Zoning
• Tracking illegal downloading
• Customs regulation
• Advertising

Find :
 • pros and cons of zoning
 • international copyright law

Figure 2   Storyboard

Drafting

When you brainstorm and use the other techniques for generating content described above, you are basically *drafting*. The drafting stage proper comes when you feel you have gathered enough information and have a clear idea where you are heading, so it is now time to expand confidently. This is when you put to practice the ideas you generated in the previous stage and see how they work in expanded form. When drafting, it helps to be receptive to influences that can provide direction and inspiration. Keep your topic in the back of your mind in your everyday activities; read, watch, listen critically, and seize all that is productive for your purposes. Also, be open to serendipity – inspiration through sudden, previously unrecognised connections. Many great scientific and technical discoveries were made accidentally, by sudden awareness of previously unseen analogies.

If you get stuck when drafting, do not attempt to complete the draft in one go. Instead, let it incubate by putting it on the 'back burner' of your mind and coming back to it later. The time lapse between giving up on a draft and coming back to it could be a few minutes, hours, overnight, or more – depending on project deadlines, of course! In the meantime, you can do something that, even though it may seem irrelevant, allows your thoughts to gestate. In fact, in professional contexts more often than not you work on many projects simultaneously, so time management, and letting go of one project to move to another become significant skills.

Table 2 gives a definition of major conceptual actions that you perform when drafting a document. These are common to both academic and professional situations.

Table 2: Writing actions	
Account for	Give reasons; explain why something has occurred.
Analyse	Take apart an idea, concept or statement in order to evaluate it. This type of answer should be methodical and logically organised.
Argue	Systematically support or reject a viewpoint by offering justification and evidence for your position while acknowledging the opposite point of view.
Assess	Judge the worth or value of something critically.
Comment on	Discuss, explain, and give your opinion on the ideas presented.
Compare	Set items side by side, show their similarities and differences, and provide a balanced description.
Criticise (or critique)	Point out strengths and weaknesses of the subject; support your judgment with evidence.
Define	Explain the precise meaning of a concept. A definition answer often follows the DEMF model: Definition, Examples, Main Theorist(s) and Further Information.
Discuss	Explain an item or concept, and then give details about it with supportive material, examples, points for and against and explanations for the points you put forward.
Evaluate	Discuss the material, and reach a conclusion either for or against the concept being discussed and evaluated.
Examine	Analyse the topic, give pros (points for) and cons (points against) or offer a critical judgment about it.
Explain	Offer a detailed and exact explanation of an idea, principle or set of reasons for a situation or an attitude.

Generate	Propose new ideas or new interpretations of available subjects.
Hypothesise	Propose a statement or set of statements that can be used as the basis for testing conclusions.
Illustrate	Provide examples to demonstrate, explain, clarify or prove the subject of the question.
Integrate	In a logically related way, draw together two or more subjects not previously connected.
Interpret	Explain the meaning of something, make it clear and explicit and evaluate it in terms of your own knowledge.
Justify	Give reasons supporting a particular position on the subject. This could be a positive or a negative position.
List	Present issues or subjects in an itemised series. In many cases, listing can be done in point form.
Outline	Give an organised ordering of information stating the main points or idea and omitting details.
Review	Examine, analyse and comment briefly on the main points of an issue.

Overcoming writer's block

If you find that it is difficult to generate ideas about a specific topic, leading to annoying and costly delay, try one or a combination of these 'unblocking' techniques.

Freewriting offers one method of clearing and opening your mind. You can freewrite by writing non-stop, on any topic, for a specific length of time. Do not stop to edit or evaluate what you are writing, and, if you cannot think of anything, keep repeating your last word or phrase until you get going again. The point of freewriting is to unblock your thought processes, and put you in the mood to express ideas in writing. The topic or relevance of what you are writing is, at this stage, put aside. Many writers find that freewriting allows them to approach their task in an uninhibited way.

Writing to the resistance means writing about why you are having trouble tackling a task, or why you are being frustrated in your investigations. This process may help you break through a puzzle, or identify more clearly what it is about the forms of evidence you are dealing with that makes them difficult. Writing to the resistance works especially in cases when you feel so perplexed or overwhelmed by a topic that you find it difficult to write about it in a systematically logical way. It may help you to trace a rational pattern in chaotic thinking.

Responding and mirroring should help you get in the mood for writing, by engaging with other texts. Read a text in the genre in which you are writing (for example, if you are writing a report, choose a report, if a magazine article, choose a magazine article), and write an informal critique of it: if you could ask the writer questions about it, what would you ask? What do you think could have been done better in the document? Rewrite a section to improve it. What is particularly effective in the document, and why? If the document asks a question, answer it. By responding this way to the text, you are building motivation and direction to work on yours.

The term for this technique – 'mirroring' – comes from the world of acting. Trainee actors learn to perform by reflecting in their behaviour what they observe in a partner – responding to a smile with a smile, to a frown with a frown, etc. This is based on the idea that any form of action is also, by extension, a form of communication, that is, it is meaningful in relation to a context and a set of participants – action is reaction. Clearly, then, this is relevant to writing too, and can fruitfully be exploited as a 'warm-up' or 'unblocking' technique.

'Blind' writing is a solution for compulsive editors. If you feel critical about every word you produce and constantly delete and rewrite the same sentence, it may be better not to see what you write. Try typing with a dark screen to help you achieve momentum and mass before crafting your output.

Tips for successful writers

As a conclusion to this chapter, here are some inspirational guidelines for effective writing. These are based on discussions with people from different countries, who make their living from writing of all kinds, professional, creative and academic. Therefore, these tips are international and based on practical, life experience.

1 *Be observant.* All kinds of writing emerge from experience, so the more experience you get in your chosen field the better a writer you will become. Also, being a good writer means being good at dealing with

people. Writing always has readers, and the more you understand people's behaviour and reactions the better a writer you will be. Remember that the writing process begins before you start writing, so keep an eye out for anything that you could use in your writing later.

2 *Record and organise different types of material.* Professional writers keep a record of ideas, objects or events that catch their eye, even if these may not seem relevant to what they are writing at the moment. Writers carry a notebook and pen, or their digital equivalents, everywhere, and many also carry a recorder to record their thoughts and observations immediately as they come. This way you are building a pool of resources that some day will find their way into your writing.

3 *Do not wait for inspiration.* Writing creates itself – rather like eating is said to arouse the appetite. Most professional writers write on a schedule to meet publishing deadlines, whether they initially feel like it or not. So start writing before you have thought out completely what you want to say. It doesn't matter if you start by writing nonsense, repetitions, fragments or mind maps. You will discover what you want to write by writing and not just by thinking. Your document will eventually write itself.

4 *Revise as you write.* Most professional writers do at least two, and sometimes many more, drafts of anything they write. The first version should never be the last version. To be a successful writer, you should see yourself both as innovator (coming up with new ideas and new connections between ideas) and editor (rearranging and cutting out parts of your text). Regarding professional writing, keep in mind that many documents are collaborative and those editing a document may not be the same as those who wrote it.

5 *Learn grammatical rules and genre conventions.* Successful writers know standard English very well. Although writing is based to a large extent on skill, imagination and knowledge, it is still a technical medium dependent on grammatical rules. Even if you want to break those rules, as many writers in fact do, you first need to know what they are. Similarly, find out what the standard conventions for different genres in your field of writing are. If working in a business context, find out about your company's house style. These rules and conventions are the tools of the trade.

6 *Get feedback.* In contrast to what some people wrongly believe, writing is not a solitary activity. A written text is meant to be read, so discuss your projects with friends and colleagues, and distribute your drafts for comments when possible and appropriate. Other people may be able to give you valuable insights on your work that you would have missed if you worked in isolation.

Activities

1 Analyse a media text (for example, an advertisement, a magazine feature article, etc.) in terms of its target audience.

2 Interpret the following briefs using the scene–content–treatment model outlined in this chapter. Plan your course of action and decide what kind of information you would need to gather to write each report.

  a You are a travel industry expert.
    A major airline, LibAir, has commissioned you to assess its competitive position in the travel industry. The airline executives want you to investigate recent developments in aircraft construction, security measures and client services, and to evaluate their airline's advantages and disadvantages in relation to those of competitors. Write a report that identifies pertinent issues and recommends a practical course of action for the airline to follow in order to remain competitive in the current travel market.

  b You are a security expert.
    The Privacy Commissioner has asked you to investigate and write a report on contemporary issues concerning privacy. With developments in surveillance technology, the spread of Internet-published information and digitally stored personal information, there is serious concern that individual rights to privacy are being eroded. The increasing presence of computer hackers and state owned satellite systems mean that individual privacy is being attacked from both private and public sectors. The Commissioner wants you to investigate the extent to which this fear is justified, to evaluate possible consequences and to suggest possible solutions. Write a report that identifies and analyses pertinent issues and puts forward a clear set of recommendations for action.

  c You are the Human Resources Manager at Law Limited, a leading national law firm.
    Law Limited has been having difficulties retaining its junior and intermediate-level lawyers. This is an industry wide problem, with law firms generally losing more than half of their junior lawyers before they reach an intermediate level (3–4 years experience). The Chief Executive of Law Limited has asked you to prepare a report investigating the problem both within the company and inter-company. Write a report that identifies pertinent issues while taking into account the interests of the company as well as the views of the junior lawyers. Outline a couple of alternative solutions, evaluate them and propose the best solution justifying your recommendation.

Style and Effect

Focus:

- Style, format and genre
- Types of style
- Clearly, accurate and concise writing
- Cohesion

Even if you have all the conceptual aspects of a written project thought out, and have a plan of the information that you want to communicate, you may find that you get stuck in some other areas. For example, you may find that you have difficulty in putting ideas into words, cannot think how to begin, or how to end, a sentence, or find that your sentences are invariably too short, too long, unclear or monotonous. Furthermore, since style differs quite drastically from spoken to written form, attempting to write as you speak can only lead to ineffective communication (unless, of course, you are writing dialogue). As the poet T. S. Eliot famously once said, 'if we spoke as we write, we would find nobody to listen; if we wrote as we speak, we would find nobody to read'. This chapter gives insights into recognising and choosing appropriate style and expression for particular genres, and in constructing sentences in an effective and clear manner.

The chapter looks at *style* in terms of *word choice* and *sentence structure*. It explains how a particular arrangement of words emphasises different elements and produces varying degrees of objectivity and subjectivity. The components of style are *balance, emphasis, degree of formality* (*register*) and *tone*. Like the clothes we wear, our hairstyle and the way we move give away much about our status, personality and cultural affiliations, choice of style and grammar tells readers whether what we say concerns them, and whether they should read it as serious, humorous, urgent and so on. Stylistic choices 'colour' writing, making the first and longest lasting impression.

A typology of style

Classifications and typologies impose sometimes artificial boundaries between elements that are often as inclusive as they are exclusive. They can be useful, however, in highlighting similarities and differences in the composition of these elements. The following typology of style is intended as a continuum, with writing addressed to a broad audience at one end, and writing addressed to a specialised audience at the other. This typology presents some criteria that could be used to discern and understand stylistic choices that produce different effects, and that are conventionally expected in different contexts of communication. Just as it is inappropriate to attend an executive board meeting in your pyjamas, so it would be inappropriate to adopt an informal style for a formal occasion and vice versa.

In many cases, written material can be classified as a certain document format. As a simple illustration of this point, think about how a shopping list looks when compared with a car manual, or a letter compared with a film script. Knowing what genre we are reading helps to clue us into what sort of language we might expect the writers to use, how they will organise their material, whether they are likely to include graphs and other visuals and so on.

For our purposes, we can distinguish three main categories of writing style: *specialist, journalistic* and *creative.* Although some genres are associated with a particular type of style, styles can be mixed, depending on the writer's intended effect, and are not strictly bound by genre conventions. The basic criteria for selecting a writing style are the audience you are addressing and the effect you intend to have on it.

Business reports tend to be written in specialist style, but their degree of formality varies according to the company's 'personality' – more hip companies would favour a less formal style than more traditional ones. National culture also plays a role in selecting a style. For instance, American, Australian and New Zealand businesses tend to use a less formal, and more direct, style than British companies, while Asian companies tend to use the most formal, and most indirect, style of English. Such factors show that cultural perceptions of politeness and interpersonal relationships are important in analysing differences in stylistic choices (for politeness in communication, see Holmes and Stubbe 2003; Watts 2003).

Journalistic style, as the title suggests, is found in journalistic texts such as magazine and newsletter articles. It is also used in public relations documents and documents that are addressed to the broad public. How 'chatty' such documents become depends on the publication and context.

Creative style is arguably the most complex because it can be found in a variety of genres. Fiction genres, especially poetry, are associated with this style, but fictional texts include a variety of styles. For example, some science fiction texts are written extensively in specialist style even though their content is based primarily on imagination.

So, what are the distinguishing features of each type of style? The following sections describe them.

Specialist style

At one end of the style continuum is specialist style, which is suitable for an audience with a specific interest in the topic. These readers may be managers, administering the business aspects of your professional field (as in reports to management or to team members), or they may have a practical interest in accessing the knowledge offered, often because they want expert advice on how to solve a problem (as in reports to clients and shareholders). Characteristics of this style are:

- strong use of quantitative or quantifiable information: where possible give numbers, facts and measurable data – but make sure you explain them
- factual tone produced by minimal use of evaluative adjectives: avoid words that show personal response, such as 'wonderful', 'horrible', 'delightful', 'heartbreaking', etc.
- use of abstract entities as agents of actions rather than people: where possible, use words that refer to things as agents in your sentence. For example, write 'The project is developing on time' instead of 'I am developing the project on time', and 'Data suggest...' instead of 'I think...'. This helps to focus on facts and observable elements rather than people
- focus on the topic rather than on readers' anticipated response towards it: avoid using direct questions, such as 'don't you think that...?' or 'wouldn't you...?', and expressions that attempt to tangle the reader in appeals to common sense, such as 'we all feel that...', 'of course, everybody knows...'. The 'you' approach is a feature of journalistic writing: avoid it in specialist style
- description and analysis of topic, presented with critical distance: describe a situation objectively, even if you have strong feelings about it
- use of complete words. Avoid the use of contractions (it's – it is, haven't – have not, etc.), as they give writing a 'spoken' or 'chatty' tone.

Here is an extract from a report written by the IT manager of an insurance company to department managers, on the dangers of new computer viruses for the functioning of the company's network. Notice the direct approach tackling the main topic immediately, the use of specifics, such as names and dates, and the impersonal presentation of facts.

> This report examines the type of computer viruses that are currently circulating and that constitute the greatest threat to the company's network system during 2014. The viruses discussed are Sircam, Love Bug and Code Red. These are especially destructive and attack the operating system. Given the insidious nature of these viruses, prevention is very important. All employees should follow these precautions:
>
> - Make sure the anti-virus software installed on all computers is functioning and updated. Check the bottom right corner of screens for an icon of a sealed computer monitor. If this is not there, contact the System Support section immediately.
> - Do not open any suspicious email attachments. Open only those attachments that you are expecting or that are clearly justified.
> - Make sure all important files are backed up so that information can be retrieved even if a virus attacks deletes files.

Journalistic style

Because it addresses a very wide audience, and comes in a variety of formats, journalistic style is more complex and harder to define. The main purposes of documents written in this style are to inform the public of a development or event, to entertain them by presenting a personal commentary on an issue that is of collective concern, or to influence and motivate them to adopt a certain attitude towards an issue. In this respect, anything that popularises a subject would use journalistic techniques to an extent. Popular science, for instance, is written in this style. In fact, even some academic or professional textbooks, including this one, are written in journalistic style, as they, too, aim to present specialist information in a readily accessible manner that can be understood by non-specialists.

Journalistic writing can vary from factual (such as reporting news stories), to informative (such as the scripting of scientific documentaries), to promotional (such as marketing products in business publications), to demagogic (such as the opinionated and often polemic style of editorials). Chapter 5 is devoted to an analysis of journalistic writing.

As regards style, the general characteristics of journalistic writing are:

- chatty tone produced by colloquial words and phrases, question–answer format and sentence fragments

- appeal to emotion and common sense
- consistent use of generalities and exaggeration
- consistent use of imperatives (sentences that begin with command words), and exclamations
- direct address to the reader: 'you' and 'we'
- dramatisation of events through use of colourful metaphors and visual language.

Here is an extract from a journalistic piece written by the same IT manager who wrote the specialist example of the previous section. This time the manager is writing for the IT column of a local newspaper, and dealing with the same topic as his report – computer viruses. Notice the chatty tone, the direct address to the reader and the use of humorous exaggeration:

> Be prepared for Armageddon. Just as you are farewelling last year's unprecedented cataclysm of computer viruses, a whole new army – better, smarter and stronger – is marching in.
>
> What can you do? Sit tight. If you don't already own anti-virus software, invest in some. If somebody sends you a love email, resist the temptation – don't open it. Love Bug is rampant. In case the worst happens, copy your files on memory sticks and CDs. Remember, do something before a virus attacks: better safe than sorry!

To better understand the difference between specialist and journalistic styles, compare the following two extracts. Both were written by biologist Frank A. Brown, but for two different publications. The first was written for a specialist scholarly journal, addressed to expert peers, while the second was published in a popular science magazine, addressed to a wider, and therefore less technically versed, audience. Both extracts deal with the same topic but present this topic differently to suit the knowledge and interests of the respective audiences.

> A deep-seated, persistent, rhythmic nature, with periods identical with or close to the major natural geophysical ones, appears increasingly to be a universal biological property. Striking published correlations of activity of hermetically sealed organisms with unpredictable weather-associated atmospheric temperature and pressure changes, and with day to day irregularities in the variations in primary cosmic and general background radiations, compel the conclusion that some, normally uncontrolled, subtle pervasive forces must be effective for living systems. The earth's natural electrostatic

field may be one contributing factor. (Published in *Biological Bulletin*, – Brown 1962.)

Everyone knows that there are individuals who are able to awaken morning after morning at the same time to within a few minutes. Are they awakened by sensory cues received unconsciously, or is there some 'biological clock' that keeps accurate account of the passage of time? Students of the behavior of animals in relation to their environment have long been interested in the biological clock question. (Published in *Scientific American* – Brown 1954.)

The first extract, written in a high degree of specialist style, is almost undecipherable by a lay audience. Some features that produce this effect are strong presence of technical jargon, long sentences, and emphasis on abstract entities and processes with no mention of human agents or personal concerns. The second extract, written in journalistic style, 'interprets' the technical information by associating it to personal, everyday experience. Some features that demonstrate this are rhetorical questions, use of metaphor ('biological clock') and generalisation ('everyone knows').

Creative style

As noted above, creative style is an umbrella term encompassing a variety of techniques, generally associated with fictional writing – although it is also used in some journalistic genres, such as 'creative non-fiction'. The main aims of creative style are: a) to draw attention to language processes themselves, rather than to events or objects in the objective world; and/or b) to evoke images in the reader's mind through linguistic symbolism such as metaphor. Creative style is not covered in this book, but it is useful to include a brief description in order to contrast it to the other stylistic types that we discuss.

For an example consider this extract from William Gibson's 1984 novel *Neuromancer* (this is the work, incidentally, that introduced the term 'cyberspace' into English):

Cyberspace. A consensual hallucination experienced daily by billions of legitimate operators, in every nation, by children being taught mathematical concepts. A graphic representation of data abstracted from the banks of every computer in the human system. Unthinkable complexity. Lines of light ranged in the nonspace of the mind, clusters and constellations of data. Like city lights, receding... (Gibson 1984: 510).

Although this extract describes an abstract concept, cyberspace, it does so by creating mental images and arousing an emotional response, rather than by detailing the technical specifics of the concept. The features that create this effect include the use of fragments (all six sentences are fragments), the strategic use of metaphor ('consensual hallucination'), analogies to common experiences ('like city lights...') and superlative expressions ('every nation', 'every computer', unthinkable complexity').

The three 'Golden Rules' of professional writing

Regardless of genre and style, effective professional writers follow three basic rules: *clarity, accuracy* and *conciseness*. These rules can be traced back to the 1970s when the Plain English campaign that was launched in most English-speaking countries helped to re-conceptualise business and government communication. The main aim of the Plain English campaign was that documents intended for the broad public should be easily understandable. The campaigners criticised the existing belief that formal writing should be technical, impersonal and passive, in order to be respectable and authoritative. Instead they emphasised the importance of communicative value: if readers cannot understand what a document says, how can they be persuaded by the content or be expected to follow the regulations described?

Since then, audience research has refined the guidelines for professional writing, and this research informs the way in which many corporate and governmental style guides are designed. Writers spend a lot of time researching and thinking about the best words and sentence structures to create the desired effect on target audiences. To be successful as a writer, and especially one with a serious public responsibility, you must have an eye for detail. As Stephen King advises, to create compelling writing that impacts on readers' perceptions, 'you must take your objective one bloody word at a time' (King 2000: 136).

Be clear

Clarity encompasses precision and conciseness. In most cases, the more precise and concise your writing is, the clearer it is. Obscure expression and verbosity are not, generally, conducive to clarity. Clarity should be assessed from the point of view of the reader, so attempt to take the reader's perspective when composing a document. Although in the planning stage you are writing for yourself, to clarify your ideas and give direction to your writing, adopt the reader's point of view when revising.

One way to assist clarity is to be as specific as possible. This is achieved by knowing exactly what you want to communicate and to whom, and by choosing relevant information to convey your message. Make sure each piece, section or chapter is about one topic only and that all information you give relates to that topic. Avoid changing the topic or including irrelevant information. Also, avoid writing in a way that forces the reader to waste time by re-reading the document to decipher 'hidden meaning' or to reverse-engineer your thinking. For example, the following announcement would have been very clear to those who wrote it, or to 'insiders', but very confusing for passers-by and visitors:

> Due to renovations, the first floor will be on the second floor, half the third floor will be on the second floor and half will remain on the third. Second floor will move to the third.

Clarity can be achieved on the text level and on the sentence level. When structuring your document, follow a logical pattern of organisation that will be easy for the reader to understand. Usually, this means going from the more general to the more specific, from assumed shared knowledge to new knowledge, from 'big picture' to details, or from definition of a problem to its analysis and then to its proposed solution. When revising the document, keep in mind that the reader should not have to go backwards or forwards to understand your message but should be able to continue reading in a linear order.

One test of the quality of professional writing is the ease with which it can be summarised. If you find a document is hard to summarise, the chances are that it needs revising to refine it of digressions, ambiguities or inconsistencies. Use this test on both your own and other people's writing.

On the sentence level, clarity is often achieved in these ways:

1 **Favour agent–action structures.** This means focusing your intended meaning on the central parts of the sentence, the subject, verb and object. Begin by naming the agent and proceed by specifying the action, what the agent does. For example, the following sentence, on the suits of players in a game, has 'the first player' as the subject of the first part of the sentence and 'the keeper' as the subject of the second. This is misleading, however, because the intended subject is actually each player's suit and not the players themselves.

   Confusing: The first player wears a special leather suit that is designed for fast movement and the ability to slip through the opponent's clutches, while the keeper wears a heavily padded suit to protect him from aggressive attacks.

Revised: The first player's special leather suit is designed for fast movement and slipping through the opponent's clutches, while the keeper's suit is heavily padded to protect him from aggressive attacks.

Also, the following sentence includes the redundant and confusing ideas of 'design' and 'ability' when the aim is to describe what a prototype does:

Confusing: The prototype is designed to ensure that it would be able to maintain consistency among all products of the same series.
Revised: The prototype ensures consistency among all products of the same series.

2 **Avoid more than two nouns in a row.** Sometimes writers try to make their writing more concise and technical by eliminating prepositions (in, of, etc.) and linking nouns in a chain. Unfortunately, this is often done at the expense of clarity and accuracy. Make sure that elegant style and clarity win over brevity and the tendency to repeat jargon indiscriminately.

Confusing: He designed a new graphics construction language.
Revised: He designed a new language for constructing graphics.

Confusing: The project includes a long term failure prevention program.
Revised: The project includes a long term program to prevent failure.
Or:
The project includes a program to prevent long term failure.

3 **Break up long sentences**, especially if they contain more than one piece of information. Usually, sentences that contain one piece of information, even if this includes details on that item, are clearer to grasp in one reading.

Confusing: Although this methodology has been tested worldwide on different formats and has been hailed as the most effective currently available, we have decided not to use it in this experiment because the present situation requires more rigorous techniques of controlling testing procedure.
Revised: This methodology has been tested worldwide on different formats and has been hailed as the most effective currently available. However, the present situation requires more rigorous techniques of controlling testing procedure. Consequently, in this experiment, we have decided not to use it.

Confusing: This is a science fiction action film set in the year 2025 about a self-centred superstar of a world sport phenomenon called

Destruktion, which has eclipsed the popularity of all sports, who is targeted by a terrorist group.

Revised: This is a science fiction action film, set in the year 2025, when a world sport phenomenon called Destruktion has eclipsed the popularity of all other sports. The film is about a self-centred superstar of this sport, who is targeted by a terrorist group.

4 **Position phrases correctly.** When you order words and phrases in a sentence, make sure that nouns agree with all their subject positions. It can be especially misleading when the noun immediately following an opening phrase cannot be identified with the noun of the phrase. This has the effect of confusing agents and actions and potentially leading to incorrect attribution of responsibility.

Confusing: As an experienced manager, my boss gives me little supervision.

Revised: Because I am an experienced manager, my boss gives me little supervision.

Be accurate

To make your writing more accurate, follow these guidelines:

1 **Favour quantification.** If you can give measurements and numbers, instead of ambiguous words, then do so.

Vague: This policy has been effective for several years.
Revised: This policy has been effective since 1995.

Vague: Many people attended the event.
Revised: About 200 people attended the event.
Or:
Attendance for the event this year was 20 per cent higher than last year.

2 **Avoid words with many meanings.** Think of a word that is specific to the meaning you intend in the sentence. For example, a commonly used word with many meanings is *over*:

During – The experiment must take place over the winter
On to – The fertiliser was spread over the field
More than – This disease affects over 10 per cent of the population
From – We collected data over three locations
Of – Apply two replications over six dilutions
To – Statistical sampling was applied over the data
Across – Sampling was stratified over taxonomic groups

Through – Dust accumulates over time
With – The company policies changed over time

Consider some examples with the word *wrong*:

Vague: The decision was wrong
Revised: The decision was financially costly for the company

Vague: This number is wrong
Revised: This number is incorrect

Vague: Cheating is wrong
Revised: Cheating is unethical

Vague: He was wearing the wrong clothes
Revised: He was dressed inappropriately.

Words that have many meanings include also evaluative adjectives whose meaning is relative to the speaker's judgment – 'nice', 'terrible', 'good', 'big', etc.:

Vague: This team contains good members.
Revised: This team contains conscientious and hard-working members.

Vague: The manager's decision was terrible.
Revised: The manager's decision was irresponsible.
Or:
The manager's decision was based on short-term profit only.

3 **Define terms** and favour specific words instead of phrases, where possible. This sharpens your writing, making it more direct. However, be careful not to offend reader by putting them in categories and labelling them. Discretion is advised.

Vague: Clear documentation pleases people and may increase the people who buy our software.
Revised: Clear documentation pleases users and may increase our clients.

Vague: Strict regulations are in place to protect against people who break into computers and steal information.
Revised: Strict regulations are in place to protect against hackers.

Be concise

The above sections show that, to be clear and accurate, you sometimes need to expand on a point, and use more words. This does not condone verbosity, however. Being direct is important in professional writing if for no other reason than, in many cases, 'time is money', and readers want to know if a document answers their question or addresses their need without having to analyse it in detail. Some writers believe that by including as many details as possible and repeating information they become clearer. Trying to 'drill in' information, however, may draw attention away from the main message and confuse the reader. In most cases, by stating your point clearly and directly at strategic sites in the document you have a better chance of getting your intended meaning across.

You can make your writing concise by avoiding long, crowded and wordy sentences, especially if they are in succession. If you write one or two long sentences, make sure the next sentence is short to break the density. Also, following these tips will help:

1 **Use the active voice where possible.** Passive sentences are wordier, and can also be confusing if they do not reveal the agent of an action.

> *Wordy*: The work was finished by the engineers before the deadline was reached.
> *Revised*: The engineers finished the work before the deadline.

> *Wordy*: The policy decision was met with disapproval by the public.
> *Revised*: The public disapproved of the policy decision.

2 **Avoid 'there is/are' at the beginning of sentences.** In many cases, we overuse these words: they are often not necessary.

> *Wordy*: There are several conclusions that we can draw from these results.
> *Revised*: We can draw several conclusions from these results.
> Or:
> From these results, we conclude…
> *Wordy*: There are several organisations that belong to the union.
> *Revised*: Several (number?) organisations belong to the union.

3 **Use modals (may, might, could, should, must) where possible.** Some harbour suspicion that modals are informal; however, this is not true. Modals modify verbs and have a clear place in language.

> *Wordy*: It is possible that the project will be funded.
> *Revised*: The project may be funded.

> *Wordy*: It is imperative that all options be considered before making a decision.
> *Revised*: All options must be considered before deciding.

4 Use verbs where possible instead of nouns. Besides making sentences concise, verbs are action-oriented and give your writing a more direct tone. Noun-centred sentences, known as *nominalisations*, have a heavy effect that makes the sentence static by reducing elements that evoke movement. Although nominalisations are still used in some technical and scientific texts, they should be avoided in energetic and people-oriented writing.

> *Heavy*: The experiments are not a demonstration of myogenesis.
> *Revised*: The experiments do not demonstrate myogenesis.

> *Heavy*: A vacuum chamber is not a requirement for this procedure.
> *Revised*: This procedure does not require a vacuum chamber.

5 Avoid weak verbs. Some verbs, instead of signaling action, depend on a noun to support them. In many cases, such verbs can be replaced by other verbs that do not require a noun. Weak verbs include *take, make, do, give, conduct, get* and *reach.*

> *Wordy*: Researchers conducted an investigation of inflation.
> *Revised*: Researchers investigated inflation.

> *Wordy*: This study serves to show the results of the investigation.
> *Revised*: This study shows the results of the investigation.

6 Use punctuation strategically. If you find that your paragraph is getting cluttered with too many wordy or long sentences, it is often possible to use punctuation to cut down on words. This is especially effective when announcing or introducing a list of items.

> *Wordy*: There are many reasons for climatic change, which include toxic pollution, deforestation and volcanic activity.
> *Revised*: There are many reasons for climatic change: toxic pollution, deforestation and volcanic activity, etc.

> *Wordy*: Most professional writing can be divided into three categories. These categories are essays, reports and articles.
> *Revised*: Most professional writing can be divided into three categories – essays, reports and articles.

7 Avoid wordy clichés. Some phrases are so commonly used in spoken language that writers have become almost unaware of their presence. Writing, nevertheless, gives you the opportunity to become more conscious of how you use language and allows for elimination of repetitive material. Table 3 lists such clichés.

Table 3: Common wordy clichés

Wordy	Concise
a majority of	many (or number)
a number of	some (or number)
at this point in time	now
basic essentials	essentials
cancel out	cancel
come to the conclusion that	conclude
completely eliminate	eliminate
due to the fact that	because
end result	result
enter into	enter
for the purpose of	to
give a summary of	summarise
has the ability to	can
have the capability to	can
higher in comparison with	higher than
in order to	to
in the absence of	without
in the event that	if
make a decision	decide
make a proposal about	propose
make an assumption about	assume
may be the mechanism responsible for	may be why
so as to	to
subsequent to	after
take action	act
there can be little doubt	definitely, certainly
with regard to	about

Effects of sentence structure

Like other media, professional writing does not aim only to inform but also to please. Correct grammar, precision and conciseness are, therefore, not the only criteria by which to judge a written text. The text should also be diplomatic, elegant and sophisticated, and should give readers the feeling of being respected at the same time as being informed or motivated.

The best way to achieve this aim is by knowing the values, knowledge and interests of your audience. This will determine your choice of going formal, impersonal, chatty, hip, 'cool' or whatever other tone you think will be most appropriate. Keep in mind that style and content are two different things; your style will have a strong effect on how the reader accepts or understands your content but will not determine what this content actually is. For example, all these sentences contain the same information, but each construction uses balance, emphasis and tone differently:

a   In the era of social media, companies have little control over information.
b   Social media have taken control over information away from companies.
c   What social media have achieved is to take control over information away from companies.
d   It is control over information that social media have taken away from companies.

The versions could be multiplied, but what this experiment shows is that you can draw attention to different parts of a topic and modify your tone by re-ordering parts of a sentence and, similarly, elements of a larger text. The changes in style in the above sentences are also a change in focus.

Sentence a) makes a loose connection between social media and loss of control over information by placing social media in an introductory phrase. Sentence b) gives much stronger agency to social media by making it the subject of the sentence. It is less equivocal than the first. Sentence c) also focuses on social media, but in this case, it places social media in the context of its results or achievements. This sentence suggests that the surrounding text would describe social media in terms of its historical or comparative aspects. Sentence d) emphasises control over information by implying that this is the most important element that social media have affected in business.

This brief analysis shows how written language creates tone by orchestrating its units (words, sentences and paragraphs) in different combinations. Assume control over this stylistic manipulation by becoming aware of it in what you write and read. The next section describes some guidelines on using sentence structure to produce different stylistic effects. Grammatical information on sentences and phrases is given in Chapter 10.

Sentences and style

Following the above guidelines, here are some tips on choosing your style:

Include variety. No document is justifiably boring, so make sure you introduce rhythm by alternating long and short sentences, using some active and some passive voice and beginning some sentences with phrases rather than with subject–verb construction. For example, this extract from a report is concise, grammatically correct and precise. However, stylistically it is displeasing to the reader and monotonous, because of its succession of simple, short sentences and lack of linking words between sentences:

> Email is the most common Internet activity. Some of the information on e-mails is of sensitive nature. A technically savvy person can intercept emails. This person then has access to the information. In fact, there is little awareness of email's lack of security among general users.

In constructing your document, use a variety of simple and complex sentences, with short, simple sentences for information you wish to emphasise. Because they condense meaning in a few words, short, simple sentences have the greatest impact on the reader. The more you expand a sentence, the more dissipated the meaning becomes. For example:

> The project team sent the data to the laboratory for testing. They expect the results back within two hours of dispatch. *It's not always so.* Sometimes they have to wait for hours, which means their whole project could be jeopardized. *It's a risky business.*

Notice how the two italicised sentences carry a lot of weight in this passage because they comment on the rest of the information. They are also the shortest of the five sentences.

Use subordination carefully. Information in a sentence can either come in the main clause or in a subordinate clause. The main clause foregrounds information; the subordinate clause diminishes information. For example, consider this sentence:

> The proposal, which was approved by the Board, will be implemented immediately.

The most important information here is in the main clause: 'The proposal will be implemented immediately'. The subordinate clause, 'which was approved by the Board' gives secondary information, or information that is assumed to be known by the audience and therefore backgrounded. When using complex sentences with one or a number of subordinate clauses, think carefully whether what you subordinate should not be given more importance by coming in a separate sentence as a main clause. Remember that what you subordinate is received by your reader, consciously or unconsciously, as secondary in relation to what you give as main information. So, consider the re-write of the above sentence:

> The proposal was approved by the Board. It will be implemented immediately.

Here the two items of information are balanced by being placed in two separate sentences – neither item is subordinated.

When writing complex sentences with more than one subordinate clause, be aware that the ways you combine main with subordinate clauses creates different effects. The different combinations are called *loose structure*, *centred structure* and *periodic structure*. Here are the effects of each.

> *Loose*: Sharks can be very dangerous when they smell blood, although they may not always be hungry.

Loose structures begin with the main clause and add subordinate clauses at the end. They project a relaxed, informal style imitating a conversation.

> *Centred*: When they smell blood, sharks can be very dangerous, although they may not always be hungry.

Centred structures begin with a subordinate clause, then give the main clause, and end with another subordinate clause. They project a tighter and more formal sentence that gives the impression you are dealing with a complicated or serious matter.

> *Periodic*: Although they may not be hungry, when they smell blood, sharks can be very dangerous.

Periodic structures begin with the subordinate clause(s) and lead to the main clause. They suggest that the information in the main clause is conditional to other factors, or that you concede a point to an opponent before asserting your opinion. Use this structure carefully, because, although it may increase the importance of the main clause, it delays it and could annoy the reader. Think about whether leading to a statement with a degree of suspense would be appropriate for the audience and purpose. This structure is more common in texts intended for oral speech, such as documentaries, than in formal report writing.

Use first- and second-person pronouns (I, my, you, we, our) differently in journalistic and specialist documents. These pronouns refer to the writer and to the reader and are important in establishing a communicative link between the two parties. Over-use of 'I' constructions, however, can give your document a simplistic or, otherwise, arrogant appearance. Similarly 'you' constructions can be inappropriately didactic or accusative, if used in cases where a more impersonal phrasing would be more appropriate. In many cases, as in formal reports for example, you are expected to focus on aspects of a situation and not on the reader's response to this situation. To decide on the best of use of pronouns, assess the nature and degree of audience complicity that you need to create.

For example, this extract is adapted from an editorial in *New Scientist* (30 June 2001). Its use of personal pronouns is typical of the demagogic variant of journalistic style. The demagogue is the enthusiastic public speaker, who tries to sway audiences with a highly emotive tone. Although fine for an editorial, this style would be highly inappropriate in business writing, say, in a formal report to a client:

> So, it turns out that poisonous polychlorinated biphenyls (PCB) are turning up in our food more often than we thought. Should we panic? PCBs are in everyday food in high concentrations and we aren't even monitoring them. It makes you wonder what else is out there.

Cohesion

Cohesion is the way segments of a text are combined to produce flow and transition from one point to another. In the hands of a competent writer, cohesion consists of a blend of repetition and variation. Cohesion exists within a sentence as well as between sentences, and, on the level of text, between paragraphs. In longer documents, such as reports, cohesion is achieved through a logical sequence of sections (more on this in Chapter 7). The rest of this section discusses cohesion at the sentence and paragraph level.

Cohesion between sentences and paragraphs is achieved in three main ways: *linkers*, *referents* and *parallel structure*.

Linkers

Linkers show the relationship between ideas or points. Your train of thought will usually seem so obvious to you as not to be worth stating. But if you do not make it clear, you will force your reader to laboriously reverse-engineer your writing to discover your meaning. In professional writing, your reader may not have the time or inclination to do that.

If, for instance, the sentence you are writing is meant to contradict the meaning of the previous sentence, signal actively to the reader that you intend a contradiction, by using 'but', 'however', 'in spite of' or some similar linking word or phrase – and make sure you use the correct grammatical structure to accommodate the linker you have used. If one sentence contains the result or consequence of a previous sentence, again, do not leave the reader to infer that you are talking about a result or consequence. Signal it by using 'consequently', 'as a result', etc. Remember to use signpost words if the relation between ideas is not obvious. Overusing such words or phrases can be tiring for the reader and can at times produce a condescending or harsh effect that may be detrimental to the quality of your document.

Table 4 gives some linkers that provide cohesion, and the relationships they express.

Table 4: Linkers and their functions	
Function	**Examples**
Adding	again, then again, also, moreover, furthermore, in addition, what is more
Contrasting	conversely, instead, on the contrary, by contrast, on the other hand, however, nevertheless
Evaluating	surprisingly, in the final analysis, paradoxically, interestingly
Explaining	namely, in other words, that is to say, better, rather
Illustrating	for example, for instance
Listing	first, second; one, two; a, b; next, then, subsequently, finally, in the end
Showing alternatives	alternatively, or again, or rather, but then, on the other hand

Showing results or effects	so, as a result, consequently, hence, now, therefore, thus
Showing similarity	equally, likewise, similarly, correspondingly, in the same way
Summarising	so, so far, altogether, overall, then

Referents

Referents are words that refer to preceding words without repeating them. **Synonyms** and **pronouns** can act as referents.

Synonyms

Words of closely related meaning can provide an effective solution to the problem of excessive repetition. If you said 'approach' in one sentence and had to repeat the idea, you might choose 'method' in the next sentence. If you said 'skill', you could then use 'ability', and so on. That would give your reader variety without changing the meaning. It indicates to the readers that you are writing about the same thing without their needing to read the same words ad nauseam.

When using synonyms, be careful not to over-use them. Overwhelming the readers with a big range of words for an object or concept can be confusing and detracts from the clarity of your document. In certain cases, especially with regard to technical terminology, it is better to repeat a term rather than replace it with a synonym.

Pronouns

If two sentences begin with the same subject, it is sufficient to use a personal pronoun in the second sentence instead of the word itself (I, he, she, it, we, you, they, this, that, these):

> The report claims that the new incentive to include all financial figures in Intranet documents has not led to an increased interest in the company's economic development. *It* adds that most stockholders do not know how to access Intranet information.

However, guard against ambiguity: sometimes the use of a pronoun instead of a noun can be confusing, especially if there are several nouns in the previous sentence to which the pronoun might refer. In this case, it is better to repeat the noun or use a demonstrative pronoun (this, that):

Incorrect: The report claims that the new incentive to include all financial figures in Intranet documents has not led to an increased interest in the company's economic development. Although *they* (?) are now available, most stockholders do not know how to access Intranet information.

Revised: The report claims that the new incentive to include all financial figures in Intranet documents has not led to an increased interest in the company's economic development. Although *these figures* are now available, most stockholders do not know how to access Intranet information

Demonstrative pronouns refer to a noun in the previous sentence or to the whole previous sentence, especially if followed by a noun:

Repetitive: The popularity of social media in business communication is increasing. The popularity of social media has been observed by many researchers and is a growing area of study.

Revised: The popularity of social media in business communication is increasing. This (popularity) has been observed by many researchers and is a growing area of study.

Parallel structure

Parallel structure adds clarity to your paragraph. Parallelism refers to the similar grammatical structure of headings and sentences within a paragraph. The more mathematically inclined will recognise the distributive law in mathematics as analogous to parallelism in language: $x(a + b) = xa + xb$. The common element must work grammatically with each of the parallel elements; the grammatically parallel elements could be substituted for each other without needing to change the rest of the sentence. Check for parallelism when you include items within one category, or balance items on one level of information.

Not parallel: These books are not primarily for reading, but they are used for reference.
Parallel: These books are not primarily for reading but for reference.

Not parallel: Not only is he a conscientious worker, but also he is very competent.
Parallel: Not only is he conscientious but also competent.

Not Parallel: Don't underestimate the value of defining technical terms. Prior knowledge on behalf of the reader should not be assumed

Parallel: Don't underestimate the value of defining technical terms. Don't assume prior knowledge on behalf of the reader

Not parallel: Possible solutions for dealing with at risk youth include implementing programmes and support measures through parent and child education, housing and physical, social and economic conditions should be changed.
Parallel: Possible solutions for dealing with at risk youth include implementing programs and support measures through parent and child education, improving housing and changing physical, social, and economic conditions.

Parallelism is very important in instructions, point lists and headings. For example, here are four introductions to a user guide for a printer:

a   Setting up the printer, maintenance, and what to do if something goes wrong are easy with Apple's step by step user guide.
b   Setting up the printer, maintaining it, and troubleshooting are easy with Apple's step-by-step user guide.
c   Printer set-up, maintenance, and troubleshooting are easy with Apple's step-by-step user guide.
d   Apple's step-by-step user guide will show you how to set up the printer, how to maintain it, and what to do if something goes wrong.

Version a) is awkward because the three elements that it lists are not parallel. The other three correct this error. Notice also how although all three are grammatically correct, there are slight differences in tone with each choice. Version c), with its noun emphasis, is the most formal version, while d), with its clause structure and second-person pronoun, is the most informal.
The following extract is analysed in terms of its cohesive devices:

Analysed example 1

Understanding the shape of the tree of life and the details of its branches is more than a quaint sideline of biology, even though the science of this quest – known as systematics – has come to be regarded by many biologists as dowdy and old fashioned, little more than stamp collecting. *But such an understanding is probably the best foundation for a larger appreciation of life*, including evolution, ecology and behaviour. As Colin Patterson, a palaeontologist at the Natural History Museum of London, says: 'To retrieve the history of life, to reconstruct the evolutionary tree, is still the aim of evolutionary biology.' *Getting it right is therefore important.*

Getting it right, however, is much harder than might be imagined. Inferring an evolutionary relationship from morphology rests on identifying anatomical features, or characters, that are shared by two species because of their common descent. *Such features* might include the shape of teeth, the form of a particular nerve canal, the number of certain flower parts, and so on. *Ironically*, the thing most likely to confound the well-intentioned systematist in identifying such characters is the power of natural selection itself. Many shared characteristics do not reflect a common ancestry, but *instead* are the result of distantly related species independently adapting their bodies to meet the demands of similar lifestyles. (Lewin 1998: 37, my emphasis.)

This is known as a parenthetical definition. It is used within a sentence to provide a brief definition of a term, and is placed between brackets or dashes. It acts a cohesive device in allowing for explanation without compromising flow as would happen if a separate sentence was inserted to explain the term.

Shows transition of contrast. Note that 'but' and 'and' at the beginning of a sentences are markers of journalistic style and should be avoided in specialist style.

Provides a supportive explanation.

Summarises an important point in the paragraph.

Repeats the concluding sentence of the previous paragraph and indicates the topic of this paragraph.

Refers to the features mentioned in the previous sentence.

Evaluates this sentence in relation to what was said before.

Emphasizes contrast.

Audience matters

The most important considerations in choosing your style are audience and purpose. If writing for complete outsiders or novices, for example, you may find that to be clear you have to use definitions and explanations that lengthen the text. If that is what would ensure reader understanding, then so be it – you cannot be as concise and direct in this situation as would be appropriate in a different situation. Also, when writing about a delicate or controversial topic, you will need to take care to avoid using phrases that are loaded with offensive connotations, especially if the audience is the general public. Phrases with offensive connotations would be suitable, however, if your purpose was to provoke! Similarly, it is sometimes impossible to be precise when quantifying a situation. In that case you could give a range, average or approximation. In all cases, choose a style that supports your message and is aligned to the situation in which your writing takes place.

In all, clarity and writer–reader complicity should guide your stylistic choices. When reading others' writing, use the guidelines given in this chapter to analyse and understand what flatters you, offends you, leaves you indifferent, angers you, enlightens you or seduces you. Then use the insights you gain to control your own writing.

Medium matters

The medium is the channel in which you transmit your message, and it is a separate decision to choosing genre and style. For example, you can submit a report by sending it through the post or you can attach it as a PDF to an email and send it electronically. The genre (report) remains the same in both cases, but the medium is different. Medium is mostly a matter of access. Which medium would reach your target audience most effectively?

Access, however, is linked to the ways readers process information perceptually. For instance, it is still easier and faster to read script off paper than it is to read it off a screen (although new digital technologies are rapidly changing this). Therefore, professional writers still work on the assumption that readers will print a long and complicated document, for easier reading. Professional editors, in fact, tend to print typescripts to proofread them, since it is easier to pick errors on a hard copy. With regard to style, this means that journalistic style, with its shorter sentences and words, is more suited to digital writing, especially writing that is generally nor printed, such as website content (more on this in Chapter 6).

Besides mental processing, space is another consideration in different media. Websites have a strict layout and typography, which affects the number of words that can 'fit' in a space. This is analogous in many ways to magazine and newspaper layout (in fact, websites were initially modelled after magazines). A rule of thumb states that a business headline should have 5–8 words or 16 characters. This has the added advantage that it fits on a Blackberry screen. Websites, magazines and newsletters are often printed in columns, so shorter paragraphs, sentences and words are best.

Activities

1 The following sentences are grammatically correct. However, they are inappropriate for professional writing because of ambiguity and/or wordiness. Re-structure the sentences to make them more suited to a professional context.

   a This program has a graphics design capability.
   b The security guards have the responsibility of checking all offices.
   c We opened the project to suggestions with a view to being able to get some ideas on the improvement of the security of the building.
   d Since we hired the new technical assistant, the quality of the equipment has improved.
   e His project will involve a big investigation into how the monetary economy has evolved.
   f There are several organisations that are concerned with the destruction of rainforests.
   g The inspecting officer can do a verification of the data when the manager has made a decision on a suitable methodology.
   h The media could not provide the public with a justification of their manipulation of the information in the news story.
   i When logging in, the data must be completed fully.
   j Non-computer background personnel can do this task.
   k To find the committee room, signs have been posted along the corridor.
   l A detailed analysis of trends and an evaluation of the relations between state and corporation is the purpose of this report.
   m Prolonged use of the battery can cause it to become drained of its energy.
   n Because there is a trend towards fewer and larger offices, it will cause an increase in the demand for computers.

2 The following sentences come from informal genres, such as conversations and email. Re-write them in specialist style to make them appropriate for a formal business report. You will need to make up some specific information.

   a The deplorable staff turnover rate could be reduced if those long-awaited fringe benefits could be introduced.
   b You can hardly imagine the effect of incentive pay on staff morale.
   c I don't understand why anyone would opt for this outrageous solution.

d Nobody likes to feel unsafe at home, so these building security measures will help to make people feel more secure.

e I think the Slick Graphics upgrade is a good, solid way to do what we want and we can also save money.

f Advertisers feed on people's greed and futile attempt to fill the emptiness of their lives with consumer objects.

3 Re-write the following sentences so that their structures are parallel.

a He has the ability both to choose a suitable course of action and he can implement his decision wisely.

b Walking quickly burns as many calories as you burn when you run slowly.

c It has been found that homo sapiens have not changed anatomically in the last 10,000 years, and also our intellectual capacities are about the same.

d The court found him guilty of insurance fraud and he has been sentenced to two years imprisonment.

e From this report it is recommended that the following initiatives be adopted: links with the Chamber of Commerce and Industry, the viability of an information technology school should be examined and also a scheme, which assists small business with accounting matters, should be established.

4 Improve the cohesion in the following paragraphs by using some of the devices described in this chapter. You may re-arrange sentences and add linkers, but do not re-write the paragraphs extensively. Keep the style and content the same as the original.

a Romantic individuality may have something to do with the sport's popularity – the fact that one undertakes a kind of Byronic solo adventure when one jumps. The jumpers do their thing in groups and form little outlaw societies in which they approve of and cheer one another. It could be the illegality of the sport that pumps them up. In an interview last April, Kappfjell said he delighted in playing outlaw and 'fooling the authorities' as he gained access to his perches. (Adapted from Rosenblatt 1999 – *note that the sport mentioned is base jumping.*)

b Complex systems are particularly good for modelling the complexities of the natural world. During the Gulf War, large quantities of oil polluted the sea. This damaged the ecosystem – but how do you go about measuring that damage and monitoring the ecosystem's recovery? Researchers needed to disentangle a complex web of interrelationships. (Adapted from Stewart 1998: 37.)

c Explorative graphics enable the user to move about a website by selecting a graphical object. This is an alternative to using text to navigate the website. They make the website more attractive while increasing download time. Excessive use of exploration graphics can confuse a user.

Short Business Documents

3

Focus:

- Everyday communication genres
- Bullet points
- Presentations

The previous chapters looked at planning and stylistic considerations relevant for different kinds of writing. Here we look at the writing that professionals do every day, and the formats of short business genres, such as memos, email and oral presentations.

The amount and kind of writing that professionals do every day vary greatly, depending on the industry, the size of the company and the person's position in it. For example, in a routine and relatively uneventful week, a Public Relations Officer in a mid-range high tech company would need to write about ten press releases about two pages long each, one proposal about four or five pages long, one presentation or speech to be delivered by a senior manager or the CEO, one press conference or media-addressed statement, and about two newsletter articles addressed to stakeholders. In addition, every day s/he would write several statements and responses, to media and stakeholders, sent mainly through email and instant messaging. If the company does not have a social media specialist, the PR Officer would also need to update the company's social media communications on Facebook and Twitter daily.

Although different genres have their own formatting conventions, there are certain writing principles that are relevant for all business genres since they reflect the rhetorical situation of workplace communication in general. Table 5 describes these principles.

These principles are consistently confirmed in research into corporate communication. For example, management communication researchers John Fielden and Ronald Dulek (1998) analysed over 2,000 documents in a corporate context and found that most were confusing and ineffective because they buried their main message and purpose by placing it in an

Table 5: General business writing principles

1 **State your purpose close to the beginning of the document**: business writing is 'top heavy'. This means that the beginning of a document is a prominent position and important information should be placed there. Don't let the reader wait for the main point – suspense is not a desirable quality in business writing.

2 **Respond to the brief/establish link with previous exchange**: remind readers why you are writing this document. Is it in response to a request? Is it an answer to a question? Is it a follow-up from a decision reached at a meeting? Establishing a link between your document and a previous communication is especially important in short documents, such as memos and email, because readers receive a number of these daily and need some context.

3 **Present information in order of its importance to the readers**: the most effective way to organise information in a business document, regardless of genre, is from most important to least important from the point of view of the reader.

4 **Chunk information into sections with a clear pattern of development**: make sure the logic of organisation of paragraphs and sections is clear to the reader and consistent throughout the document.

5 **Use listing and bullet-points to condense and highlight information**: if not over-used, bullet points can be a strategic device for summarising and emphasising information, as well as a technique for making your document more concise.

6 **Put information of questionable or partial importance into an attachment**: Short documents must have one main message. Any additional information should go in a separate attached document. Reports also have the advantage of allowing you to attach appendices with additional information. This is especially important when you have mixed audiences, with some readers having more knowledge of your topic and others needing more detail and explanation.

7 **Where appropriate, state clearly what action you want the reader to take**: if the document requires action, make sure this is explicit and not implied. Readers' requested action usually comes at the end of a document – in the closing line in memos and email, and in the recommendations in a formal report.

inconspicuous position. This forced the reader to reread sections in an attempt to interpret the writer's intention. To remedy this, Fielden and Dulek propose a 'bottom-line' approach to business writing, by organising information so that the main message and purpose of the document are stated first, before any justifications, explanations or reasoning. This way, all the information that follows becomes meaningful, because it is framed by the main point (see also Gunnarsson 2009; Garzone and Archibald 2010).

Short reports

The report is the most common genre in business writing, divided into various sub-genres. Many reports are analytical, evaluating and interpreting facts and ideas (they are the focus of Chapter 7). Other reports are descriptive, stating facts without any analysis. Objectivity and good summarising skills are necessary to produce clear and useful descriptive reports. Here are some types of descriptive reports and their functions:

Agendas

Agendas for committee meetings list the topics for discussion at the meeting. An agenda is circulated prior to the meeting to people who are scheduled to attend. Included items are the date, time and venue of the meeting, and the topics to be discussed. The second topic, after apologies of absentees, is a discussion of whether the tasks allocated at the previous meeting have been actioned – facilitating continuity in meetings and, by extension, in the progress of a project or the management of a section.

The following is an example of an agenda for a meeting with engineers and project managers on the development of a new product.

AGENDA

Date: 23 August 2012
Time: 11:00–12:00
Venue: Board Room B

Items:
1. Apologies
2. Matters arising from minutes of last meeting
3. Brief discussion of project progress
4. Product specifications
5. Product architecture
6. Any Other Business (AOB)

Minutes

Minutes contain a summary of discussions held at meetings. The committee secretary is responsible for taking notes at the meeting, revising them into a minutes document and circulating the document to committee members. Minutes should include information on tasks allocated to project or section members to action. Here are the minutes of the meeting following the above agenda:

Minutes of Meeting 23 August 2012

Present: John Amos, Grace Chung, Mary Willis, Steve Johnson, Adam Reeves
Apologies: George Craig, Petar Sladic

1. Progress:
   Contacted South American representative
   Agreed on collaboration plan with Dan Jones, local hobbyist
   Have not yet contacted Mario Gracci
   Have not contacted colleagues at UC Davis, and have not identified specific contact target yet
   Finalised major decision: we will obtain all raw materials from Venezuela
2. Product Specifications:
   Discussed marketing, engineering, and manufacturing specs of final product – brandy (tentative plan attached)
   Discussed estimated engineering specs of crusher (specs attached)
3. Product Architecture:
   Identified and defined major functional elements in project
   Identified sub-elements in each major block
   Identified physical components associated with each block
   Discussed crusher in detail – decided on a screw-type system
4. By next meeting, 10 December 2012:
   Adam Reeves to contact Mario Gracci
   Mary Ho to initiate contact with UC Davis and gauge interest in collaborating
   Team members to bring prototype of crusher for analysis and discussion

---

Progress reports

Progress reports state tasks completed to date within a project. Progress reports compare actual progress against planned progress in terms of cost, resource use and level of performance. Writing progress reports is an essential part of project management. With regular and timely progress reports, problems can be addressed and corrected before they damage the outcome of the project. Ideally, progress reports are written into project design as a formal requirement. For example, a systems analyst might be required to report to the project team or project manager every three weeks. This procedure reduces the risk of confusion, misunderstandings and delays.

When writing a progress report, consider:

Who to report to: Progress reports are typically addressed to both sectors of the project team, the project steering committee, who oversee the project, and the project implementation group, who put the project design into operation.

When to communicate: Project reports are generally required regularly.

What to communicate: Headings for the report may include the following:

- major issues
- key achievements
- targets
- progress against schedule (indicate whether the project is progressing according to plan)
- resource summary against plan (compare the utilisation of resources against planned use at this stage)
- major tasks remaining
- forecast
- additional comments/notation (for example, explain any deviations from the project plan)

How to communicate: As with all professional communication, expression in the report should be accurate, concise and unambiguous. It should be formatted using the house style of the company.

Contracts and licence agreements

Contracts and *licence agreements* list obligations and privileges that bind two or more parties, and describe the conditions and rules that underlie the transactions of the signing parties. The legal and non-negotiative nature of such documents gives them the highest degree of formality of all descriptive reports.

Here is an extract from a licence agreement:

Everyday communication documents

Business letters

In addition to reports, much professional communication takes place through shorter documents, such as letters and memos. These two documents are very similar in many respects. Their main difference lies in their recipients: letters tend to be addressed to readers outside the writer's organisation, while memos are written for colleagues and employees within the organisation.

Business letters generally serve the following functions:

- They accompany a report (as in a letter of transmittal), a packaged product or advertising material (such as a brochure).
- They confirm a previous communication between writer and reader by stating the decisions or agreements that were made.
- They introduce a candidate's application for a professional position (as in a cover letter to a job application).
- They notify the recipient of the outcome of his/her application.
- They notify the recipient of changes or developments made in an established relationship (such as writing to shareholders to inform them of a new method of accessing financial data, or notifying employers of resignation).
- They carry a formal complaint or warning.
- They congratulate the recipient on a success, such as a promotion, or offer sympathy on a loss.
- They thank the recipient for his/her support, or continued support.

Letters also used to be written to request information, and this could well still be the case in more traditional contexts. However, in most modern day situations, this function of letter writing has been replaced with phone communication and email. The use and frequency of letters in a company depend on the company culture. Letters are more frequent in traditional companies, but are being replaced by the digital medium in many progressive companies. They generally draw attention to something, whether that is an agreement, product or longer document, and should do this succinctly and directly.

The standard length of a business letter is one page. Only under special circumstances should you go to one and a half or two pages. For any situation requiring a longer document, write a short report. The standard order of items in a business letter is as follows:

1 Use letterhead for the sender company's name and address. If you are writing as an individual and have no letterhead, include your name and address as the first item on the top left of the page.
2 Follow by date and then by the recipient's name, position and address. Always try to address readers personally. Avoid addressing them by the impersonal Dear Sir or Madam. If need be, phone the company to find out the person's name. If you cannot find the recipient's name, use their tile, such as Dear Public Relations Officer, or Dear Human Resources Manager. Use a title (Mr, Ms) and then the recipient's surname. Use a first name only if you know the recipient well. Polite forms of address differ worldwide, so the safest option would be the neutral title plus surname.
3 The first sentence should state the nature of the letter. The best way is to write a short sentence beginning with 'Here is…' or 'This is to…'. The word Re (short for regarding) followed by a title summarising the purpose of the letter is also often used.
4 Follow with two or three paragraphs of two to four sentences each, with the main content. Be as concise as possible, and avoid repetition and elaborate descriptions or justifications. End with a sentence indicating further action that you or the reader should take.
5 The most widespread courteous close is 'yours sincerely'. Although 'yours truly' and 'yours faithfully,' and the less formal 'Cordially,' are also used extensively, 'yours sincerely' is an internationally accepted standard. If the recipient is a close associate, you could go for the friendlier, 'Regards' or 'Best wishes'.
6 Type your name after your signature and follow by your position title.

As regards spacing, leave double space between each section. You can leave more space if the letter is short and there is a lot of white space on the page, but make sure you do not leave too many gaps between sections as this gives a fragmented appearance.

Analysed example 2 is the letter of transmittal of a report investigating career opportunities for law graduates. The report was commissioned by a career consulting company and written by the president of a law students' society.

Memoranda (memos)

Memos are internal documents, written to colleagues, superiors or subordinates within a company. There are a few cases where memos are sent to another company, notably when a *Memorandum of Understanding* is written to formalise an agreement between the two companies.

Memos are rapidly being replaced with email. The use and frequency of memos in a company depend on the company's culture. Since memos are an older genre than email, they tend to be associated with more traditional communication. In many cases, memos are considered a little more formal than email. Often they are attached to email as a PDF or Word document, especially in cases where it is expected that they will be printed or saved in a folder and recorded as a formal notification. Memos were the template for email when it was first introduced, so the two can be seen as variants of the same genre transmitted in a different medium. Both memos and email use the same header, known as a *memo header*: To, From, Date, Subject.

Memos are sent for a great range of reasons that involve some form of notification. They generally serve these functions:

- They confirm in writing the results of an oral communication, often also providing more detail on the issues discussed.
- They inform the recipient of the stage reached in a developmental procedure. In this case, they function as informal progress reports.
- They carry a formal request, reminder (memorandum is actually a Latin word for reminder) or suggestion.
- They notify employees of a change or development in an established course of action (for example, if set hours for coffee and lunch breaks are implemented or changed).
- They accompany and introduce documentation, such as internal reports.

Companies often have house style templates for internal memos. If not, follow these guidelines:

- Always use a 'memo header': To, From, Date, Subject.
- Like with letters, aim for one page and do not exceed two pages.

Analysed example 2

Law Students' Society
4 Gladstone Terrace
X City, Y Country

Catherine Hayes
Manager
Bellevue Career Counsellors
Street Address
City

28 May 2013

Dear Ms Hayes,

Please find attached the report regarding the occupational possibilities of Law Majors that you requested on 24 March 2013. In accordance with your specifications, the report includes information on employment opportunities, pay rates and trends – areas interesting to graduates. Also, the report incorporates information for prospective students, such as advice on appropriate choice of courses and study planning.

The report outlines possible career options for law graduates and examines advantages of the profession such as the wide range of work available, the flexibility within the occupation and the high levels of remuneration. Disadvantages such as high stress levels and competition are also considered.

Recommendations include advice concerning appropriate professional development training, membership in professional associations, and publicity.

I hope this report will be useful for Bellevue's further work on career advice to students and graduates. Please feel free to contact me if you have questions about the report or require additional information.

Yours sincerely,

Franziska Federle
President, Law Students' Society

Recipient's name

First sentence states directly the purpose of the letter.

This being a letter of transmittal, it summarises the main contents of the report, and connects them with the client's specifications

The second paragraph goes into more detail on report contents.

The body of the letter ends with a note on recommendations. In other types of letters, this would be replaced with action to be taken by either the recipient and/or the writer.

The letter ends with an offer to assist further should it be required.

- Begin with a personal address, especially if you are writing to one person or to group members with whom you work closely. A memo is still a relatively informal piece of communication, so beginning with 'Dear X', or 'Dear colleagues' is more palatable than an abrupt beginning. However, if you are writing to many readers who do not fall into one particular category, leave the personal address out.
- Tie your topic to a concern you expect your reader to share or to a subject you have previously discussed. For example, you could start by writing 'As you know…' or 'Following our meeting…'. Do not begin abruptly with a new piece of information stated out of context.
- If appropriate, include a closing remark indicating further action, such as 'Please get back to me on this question as soon as possible'. However, a closing tie is not necessary in a memo and you can, in fact, end with your last paragraph.
- A memo is a short text that states facts, so use bullet points and lists to summarise and classify information. Avoid wordiness and detailed specifications and justifications (but you can write a memo to point the reader to a document that gives these detailed specifications and justifications). Optionally use headings, if they assist communication by signposting information.

Analysed example 3 is a memo written by the Staff Welfare Officer to the Human Resources Manager of the Ministry of the Interior. The memo informs the manager of the results reached in a feasibility analysis carried out by the Staff Welfare Officer regarding coffee breaks. Note how it also acts as an informal progress report.

Email

Email has one definite quality: it is fast. For professional situations, this is both an advantage and a drawback. The advantage is that your message can reach a number of recipients in different parts of the world in seconds – saving you both time and the cost of courier or airmail. Also, email can make a message public (read by many readers simultaneously), thereby opening it up to more constructive feedback. The drawback is that, because of its ease and simplicity, email often tends to be associated with speech rather than written language, which can lead to bad audience dynamics and miscommunication. When sending email as part of a professional communication, keep in mind these two points:

1 An email message is a written text. It is, therefore, bound by the conventions of writing, as discussed in this book. That is, your audience

Analysed example 3

TO: Greg Taylor, Human Resources Manager
FROM: John Masters, Staff Welfare Coordinator
DATE: 25 November 2012
SUBJECT: Coffee Breaks

Greg,
As you requested in our phone conversation last Friday, here is a summary of the issue and recommendations developed in relation to the current problem of coffee breaks. These issues and recommendations will be part of the formal report that I will submit to the Human Resources Committee on 15 January.

The Issue
Currently there is no provision of morning or afternoon coffee breaks for staff at the Ministry of the Interior. However, recent surveys and monitoring have indicated that approximately 70% per cent of staff take unofficial breaks of between 20 and 40 minutes duration each day. Other than causing work disruption, this also leaves staff that do not take breaks feeling disgruntled.

The issue for the Ministry of the Interior is whether it should implement an official morning and afternoon break policy, and, if so, on what conditions.

Recommendations
Studies have shown that 20-minute morning and afternoon breaks have a measurable positive effect on labour efficiency. This is reflected in the fact that three

The first sentence links this communication with a previous one that initiated it. The recipient is, therefore, given context for the memo.

The second sentence gives more context by stating the overall purpose of the document.

The headings signal the organisation of content

and purpose should determine the relative formality, the style and the amount of detail. Contrary to what is sometimes assumed, the Internet does not level status distinctions; you are still writing to someone with a specific position of power and authority in relation to your own. Reflect this in your writing. Also, the ease with which a message can be transmitted and deleted does not justify sloppy composition, with quarters of businesses nationwide have daily break policies.

The formal report in response to this issue will contain these recommendations, briefly outlined here:

1. The Ministry of the Interior should implement an official morning and afternoon break policy. This recommendation is legal and within the powers of the commissioners to authorise.
2. The breaks should be 20 minutes long and staff should be deducted one hour's pay if their break period is longer than this (except in special circumstances).
3. No more than half the employees in any department should be on a break at one time.
4. The breaks cannot be exchanged for time off at either end of the working day.
5. The Ministry should establish a canteen on the premises to provide a facility where staff can purchase food and beverages. There is currently no such facility close to the Ministry. I have obtained the relevant costs and am currently conducting negotiations for final pricing.

Please contact me if you have any other questions at this stage.

John

> The beginning of this section summarises the findings that justify the recommendations.

> The last sentence avoids an abrupt ending by offering further communication.

misspelt words and ungrammatical sentences. In fact, a very common complaint with business email is that the writer seems abrupt and disrespectful and the message is hastily put together. Therefore, implement the guidelines for revision and editing given in this book.

2 Email does not replace hard copy. Printed and signed documents are still considered more binding and formal than soft copy. For example,

although you may email a formal report for fast transmission, make sure you also send a hard copy to formalise the communication. One reason for this is that it is still easier to lose documents in cyberspace than if they are in tangible form. Another reason is that electronic communication depends on availability of software and hardware, whereas print can fall back on the universality and reliability of paper. Your best option for certain transmission is to send your document in both forms.

Here are some general guidelines on writing effective business email:

1 **Begin with an opening address**: this could be 'Dear...' for more formal correspondence, or 'Hello...' for less formal. You can omit an opening address if the message is one in a series of reply exchanges on a topic.

2 **Place your main message as close to the beginning as possible**. Do not force the reader to read the whole message to understand what it is about. Give as much information as possible about yourself (if necessary) and your main point at the beginning to put the reader in perspective. Any details you then proceed to give will be more meaningful.

3 **Write in full words and sentences.** Do not use abbreviated words, unless they are acronyms – email is not text messaging.

4 **Do not use upper case to emphasise.** Words and sentences written in upper case fonts are perceived as equivalent to shouting, not emphasis. If you want to emphasise, do so by using appropriate terminology.

5 **End by clearly stating what action you request or expect the reader to take** in response to your message, and close the message politely.

6 **Revise the message before you send it**, paying close attention to spelling, word choice and repetition.

7 **Sign your message** with your name and affiliation as appropriate: often, the email address is not enough for the recipient to know who you are.

8 **Write short paragraphs** (no more than three sentences). It is more difficult to read from a computer monitor than it is from paper, so you facilitate communication by making the text as simple as possible.

9 **Do not use headings, tables or formatted text in the body of the email**. The reason for this is that email text is based on code – HTML (Hypertext Mark-up Language). This means that layout and formatting may not display as you intended. If you want to send graphs and tables, attach them as Word or PDF documents (and don't forget to actually attach the document!)

10 **Think carefully before you copy secondary audiences.** The ease with which email can be sent increases the temptation to copy a number of recipients. However, some content may be inappropriate or offensive to some audiences and this risk should be considered. Similarly, always be discreet when writing about a third party in an email. This person may well be copied your message at some stage in the sometimes long and convoluted circulation of email messages. The nature of the digital medium makes it very easy to make private information public. Also, if you are copying recipients outside your company who do not know each other, blind-copy them in order to keep their email addresses confidential.

In cases where your message is a binding contract, or includes information that should be recorded, consider submitting it in a different document, such as a letter, a contract, a written agreement or a report. Submit these as PDFs or Word documents or in hard copy. For formal, developmental procedures where the actual document is important, and not just the action it recommends, make sure a permanent copy is available, such as a brochure or content on a website – and maybe signal its existence by an email message.

Below is the body of an email written by an information analyst of a small IT company to her manager to complain about ineffective duty allocation. The email is tactless, unclear and contentious: it's obvious the writer did not revise it and wrote it while in an emotional state. The email has bad audience dynamics, and the writer is defeating her own purpose to implement changes in duty allocation by confusing and antagonising the recipient of the message.

> Positions in the corporation have multiplied to such an extent over the last two years that human resources have no longer any idea who is doing what. I have to do so much that is not directly in my area that I hardly have any time to do my job. Only last week I had to prepare three press releases for new products and to respond to questions e-mailed to me by the marketing department because I didn't know who to refer them to. None of this is stuff I have to do. My job is to produce reports for management and for clients. I should not be at all involved in the selling area. If you want me to do my job properly, you should contact the human resources manager and tell him to do something about it. We should all get detailed job descriptions, our own and other people's so that we can refer requests to the relevant people within the company.

The email is ineffective in these areas:

- It begins abruptly with no introductory statement to define the context.
- It constantly repeats the writer's personal problem but does not show how this problem affects the whole company and how its correction would benefit everybody.
- It focuses on the problem but makes very little attempt to propose solutions.
- It is written in one chunk with no section or paragraph breaks. This makes it even more unpalatable and overbearing.

Analysed example 4 is a suggested revision:

Analysed example 4

Dear Dave,

I would like to draw your attention to a problem that affects staff efficiency as well as time and resource management.

As you know, over the last two years, positions in the company have multiplied. This has led to confusion in duty allocation, with staff not knowing who to contact for specific tasks. As a result, many staff members divert their time and energy to tasks that are not officially in their area. For example, I often have to deal with the marketing department for sales enquiries, although this is not within the scope of my position. As you can understand, this situation is counterproductive and time consuming, and works against the company's best interests.

I propose that we organise a meeting with representatives from Human Resources to discuss possible solutions.

Please get back to me with your views on this matter, or if you need more information.

States the purpose and main point in the first sentence.

Establishes rapport with the reader through shared knowledge.

Gives background to the situation that created the problem.

Gives personal situation as an example, not as the main focus of the message.

Links personal situation with the company's interests.

Makes a practical suggestion.

Concludes with a request for reader action.

Writing in bullets

With the exception of email, the other short business genres described above (as well as longer reports, of course) include bullet points in their layout. This section gives some general advice on using bullet points effectively. Bullets and numbered lists are powerful devices to condense and highlight information in reports. They make a text more concise while allowing you to cover a wide area. Points also stand out from the rest of the text and draw the reader's attention to the issues you are discussing. They enable you to show your awareness of issues without needing to discuss them in depth. Use bullet points for items of roughly equal value; use numbered lists for items with priority ranking.

Bullet points list information that belongs to one logical category. For this reason, they should not list random or unrelated items. If placed within a report or memo, they should follow from a lead sentence, and be structured as endings of that sentence, with each point suggesting an alternative completion of the sentence. The only cases when bullet points can follow directly from a heading, without an introductory sentence, are in CVs and presentation slides. Headings describe the content of a whole section and should not be used as an introduction to a list of bullet points in other genres. Bullet points could be complete sentences or phrases, but in either case, the rule of being part of a logical category would apply: they should present different aspects of the same category of information. They are an additive, not a developmental or procedural, technique: they accumulate information on a topic but do not develop the discussion from one topic to another.

Compare the following extracts; the first is written in a block paragraph, and the other uses bullet points. Both are correctly written, so their appropriateness is determined by context and purpose. For example, the bullet-pointed version lends itself more readily to a document where each point is taken up and discussed further in subsequent sections.

A. The department must make a reasonable effort to make stakeholders aware that information is being collected and the purpose for which it is collected. Also, the department must indicate who the intended recipients are, and provide details on its own structure. Another responsibility of the department is to notify the stakeholders of the legal requirements of the information (i.e. whether it is mandatory or voluntary), and the consequences of not providing it. Finally, the department must clarify what access stakeholders will have to the information to correct it, if necessary.

B. The department must make a reasonable effort to make the stakeholders aware of the:
   - fact that information is being collected
   - purpose for which the information is being collected
   - details of the department collecting the information

- legal requirement of the information
- consequences of not providing the information
- rights of access and correction of that information.

If bullet points are overused, they can make writing choppy and may leave the reader without a strong grasp of the main message. Other common problems with bullet points include confusing items in a series, using bullets to develop a sequence of events and neglecting parallel structure. For example, the following list is incorrect because the first point is a heading, the second is an explanation of the heading and the third is a prescription of what should be done; the points do not list items in a category and should not be formatted as bullet points.

- Confusing levels of hierarchy.
- This disrupts the flow of information.
- Points should follow from lead sentence.

In the following incorrect list the points actually describe a chronological sequence of events and should be presented in paragraph form.

- The project investigates the high staff turnover in the company.
- We collected data from surveys and interviews conducted over a period of two years.
- Exit surveys showed a dissatisfaction with promotion opportunities.
- It is obvious that measures need to be taken to prevent such staffing issues.

Parallel structure is very important in bullets because the similar grammatical structure of all points reflects the fact that they belong to the same logical category. For example, the following list lacks parallel structure and is incorrect:

Suggestions for improvement include:
- More incentives for initiative should be given
- Salary increase
- we should review current recruitment methods
- developing a mentoring scheme

This problem can be corrected by choosing one structure and keeping it consistent in all points, as in the following list (notice also the consistency in using upper case first letter for each point):

Suggestions for improvement include:
- Giving more incentives for initiative
- Increasing salary

- Reviewing current recruitment methods
- Developing a mentoring scheme

Consistency is very important in bullets and numbered lists, and this extends to the use of punctuation. Companies usually have their own house style on punctuation in bullet points, but it is becoming increasingly common practice to omit any punctuation at the end of each bullet point unless the point is a complete sentence. Semi-colons at the end of bullets are becoming outdated, although they are still used in more traditional companies. Using upper or lower case for the first letter of each point usually depends on the content of the points: points that complete the introductory sentence tend to take lower case, whereas those that list independent items tend to take upper case. Whichever option you follow, make sure you are consistent throughout your document.

Bad news messages

During their careers, professionals will find themselves in situations where they are required to communicate negative messages, also known as 'bad news' messages. This can raise complicated issues because such messages are often preceded or followed by conflict with peers, managers, employees and/or the public. Bad news can be carried by different genres, both short and long, such as letters, reports and even the more 'upbeat' genres, such as press releases. Some situations that involve the writing of bad news messages include:

- An accident has occurred that caused deaths and/or environmental damage.
- Technical products have been found to contain faults and deficiencies.
- A company needs to cut down on jobs and make employees redundant.
- A company did not make a profit and is in financial difficulties.
- A project team has exceeded budget or did not meet project milestones.
- A company is not renewing its contract with a collaborating company.
- A proposal is rejected.
- Customers complain about problems associated with a product.

The gravity of the bad news, of course, varies with each situation: an accident involving equipment malfunction that has caused environmental damage is much more serious, and would require much more justification, than a customer's complaint that the company's retail outlets do not open on public holidays. In fact, there is a whole field of organisational communication known as *crisis communication*, which examines the public relations and risk management strategies of companies facing serious failures.

Below are some tested and widely recommended actions to follow when faced with a public relations crisis (*crisis management*):

Respond quickly: Things get quickly out of hand in business crises, so a company facing an accusation or a failure should respond immediately, or as quickly as possible. Research has consistently shown that delays sway public opinion against the company, and it is more difficult to repair reputation damage after time has passed.

Accept responsibility: It is important to tell the truth and not attempt to conceal faults, or to deflect responsibility. After a crisis, image restoration becomes essential, so defensive tactics would not help. Claiming responsibility for mistakes enhances the company's damaged integrity.

Avoid laying blame and scapegoating: Similar to the above point, don't focus on finding someone to blame. Instead, focus on facts where possible. Usually crises and damage are the outcome of many individuals' actions and cannot be reduced to one person's decisions. It is more constructive to try to find the causes of the damage, not so as to punish individuals, but so as to revise the system that enabled the problem to occur in the first place.

Apologise: Victims of disasters and the public appreciate apology. An apology shows recognition and respect for people's feelings and losses, and should be an immediate response to a crisis.

Describe measures taken to remedy the situation: Apologies are empty without actions. Show that your company is taking measures to fix the problem. In cases where people have suffered loss, compensation is a measure to alleviate the situation. In cases where there is on-going damage (such as in oils spills), explain clearly how the company is taking the most appropriate actions regardless of cost.

Be constructive: Fixing a problem is important, but not enough. Show also that the company is taking long-term measures to ensure that the problem is not repeated in the future. Show foresight and the willingness to learn from mistakes.

Below are some tested and widely recommended actions that can prevent a problem from escalating into a disaster (*risk management*):

Do not downplay an identified problem: If you suspect that there is a problem somewhere that will worsen if not fixed, make this known to management. Even if you are not sure the problem is serious, it is better to work on the premise of 'better safe than sorry'. If a situation seems urgent to you as an expert, do not hesitate to communicate this urgency to decision makers. This approach can help to prevent costly and even fatal outcomes, and is the reason that pessimists generally make better risk managers than optimists.

Communicate your message to the appropriate individuals in the most effective genre and style: When communicating bad news or possible dangers to management or decision makers, make sure you present your reasons in ways that they will understand.

If you are in a management position, make sure that there are communication channels and feedback mechanisms between all ranks of employees, and that employees are made aware of these and are encouraged to use them without fear of penalty.

Consider two emails written by public relations officers and sent by customer service representatives. Both are from the cosmetics industry (names have been changed), and both convey bad news of a different kind to clients. Analysed example 5 is written by a UK-based company in response to a customer complaint about a product discontinuation. Analysed example 6 is written by a US-based company in response to a customer request to order products online and have them shipped to an international location. In addition to the techniques of apology, justification and constructive action, notice the differences in register (degree of formality). Analysed example 5 is more formal, representing the audience dynamics favoured in UK companies, whereas example 6 is more informal and direct, which is more characteristic of North American (as well as Australian and New Zealand) companies. Keep in mind that the bad news discussed in these emails is low key and does not involve issues of serious concern to the reputation of the company.

Presentations

Presentations are a staple of business communication. Their combination of physical presence with text and visuals enables the presenter to establish a relationship with his/her audience and to promote his/her aims. Presentations are a *multimodal* genre, which allows the presenter to showcase the qualities of a product, new idea or service in an appealing

Analysed example 5

Example A (UK-based cosmetics company)

Dear Ms Smith

Thank you for taking the time to email ForeverBeauty Ltd.

We are sorry to hear of your disappointment following the discontinuation of X product from the ForeverBeauty Skincare range. This particular range of products was discontinued because it did not receive the response that we have come to expect from our valued customers and for this we apologise.

In view of this I would like to recommend that you visit a ForeverBeauty Specialist at your nearest department store who will be pleased to advise on your skin care requirements on a one to one basis.

Your nearest ForeverBeauty counter can be found at (Link to Map).

In the meantime, please accept our sincere apologies for any inconvenience that you have been caused and we hope that you will continue to enjoy the benefits of ForeverBeauty products for many years to come.

With kind regards
Customer Relations
ForeverBeauty Ltd

Annotations:

Formal form of address.

Sets contexts: link with previous communication.

Apology and recognition of client's feelings.

Justification of company action and repetition of apology.

Constructive action recommended to the client to possibly remedy the situation and to assist in client's continued custom.

Repetition of apology and invitation to continue relationship.

Impersonal close.

and creative manner. They are used in countless business situations, such as presenting a business plan to potential investors, presenting the particulars of a new advertising campaign to management, presenting progress on a project or presenting the findings of an investigation – to name just a few situations.

What makes a good presentation? In the final analysis, the best way to answer this question is by attending presentations and seeing which stand out as impressive, which are competent but unexceptional and which are

Analysed example 6

Example B (US-based cosmetics company)

Dear Jim,

Thank you for your inquiry. Unfortunately, Cityscape does not ship orders internationally. In an effort to prevent identity theft, we must adhere to strict security guidelines for account verification. At this time, we are unable to verify information for international credit card accounts. Additionally, UPS has certain shipping restrictions that will not allow us to ship some of our products internationally.

We are currently looking into system options that will allow us to ship to select countries outside of the United States. However, there isn't an expected date for this. If you haven't already done so, please sign up for our Newsletter (see the link after my signature). We will be notifying our customers via the Newsletter when there's a change in this process.

Our current international locations include Canada, France, Italy, Ireland, Malaysia, Netherlands, Puerto Rico, Singapore, Spain, United Arab Emirates and the UK. We add new retail partners and locations all the time, so check back soon.

We have international retail partners that sell many of our most popular products. Click here for a current list of store locations.

We appreciate your interest in purchasing products from Cityscape. If you need any further assistance, please don't hesitate to let us know. That's what we're here for!

Thank you,

Martha

Cityscape Customer Service

Annotations:

First-person, friendly form of address.

Direct negative statement.

Detailed explanation and justification for company action.

Constructive action taken by the company to remedy the situation.

Constructive action recommended to the client that will also enable continuation of relationship.

More information on problem situation and optimistic outlook.

downright boring and confusing. You can then analyse the characteristics of each, emulate the ones that produce effective results, and avoid the ones that lead to failure, while keeping in mind that quality should be assessed according to the criteria of each industry. Being an attentive member of the audience will give you invaluable tips on being a master speaker. The following guidelines are based on tested observations and discussions with seasoned presenters.

The most common digital tools used for business presentations are currently PowerPoint, Keynote and Prezzi. All have advantages and disadvantages, and all can suffer from two common misuses caused by over-reliance. The first misuse occurs when the presenter relies on the digital tool to carry through the presentation (also known as *death by PowerPoint*). This happens when the speaker 'kills' the topic (not to mention the audience) by relying inordinately on slides. Some speakers have been known to write slides to fill an hour's talk – which can make up about 90 slides! In fact, the best way to conceptualise a presentation is as a speech genre with the digital tool as an aid in delivering this speech, a means to an end, not the end itself.

The second misuse occurs when the speaker uses the slides as transcripts and reads them out to the audience (also known as *PowerPoint karaoke*). In this case, the slides become the centrepiece of the talk, not the speaker. However, although focusing on one or two slides to analyse information is acceptable (especially if the slides contain financial data or other important graphical information), relying on the slides to carry the whole interaction is not. If you expect the audience to read a lot of data during your talk, consider giving handouts or sending out some written information before the talk, to prepare the audience. Also, for complex arguments, elaborate explanations and detailed justifications, complement presentations with written material that does not have to be read off a screen.

In order to understand the role of business presentations within the general genre of public speech consider some differences between spoken and written information:

1 **Spoken information is more difficult to retain.** This is why listeners need to take notes or be given written material to summarise, highlight and reinforce the main information presented.
2 **Attention tends to fluctuate when listening.** Distractions are more pronounced in oral communication contexts than in written. When reading, one can always reread information; when listening this is not always possible.
3 **Spoken information is coloured by the speaker's physical presence.** The speaker him/herself may be a distraction, which is why speakers

should take care to dress, speak and move in ways that complement the content of their speech, not in ways that draw attention away from it. When delivering an oral presentation take care to present a strong and confident presence (unassuming speakers tend to diminish the importance of what they are saying), with enough control over mannerisms and voice projection, so that you do not become the centre of attention (unless that is your intention), drawing attention from the content of your presentation.

4 **Speaker's presence enables clarification.** This is an advantage in speaking because listeners can ask for explanations and otherwise interact with the speaker.

At the same time, oral and written information is governed by certain similarities. In both written documents and oral presentations the following guidelines are valid:

1 **Take the audience from what they know to what they do not know.** People become involved in the interaction if the presentation begins with common ground (i.e. information that is shared between speaker and audience) and then presents the new information or findings against this background.

2 **Have an overall message sustained throughout.** A presentation is a document. Therefore, do not try to cram too much information in it, especially if it does not relate directly to the main message of the presentation. If you have a lot to say, produce different documents with a main message in each, or give a series of presentations. At the end of your talk, the audience should be able to clearly summarise what the talk was about.

3 **Establish a pattern of organisation.** Be consistent through the presentation, so that the audience can recognise your logic of organisation and follow it better. For example, if you decide to present a topic in its chronological development, sustain this throughout, or indicate and justify the point where you change. Similarly, if going from most important to least important, sustain it and do not suddenly include an important point towards the end where it is more likely to be misunderstood as a minor detail because of its position.

4 **Balance innovation with expectation.** People generally listen and read to learn something new that they can understand. Therefore, make sure your content is original enough to be compelling and interesting, and understandable enough so that the audience do not lose their way.

When designing slides or screenshots, follow these important tips:

1 **Avoid visual clutter**: include ample white space; in fact, five points or fewer on a slide is a good way to go.
2 **Avoid blaring colours and contrasts**: include informative items on your slides, and avoid irrelevant or distractive items, such as ornamental images or intense colours.
3 **Choose clearly visible fonts**: remember that readers need to be able to read your text so make it easy for them. 18 point font or larger is advisable.
4 **Take care when designing graphs:** numbers and graphs are harder to read off a slide than text, so, if you use graphs ensure that they are clearly visible.

Ordering information in presentations

What you say and how you say it depends on your purpose, audience and time limits. An analysis of these should give you the background and confidence necessary to create an effective talk that answers the audience's questions and wins them over. However, here are some general guidelines that are valid for many occasions.

1 Begin with 'bottom line' in business contexts and with hypothesis/ objectives in research contexts: this puts the audience in perspective and directs their attention – they know why it is important to listen.
2 Give only as much background as necessary: since listeners cannot retain as much information as readers, limit background details to the essential.
3 Avoid an overly linear sequence: especially in longer (one hour or more) presentations, divide your content into sections. At the end of each section, summarise briefly and introduce the next section. This is useful because listeners may get distracted and lose your thread; by including appropriate section endings and beginnings within the talk, you allow them to catch up.
4 End on a high note: the audience is more likely to remember your presentation if it ends on a strong point rather than just fading away or ending abruptly, especially if you are competing with other presenters for attention.

Activities

Here is a memo written by a software developer to the Public Relations Manager of a corporation. The memo concerns a new networking system, called Wizz, currently on trial at the corporation. The writer of the memo has made the common error of 'writing as he thinks', which means the memo lacks organisation and focus. Read the memo and make a list of the problems it has in communicating a clear message. Especially, answer these questions:

- Does the memo have a main message? If yes, summarise it.
- What is the implied event that triggered the writing of the memo? What problem is the memo concerned with?
- What action does the writer expect the reader to take after reading the memo? Is this action clearly delineated?
- What problems are there with content organisation and cohesion?
- What are some problems with style and sentence structure that contribute to the lack of clarity?

After answering these questions, write a revised version of the memo.

To: Michelle Lanier
From: David Atkinson
Date: 10 June 2013

The Wizz system is designed to help with the job of managing a large number of company stakeholders' access to the computer resources of the corporation. This includes configuring the network accounts up in the first place and removing the accounts at appropriate times. As it is currently implemented the system is very incomplete and is useful only as a way for any network administration staff to track how they have set up the computers.

We've had great input into developing what Wizz should be, but much less input at how Wizz should do this. Unless we have specific regulation on how to use to use it, unless we give users specific instructions, unless we get specific feedback on what problems there are, we won't know if Wizz is the best solution to the problem. Using someone who is not the designer of a component to implement it, is a test on the correctness of the design as it is likely to show up any short falls in it. For this reason the different approaches of a whole team of developers is valuable, based on their different interpretations or scepticism as well as their ability at solving a particular problem.

In general the Wizz software developed may be the highest quality system we have ever used. The process would work better if we had ways to get specific feedback. For this reason I don't regard the system as a total success, but feel it is a valuable experiment.

Research Methods

Focus:

- Types of research
- Types of sources
- Legal and ethical issues in using sources

In many cases, creating professional documents means finding information, assessing its relevance for your purpose, and integrating it in your text. Analysing the information that you find not only provides you with facts and usable data, but also makes you aware of the effects of different styles and writing strategies on audiences. As all good writers are by definition also good readers, text-analysis skills are essential in highlighting the structures and methods of organisation in which a writer presents ideas. Being able to understand facts, issues and arguments is fundamental for successful participation in any kind of professional activity. Correlatively, being able to critically analyse the shortcomings and ambiguities of a document assists in avoiding such problems in your own writing.

This chapter considers the role of research in business writing, and describes how information can be accessed and analysed. It begins with a description of types of research, goes on to explain how sources may be evaluated, and continues with an overview of legal and ethical concerns in using sources.

Types of research

The research process

Regardless of the type of information you require to tackle your project, five steps are essential in the data-gathering process:

1 Identify the information that you require.
2 Identify potential sources of information.
3 Decide upon appropriate search strategies.

4 Evaluate the source and content of the information that you find.
5 Use the information.

Primary and secondary research

Research is divided into *primary* and *secondary*. Primary research includes direct observation, preparing questionnaires and interviewing, undertaking fieldwork and conducting experiments. Secondary research includes the consultation of printed and electronically transmitted material. Primary research leads to the presentation of empirical data, has a more applied focus and is, therefore, generally written in an analytical and descriptive fashion. Secondary research searches for historical backgrounds, different points of view on an issue, recorded precedents of a situation and theoretical perspectives. As a result, it generally lends itself to techniques of synthesis, interpretation and evaluation.

Primary research: focus groups, interviews, user observation and surveys

Primary research consists of the knowledge you have obtained through first-hand experience. It includes research associated with laboratory experiments, market research carried out with focus groups and statistical evaluations based on responses to set questions. Here we focus on some points to consider when collecting primary data by conducting interviews.

Because work in professional contexts often means developing products and services for the market, or dealing directly with the public, the ability to detect client needs and responses is very important. An effective way to monitor client reactions to a decision or product is by means of controlled interviews. In fact, many corporations have the interviewing process built into their marketing and public relations procedures through *focus groups*. These tend to be organised at transitional periods of a product or project's development (known as the life-cycle of product development), and involve inviting a selected sample of the target audience, and discussing with them specific problems, needs and expectations. Focus groups have a *facilitator*, who asks questions and generally leads and monitors the discussion and responses.

Focus groups bring facilitator and group in a face-to-face situation that allows for more negotiation of questions and enables members of the target group to interact and respond to each other's comments. The company thus receives feedback on the value and usability of a product, on ways that would make the product more appealing and competitive, and on common complaints regarding the product's design. They can subsequently make alterations that make the product more functional and/or more attractive, and thereby increase their customer numbers. Famous examples of product change as a result of focus group feedback abound: one of these is the development of the now widespread flip top for toothpaste tubes to replace the previously common screw top, which, as focus groups revealed, used to annoy consumers.

The physical proximity that characterises the focus group situation brings into play non-verbal communication, such as body language, and conversational aspects, such as intonation, turn-taking and silence gaps, all of which contribute to the feedback received during the interaction. However, the success of the discussion depends to a large extent on the quality of the questions asked. Whether in person-to-person communication or in surveys, make the most of questions by taking the following points into account:

- Research your target audience following the guidelines given in Chapter 1. You should have a clear idea of who you are communicating to before deciding on questionnaires and methods of interviewing.
- Decide whether it is appropriate to administer the questionnaire one-to-one, in a focus group, by mail or by email.
- Decide how you are going to approach the respondents to obtain consent.
- Decide if the information will be confidential or not, and make sure respondents know too. Usually, the researchers do not include the name of respondents in any published findings; however, if they do, they may need formal consent, as in a signed release.
- Decide whether the information you seek is best obtained by open or closed questions, or a mixture of both. Open questions start with the five Ws and one H (*What? Why? Where? Who? When? How?*), and require the respondent to create a response. Closed questions give only a set number of options; the respondent ticks boxes or ranks items on a scale.
- Make sure that your questions are not ambiguous. Will your respondent understand what you are asking for?
- Make sure that each question asks for one piece of information only.
- Make the questionnaire attractive and easy to use by including headings, a clear layout and an effective sequencing of questions to enable a linear progression and prevent returning to previous questions in zigzag.

- Keep questions short, and try them out on someone first.

When conducting interviews face-to-face, or in focus groups, keep the following factors in mind:

- Allow the interviewee time to respond. Do not be afraid of silence.
- Maintain eye contact, be professional and impartial. Do not antagonise your interviewee or make personally intrusive remarks.
- Avoid leading questions (questions that presume an answer in advance, such as 'Don't you think it's true that...'? and 'wouldn't you say that...?').
- Ask easy questions first to build rapport, trust and connection between yourself and the interviewee. Ask short, impersonal and general questions first. Leave difficult or sensitive questions for the latter part of the interview.

If you are dealing with people or animals, do not launch into your research without considering the ethical consequences of your action. Will you be harming your subjects? Engaging in unethical activities? Dealing with confidential information? In many cases, you may need to submit your proposal to an ethics committee for approval before conducting primary research. In other cases, you may need to obtain releases of information, or sign confidentiality agreements.

In cases where the feedback that you wish to obtain is related to usability of equipment or tools, *user observation* is a popular method of primary research. This involves inviting a sample group of target users of the product to try out the product by following the instructions on the provided documentation. Engineers, designers and communication specialists observe the users, and note points of misunderstanding and glitches, as well as the areas where the product was used effectively without problems. They then decide if problematic areas are in design or in documentation (or a combination), and make a plan to amend and revise the product and its documentation.

If the information you require involves a large number of respondents and statistical data, *surveys* are a useful method. Table 6 shows the question categories of surveys, with examples of each category:

Table 6: Survey questions

1 An open-ended question – this allows respondents to supply their own answer with little guidance:

> Who would you like to see as the corporation's Chief Executive Officer?

2 A closed-ended question with unordered answer categories – this provides several possible answers and asks respondents to select one:

> Who would you like to see as the corporation's Chief Executive Officer?
>
> a. *Smith*
> b. *Jones*
> c. *O'Neill*
> d. *Robinson*

3 A closed-ended question with ordered answer categories – this provides several possible answers and asks respondents to rate each according to degrees of intensity:

> For each of these candidates, please indicate how much you would like that individual to be the corporation's Chief Executive Officer.
>
> | | Strongly favour | Somewhat favour | Somewhat oppose | Strongly oppose |
> |---|---|---|---|---|
> | a. *Smith* | 1 | 2 | 3 | 4 |
> | b. *Jones* | 1 | 2 | 3 | 4 |
> | c. *O'Neill* | 1 | 2 | 3 | 4 |
> | d. *Robinson* | 1 | 2 | 3 | 4 |
> | e. *Patel* | 1 | 2 | 3 | 4 |

4 A partially closed-ended question – this provides several possible answers, but also allows respondents to select a different answer if required:

> Who would you like to see as the corporation's Chief Executive Officer?
>
> a. *Smith*
> b. *Jones*
> c. *O'Neill*
> d. *Robinson*
> e. *Patel*
> f. Other (specify)

5 Ladder-scale question – this provides a scale on which respondents can rate the performance or degree of probability:

> On a scale from 0 to 10, where 0 means you rate the job the CEO is doing as extremely poor and 10 means you rate the job the CEO is doing as extremely good, how would you rate the job CEO X is doing?
>
> Extremely   Extremely
> poor   good
>
>   0   1   2   3   4   5   6   7   8   9   10

6 Lickert-scale question – this asks respondents to evaluate the likelihood of particular actions:

> How likely do you think you will be to support the election of X as the corporation's new Chief Executive Officer?
>
> a. Very likely
> b. Somewhat likely
> c. Neither likely nor unlikely
> d. Somewhat unlikely
> e. Very unlikely

7 Semantic differential question: this asks respondents to give impressionistic answers to a particular object by selecting specific positions in relation to pairs of contrastive adjectives on a scale of one to seven. The aim is to locate the meaning of the object in three dimensions: evaluation (e.g. good–bad), potency (e.g. strong–weak), and activity (e.g. active–passive). This method is useful in studying emotional reactions and attitudes and gauging the differences in outlook between cultural groups.

> How would you characterise X as the corporation's CEO?
>
> Good ——————————————————————— Bad
>
> Strong ——————————————————————— Weak
>
> Decisive ——————————————————————— Indecisive
>
> Moral ——————————————————————— Immoral
>
> Intelligent ——————————————————————— Stupid

Secondary research: print and electronic sources

Secondary research refers to the activity of obtaining information from published sources, including books, journal articles, newspaper and magazine articles, government publications, corporate publications and online journals. Different sources are valid for different subjects, and professionals know what these are by being immersed in their fields, and through experience. Strategies to help you keep up-to-date with current developments in your field include networking with relevant groups, and joining professional associations. In addition, many organisations and professional bodies require their members to regularly update their knowledge and qualifications through professional development training.

Depending on your position in a company, very often the writing you will need to do falls into two broad categories: routine documents, such as press releases and information statements (for PR and communication officers), and urgent responses, such as response to crisis. For both these categories, the first port of call is the company's databases. Companies record their history of document production, their *corporate memory*, so new employees do not have to 're-invent the wheel' by writing everything from scratch; they can recycle existing statements and phrases. In fact, many companies have databases of statements that they encourage, if not require, employees to use in their texts. For example, if you are a PR Officer or Media Liaison and there's been an accident with a company truck overturning on a highway, you will need to rapidly produce a statement informing the media and the public. The company's database will have some information on how to organise your statement in such a situation. For instance, it might say that you need to begin by specifying that this was 'an isolated incident' (if it actually was, of course), continue by describing what happened, then emphasise that there was 'no environmental damage or deaths' and end by listing the measures taken to fix this problem and prevent it from happening in the future.

Besides recorded corporate memory found in company databases and style manuals, work projects may require you to investigate specific topics and problems. Before identifying potential sources or starting any form of research, you should have a clear idea of your objectives. This comes with audience, purpose and genre analysis. Once this is done, and you have some idea of what you are looking for, adapt the following procedure according to the requirements of your topic:

Search for journals in your topic. For example, if your research is on surveillance technologies, check journals on video and photographic equipment, on new media technologies and on privacy issues. Many of these have online access, and most allow you to search inside the publications to see if they have published articles in your topic of interest.

Do a Google Scholar search using keywords associated with the topic. Google Scholar is much more likely to direct you to trustworthy, expert work, as opposed to Google standard, which will give you too many hits, most of which are not likely to be of the quality you require. When searching, use a variety of keywords associated with the topic. For example, if you are researching 'smoking', look for 'tobacco', 'nicotine', 'lung diseases', 'cigarettes', etc.

Search reference material, such as dictionaries, thesauri, encyclopedias. A considerable number of these can be found online. However, if your work consists to a large extent of writing, you will find that building a library of reference material will prove very useful for your tasks. The market abounds in dictionaries of various sorts – quotations, humour, famous speeches, clichés, etc. – and a good collection of these will often prove instrumental in helping you come up with the right idea. Reference material will also point you to the right direction even when it does not itself offer the answer to your question. The online encyclopedia *Wikipedia* (www.wikipedia.org), for example, provides information of varying quality and depth; it can, however, direct you to the sources that may be more suited to your requirements.

Do a library search. Many organisations are affiliated with research institutions and universities that have substantial libraries. Others subscribe to online database services, such as the Online Computer Library Center (OCLC), the Research Libraries Information Network (RLIN) and DIALOG, which cover a wide range of subjects and can be searched by keywords. Search library catalogues for names of experts in your topic; search databases for keywords of the topic. Databases such as *ProQuest* will give you a range of sources, while *LexisNexis* will point you to popular sources, such as newspaper articles.

Get company annual reports, government reports, newsletters and information material from institutions and corporations that are related to your topic. These are often available online, although you may need to subscribe. Even if these documents defend the interests of the issuing organisations, they can still offer valuable factual information.

Follow up articles and books that are included in the references and bibliography sections of published material.

Search press releases and news sections of corporate and governmental websites for current information and recent developments. Almost all organisations contain a page on their websites where they publicise their breaking news. This is usually called 'For Journalists' or 'Press Room', and it is where you can get press releases and information on new products. If you work in the fields of science and technology, a central source of press releases is www.eurekalert.org.

Search social media sites. Most organisations have Facebook, Twitter and YouTube sites and these have updated information on developments, products, etc. that might be useful in your project. The advantage of information found in social media sites is that it is current; the disadvantage is that it is often not well thought-out and not detailed. Social media sites will also indicate the public's response to an issue.

Contact professionals for advice on major publications and journal titles in specific fields. These professionals include academic staff in university departments, editors of key journals in your specialty, staff in research institutions and public relations representatives of relevant companies. Your networks can be very useful in research. Many professionals belong to online social networks that allow them to connect with other professionals in different fields internationally and keep up with developments in their field. For example, www.LinkedIn.com is a major social networking site for professionals.

Browse library bookshelves with the call number related to your topic. You may well serendipitously come across useful material that you would not have otherwise planned to get. Also, **browse the catalogues of publishers** that deal with your topic for recent publications.

   Clearly, sources abound. In most instances, there is a higher risk that you will suffer from information overload than from a shortage of data. The problem now becomes which sources to use and which to avoid – the topic of the next section.

Evaluating sources

In truth, there is no totally foolproof way to establish the credibility of a text. New data constantly emerge that destroy previously accepted 'truths', bias is insidious and mistakes are made. One safeguard for credibility is to ensure that the text has been accepted by the community in which it belongs, as happens, for example, with peer-reviewed material.

Peer reviewed articles have been read and approved by experts in the field prior to publication. The peer review process takes place in the following stages. First, a writer submits his or her text to the editor of a journal or a publishing company. The editor, in turn, sends it to reviewers who are familiar with the knowledge in the field. If the information provided in the text is acceptable, the reviewers recommend that the article proceed to publication. The reviewers could also recommend revisions and amendments to the text, and they could also advise that the text is not worthy of publication.

This method, however, is also inconclusive. Both Galileo's and Einstein's theories, for example, were rejected by the scientific community when they were first formulated.

In other cases, one *discourse community* (group of specialists who share the same way of writing and talking about things) may find fault with a text where another will not. This is a symptom of the diversification of knowledge and the multiplication of specialties, even within one discipline. An author may send an article to a journal, for instance, and have it criticised and rejected by reviewers. S/he may then send the same article to another journal, where it is accepted without hesitation. This shows that knowledge is regulated according to the cultural values of specific groups, who set the criteria for its assessment. Attaining expertise in a professional or scholarly field, therefore, in many ways means being accepted by the community that is formed around this field. It also means that, as a writer, you should not be discouraged by an initial cold reception to your work, but should continue looking for your 'niche'; and, as a researcher, you should be aware that publications reflect certain perspectives, and follow a particular tradition of thought.

Keeping all this in mind, when deciding whether an information source is likely to be accurate and reliable, consider the following factors:

- Has the information been peer-reviewed? This will show you at least if a community of specialists have accepted it as 'true'.
- How prestigious or credible is the information source? Publications with a reputation for impartiality and rigour would be more selective of their material.
- Does the writer give references for information cited? Are these references accurate? An article that is based on personal opinion only may make a good editorial, but it would not provide a solid basis for an objective and comprehensive assessment of an issue.
- Has the writer considered a range of information sources, or merely relied on a small number of sources? Are the information sources

themselves reliable? Writers should not only show rigour in their own thinking, but also ensure that the sources they rely on have done the same.

- What organisation does the writer belong to? What is the reputation of this organisation? Non-profit organisations may have ideological biases just as 'big business' may have financial biases, and the possibility of these biases should be taken into account when assessing the information.

- What organisation funded the research? Many funding organisations have vested or political interests in assisting certain forms of research, as opposed to others. Learn as much as you can on the values and political structure of research funding agencies.

- Did the writer conduct primary research? If so, does the writer state what kind of research was conducted and how it was conducted? Is the sample population typical or exceptional in some way? If a questionnaire was used, was it anonymous? Was the interview conducted face-to-face, by mail or by email? Are copies of the questionnaire included? The results of primary research depend strictly on the methods used.

Types of sources

Following the above discussion, and keeping in mind that the boundaries between types are not always clear-cut, I propose the following typology of sources, going from most to least authoritative. These should be seen on a continuum, with each category encompassing different levels.

A. Scholarly

Scholarly sources include academic or research-based journals, research monographs, university textbooks and anthologies of essays on academic disciplines. Most scholarly journals are published by universities or professional bodies, and scholarly books are published by publishers specialising in 'serious' work. These sources are written in language specific to their discipline (insider language, or jargon) and always cite their own sources. Writers of such sources make a conscious effort to make their assumptions explicit and to persuade the readers with logical and systematic reasoning, rather than emotive appeals or generalisations. The audience for such documents is peers and students being initiated into the conventions and language expectations of the discipline. Consequently, the style and terminology of these sources is not 'easy' or obvious for outsiders.

Scholarly sources are the most authoritative because their authors, in most cases, have a professional commitment to maintaining open debates, while acknowledging and building on previously received knowledge.

B. Specialist

Specialist sources include magazines on science, technology and social topics, and serious non-fiction, such as popular science. The aim of such documents is usually to inform a non-specialist public of technical topics in an accessible way, and thereby to publicise or popularise otherwise daunting or overly complex concepts. The intended audience of this type of source would be an educated and informed reader with no or little expertise on the topic presented, but with a commitment to gaining new knowledge, and, consequently, with a longer attention span than a reader of lower-level documents.

Authors of specialist documents often attempt to entertain as well as inform, and therefore tend to rely more strongly on analogy, metaphor and dramatisation than authors of scholarly documents. They do, however, cite sources, although the technique of integrating these in the text may be different from that in scholarly documents, which use formal referencing styles. Serious non-fiction often uses similar techniques of referencing to scholarly work. Specialist magazine articles, in contrast, name researchers and their professional positions in the body of the articles, rather than in endnotes or end-of-text references. In addition, in magazines of this type, the role of visuals becomes important, with attention being paid to aesthetics of layout and design (more on feature journalism in Chapter 5).

Specialist documents are an excellent source of information on a rather superficial level. If more depth or analysis is needed, such documents can refer you to the original, more formal sources.

C. Public

These sources include governmental, corporate and legal documents, such as public statements issued by government agencies, and corporate information, as can be found in organisational websites and public relations material. As these documents are generally addressed to the general public, the language is clear and unambiguous, and concepts are made as simple as possible. This is especially so with government and business documents since the Plain English campaign, which foregrounded reader-based aspects of communication and propounded a direct and informal approach to public writing.

Documents belonging to this category tend to assume a low attention span, and do not expand on a topic more than is necessary to get their point across. Many have a promotional edge, and, even when they are not selling a product, they support the issuing organisation's interests – as happens with press releases, for example. Public documents are usually a good source of facts (often the only source of facts about a corporation or government policy), but should always be read critically, and interpreted according to the requirements of a specific project.

This category includes (non-tabloid) local newspapers and non-specialised, general interest magazines, as they too address the general public, aiming to appeal to the low common denominator of a community's interests and sensibilities.

D. Sensationalist

Sensationalist sources base their information on rumour, fabrication or exaggeration, rather than on any form of empirical or interpretative research, and are, therefore, the least credible type. In fact, they do not merit to be classified as sources of research at all, unless you use them as examples of the distortion of information in the popularisation of knowledge. Many popular magazines and newspapers fall into this category, especially the ones that appeal to thrill and sensation as opposed to any form of truth or reflection. These sources should be avoided in business writing, unless your aim is to analyse the way they use language.

The Internet

Today information on any subject can be retrieved in a wide variety of formats and through a range of channels. The plethora of information can make it difficult for researchers or investigators to decide on which sources to use. The temptation for many is to automatically search the Internet. Although this can be productive, be cautious to avoid potential problems.

It is difficult to estimate how much information, and how many documents are available through the Internet at any one time. Whatever number people might estimate, one minute after the estimation there will be more. The size of the Internet in terms of the amount of information contained is one of the factors that, while making it a strong support for learning, can also limit its potential. Sometimes there is just too much information to be found, which makes assessing the credibility of information difficult, and can also be extremely time consuming.

Those who received primary and secondary education before the 1990s are accustomed to consulting (and trusting) textbooks and encyclopedias for facts about specific events. This attitude is now being seriously challenged by the quantity and quality of information on the Internet. If you do an Internet search for the answers to seemingly straightforward factual questions such as 'Who invented the microscope?' and 'In what year was the telescope invented?' you may come up with some surprises. You will probably find a range of names and dates offered as the right answer, depending on such factors as different definitions, different methodologies of research, different interpretations of events – even personal preference! This suggests that, because of its lack of control over what is published, the Internet is not always a reliable source of information – but it can certainly give you alternative views and different sides to an issue that you may wish to investigate further.

One way to avoid such problems is by recognising that the Internet, besides being a source, is, in fact, a medium. This means that although sources of information may be transmitted through the Internet, they can still be evaluated with reference to the typology proposed earlier, like print sources. The presence of 'walled gardens' on the Internet is a case in point. For example, many sites are encrypted, and require a special password to access the information they contain. An example of this is digital libraries, which require subscription for access. In fact, many digital libraries from scholarly institutions or reputable publishers have valuable resources online, but limit their access to subscribers or members.

Many scholarly and specialist journals offer the option to access materials both online and in print. This is the case, for instance, with many business publications, such as *The Economist* (http://www.economist.com/) and *Time* (http://www.time.com/time/magazine), as well as popular science publications *New Scientist* (www.newscientist.com) and *Scientific American* (www.sciam.com), which have both online and print versions. An interesting additional element to using the Internet as a medium in such cases is the option to open articles to discussion and comment. In fact, often writers of articles enter the interactive discussion to offer clarifications on points they have made in their articles and to respond to reader feedback.

Similarly, broadcast companies transmit news stories online as well as through the older media of radio and television (see, for example, www.bbc.com and www.cnn.com). Finally, government agencies and corporations publish information on their policies and products online, and these can be very useful when you search for facts and figures and for contacts from whom to obtain more details.

Other Internet sources include:

Blogs and wikis: these are popular online forums for discussion and collaboration. Easily designed with authoring tools that can be downloaded from sites such as www.blogger.com, blogs enable users to interact in real-time to exchange ideas and opinions, or to produce collaborative documents where all writers contribute and can edit each others' work. Blogs can be very productive in their interactive and collaborative function. However, they should not be used as the sole or main source of information because their informality and experimental nature generally does not lead to definite information, but, rather, to work in progress, or to directions that need more exploring through other means.

Blogs (originally weblogs) are authored by individuals or groups, and have a serial nature, offering commentary on a particular topic. The credibility of this commentary, as in other media, depends on the reputation and expertise of the blogger. In contrast, wikis are not serial, but collaborative. Some wikis are open and some are closed. However, wikis generally allow the community to add, edit and restructure contents. High-quality wikis have communities of volunteers to continually check and edit content to ensure credibility. They generally also attribute edits and changes to particular individuals, and may also include a change history with comments and discussion showing the rationale of the changes. Wikipedia is an example of this.

Discussion groups: you can find discussion groups on practically any topic imaginable. These can be useful in exchanging information with similar-interest peers, who may direct you to the information you need for a project. At the same time, remember that, however insightful the information you obtain may be, it does not represent all the input the topic can generate and requires careful scrutiny and balance with material from other sources. For straightforward topics, discussion groups can be useful in encouraging and documenting questions and answers. Also, in finding the answer to a query about a narrow topic, discussion groups may be the best resource.

Personal websites: these are the least credible of Internet sources, and could, in fact, be placed in the sensationalist category. The Internet's decentralised and open structure allows anyone with server space and minimal technical knowledge to set up a site and post whatever they want on it, so the best advice is to avoid personal websites altogether for research purposes (unless personal websites are the topic of your research).

Table 7 lists some questions to ask when deciding if an Internet source is credible.

Table 7: Checklist for evaluating Internet sources

1 Is the information presented on the site comprehensive and unbiased? Does it describe clearly where the information came from and what its purpose is? Sites that present opinions based on personal experience or belief should be avoided when credible data are required.

2 What is the style and quality of writing of the site? No organisation that takes itself seriously would condone sloppy or ungrammatical writing, so if you find this in the site, be careful. As with other types of written communication, the text of a site should use the terminology and style that are recognised and used by its target audience.

3 Does the site clearly state its purpose? Sites whose purpose is ambiguous or hard to find, may be of dubious value.

4 Does the site include author's name and affiliation? Does the author have credentials in the field that he/she is writing? Suspect anonymous sites (unless they are sponsored by a well-known organisation).

5 Does the site include a date of updating? Like with all publications, the date that the information was last reviewed is vital in assessing its reliability.

6 Does the site have links to other sites and/or references to other sources? What is the value and reputation of these other sources? Links function like references in printed texts, allowing the reader to obtain further information or different points of view on a topic. A site that is self-sufficient is more likely to be based on personal, unsupported, opinion.

Searching the Internet

Search engines

Currently, there are more than 100 search engines that can be used to locate information on the Internet. An important feature of search engines is their increasingly commercial nature. For example, many engines will place prominently paid advertisements related to a search, according to criteria set by advertisers. Advertisements should be distinguished from search results, and some engines make this difficult. Also, some engines are suspected of reducing or eliminating search results for products or services that compete with those owned by the search engine company. Finally, some search engines censor results to appease political authorities in some countries.

Another important issue is that many websites actually exist for the sole purpose of being found in search results. These often have many words that people might search for, and contain advertisements or links to other sites. Some of these sites promise their content only to those who register with an e-mail address, which then leads to spam advertising messages.

Therefore, choosing the right search engine can mean the difference between finding a lot of useful information and a lot of useless information. Users should have some awareness of the qualities of the different engines so that they can choose the one that best meets their needs.

Searching Tips

The following tips are generally valid for many search engines and searching activities on the Internet.

1 **Use multiple words**: You will get more refined results from several words than from a single word. For example, 'Detective Sherlock Holmes' will yield more relevant results than 'Sherlock Holmes' or 'detectives'.
2 **Use similar words**: The more similar words you use in a search, the more results you will get back; for example, 'restaurant, cafe, bistro'.
3 **Capitalise when appropriate**: Capitalise proper nouns. Capitalised names that are adjacent are generally treated as a single name and not as two separate words.
4 **Use quotation marks to set off phrases**: Use quotation marks to find words that are part of a set phrase; for example, 'deep blue sea'. Otherwise, you may get pages that include the word 'deep', the word 'blue' and the word 'sea'.

Copyright and plagiarism

The general context

When thinking about research, the terms *copyright* and *plagiarism* come to mind. Plagiarism means copying or in some way reproducing someone else's work without giving them credit or acknowledgement. In many ways, it is a form of stealing – consistent with the etymological root of 'plagiarism', which in Latin means 'kidnapping'. In our era of collaborative writing and digital remix, however, things are not as simple as they sound. It is sometimes unclear where the boundaries between one's own and someone else's work lie. This section attempts to shed light on some pertinent issues.

Using another's work without permission and/or credit signals one of three different situations: *copyright breach, plagiarism* or *invasion of privacy* (Leval 1990; Branscum 1991; Howard 2003).

Copyright is a legal issue. If you use without permission work that has been published in a tangible medium or patented, you breach copyright and are liable to, often very costly, lawsuits. Any item that has been formally published or registered with a recognised organisation is protected by copyright law, and this includes Internet sources. Copyright law originated in England to protect the printing trade. Since then, it has become part of a set of laws, together with *patent law* and *trademark law*, that regulate *Intellectual Property* (IP). Copyrighted items include scientific articles, novels and other literary works; drawings, paintings, photographs, films and other audiovisual work; musical compositions; and software. As copyright laws tend to change regularly, it is always advisable to check the copyright status of an item you want to use (www.rightsdirect.com). To complicate matters further, copyright is regulated by the laws of each country, although there are some general international principles. For instance, more than 160 countries have signed the Berne Convention, administered by the World Intellectual Property Organization (WIPO), which sets some basic standards for copyright protection.

Copyright expires after a certain amount of time, when the work becomes part of the *public domain*. Countries set a different timeline for this, but a generally accepted principle is that for works created after 1977, the term of copyright protection is the life of the author with 70 additional years for individuals (known as 'life plus 70') and 95 years for corporate authors (http://www.wipo.int/treaties/en/ip/berne/index.html).

Copyright law was designed to protect the rights of producers of literary and artistic artefacts. After all, these individuals make a living from their products, and these products should be protected to encourage their producers to continue creating. However, public access to such artefacts also needs legal protection, so *fair use* or *fair dealing* was created as an amendment to copyright law. This entails using a part of a work for purposes that benefit the public good, such as education. According to 'fair use' or 'fair dealing', you may use another's work without permission if:

- you are using only a fraction (usually 10 per cent) and not the complete item
- you give credit to the original source
- the item has been published, and is, therefore, not private
  the purpose is educational
- your use of the material will not affect the market value of the original.

Many government documents are considered public property (government employees are paid from taxes), and are not copyrighted. This does not mean to say, however, that you can copy material from them without citing the source – this would be *plagiarism*, even though it is not copyright breach.

If you reproduce a work or part of a work without acknowledging the original creator, and present it as being your own, you are plagiarising, even in cases when the work is not copyrighted and is in the public domain. For example, Shakespeare's work is now in the public domain; however, if you copy a part of it and present it as your own, you are plagiarising the work, even if you are not liable to legal action for doing so. With plagiarism we leave the domain of law and enter the domain of ethics.

Copyright protects only the tangible expression of an idea – not the idea itself. In contrast, plagiarism regulations cover the unacknowledged reproduction of the idea itself. Knowledge and ideas are academic and artistic currency: through the exchange of ideas, the academic and artistic communities sustain themselves and contribute to the well-being of society as a whole. Individual scholars and artists produce and publish ideas for their livelihood, and any unacknowledged use of their hard work is both injury and insult. This accounts for the heavy penalties universities impose on students convicted of plagiarism; although legal sanctions may not apply if the work is not copyrighted, the ethical violation carries an equally serious consequence – exclusion (temporary or permanent) from the community.

Plagiarism can be avoided by:

- summarising: expressing in your own words the gist of a document, and citing the source
- paraphrasing: expressing in your own words the gist of a part of an idea, and citing the source
- quoting: copying the exact words of a section of the original document, putting them in quotation marks to set them off from your own words and citing the source. A rule of thumb is to quote if you copy more than four words in a row from a text.

All ideas taken from other texts need referencing. The only exception is *common knowledge*. Common knowledge consists of propositions and statements that did not originate with the writer (or speaker), but that are accepted facts in the wider community. Examples include such propositions as 'Rome is the capital of Italy', 'The Sun is a star' and 'two plus two equals four'. This, however, is not always so straightforward, because knowledge, in many cases, depends on the community in which it is used. A proposition that may be considered common knowledge among quantum physicists, for example, may not be so among another group. This is why, as with other aspects of writing, analysing your audience and purpose will point you to the right direction on ways to integrate knowledge in your document, and on when to cite a source. The rule of thumb, though, is that when in doubt, always cite.

Finally, when using another's work you may also be *invading their privacy* – a legally sanctioned offence. This generally occurs when you publicise information that the originator kept personal or private. If you publish your roommate's journal on the Internet, for example, you are infringing on their privacy. If you publish the journal and present it as your own, you are also plagiarising! In professional contexts, privacy issues often arise with email and Internet use. It is contestable if a manager has the right to 'spy' on employees' email exchanges and the sites they visit on the Internet. For some, the manager does have this right, since the employees are using computers, Internet provision and time supplied by the company. For others, email is private if it is not exchanged for professional purposes, and should not be accessed by employers, even if the employee exchanges it during work hours. The debate continues on such issues.

Plagiarism and copyright in business contexts

As the last example shows, the professional world presents a challenge to conventions regarding plagiarism and privacy. One reason for this is that the IP of a company can be used in different ways by employees. Since companies have the legal status of persons, they can own IP, and this can be used in different texts produced by the company. Employees who write material that finds its way into recorded corporate memory generally do not have ownership of this material. In fact, in many instances, new recruits sign contracts releasing all the work they produce to the company, which then becomes the sole copyright owner.

One example of text that is considered common property within a company is *boilerplate text* – standardised writing that can be reproduced verbatim, or with minor alterations, for different audiences and documents. For instance, letters sent to clients to inform them of company developments or changes work on the boilerplate model – all recipients get basically the same letter, with only the opening address differing. Similarly, a lab whose members often apply for funding may have a set description of the lab and its operations, which individual members must use, unchanged, in their proposals. In such cases, the individual whose name appears on the document is not the same as the one who wrote a section of the document. This is accepted practice in business and is not considered plagiarism in this context.

Public relations documents are also often anonymous, attributed to anyone who may be a PR officer at a particular time, or written by someone other than the person whose name appears on the document. For instance, corporate websites and promotional material, such as brochures, often contain segments written by different individuals, and they can be updated by rewriting some sections, reorganising information by cutting and pasting from different sections, etc. – all without acknowledging the original source. Press releases contain the name of a media relations officer from whom the press can obtain more information, but this does not mean the release was written by that person. Furthermore, speeches and articles of Chief Executive Officers (CEOs), and other senior personnel, are, more often than not, written by the company's professional writers, but presented as the CEO's own words. The original writer in these cases has nothing to show but financial reward and secret pride!

In the corporate world, the company takes precedence over the individual in matters of production. This is acknowledged as business convention, so the CEO who puts his/her name on an article written by his/her writers is not morally or legally reprehensible. In such instances, the corporation is seen as a body ('body' being, in fact, the etymology of 'corporation'), and acting as an individual. Stepping outside the boundaries of a company, however, would transgress this convention. If a writer of company *X*, for example, uses material that a writer of company *Y* wrote, s/he is plagiarising, not to mention breaching copyright, if the work was published. Similarly, circulating published material, such as news stories or scientific articles, among members of a project team constitutes copyright breach, regardless of the fact that the material does not leave the company confines. In such cases, permission should be sought from the copyright owners to distribute the material, or, alternatively, the distributor should send out the link or reference to the article for each team member to access individually.

On-going writing projects in business contexts are generally open to rewriting, and, therefore, have many writers, who most often remain anonymous, or have a group or position title. These projects include style manuals, which are regularly updated and changed. It should be noted that this situation is not unique to companies. The creative industries have similar methods. For example, a Hollywood film can have several writers, and the final product shown on screen could be the result of a rewrite done by someone who had no contact with the writer of the first version.

However, some business documents, especially those that involve major finalisable projects, follow rules akin to those of academic contexts. For example, proposals to management for funding and/or approval of a project always include writers' names, and so do reports describing the results of an investigation. The accountability involved in such writing makes it necessary to frame the writing in more personal terms and associate it with its actual author. Accordingly, in such reports, the writers also are expected to cite their sources of information, and to quote, summarise and paraphrase as appropriate. In such situations, the rules of referencing apply, both for sources within the document and for the document itself when used as a source.

Besides giving credit where it is due, citing sources, in both professional and academic contexts, enhances a writer's accountability. As a researcher and problem solver, refer to sources to:

- show you have consulted relevant material and can advise authoritatively
- support your findings and recommendations by linking them with independent data
- enable readers to follow up material for more information.

Activities

1 Watch or listen to a television or radio interview, and notice how it was conducted. How did the interview compare with the guidelines given in this chapter? How would a different approach have produced other results? Write a short report with the results of your investigation.
2 Discuss the ways that you could use the following sources of information in a formal business report. Decide what other sources you would need to consult to complement these.

   1 A university textbook on software engineering.
   2 A report on smoking published by an anti-smoking organisation.
   3 A *Discovery Channel* documentary.
   4 An article on cosmetic surgery published in *Vogue*.
   5 Information on cosmetic surgery published on a plastic surgeon's website.
   6 An article on globalisation written by a left wing radical.
   7 Data published on an academic's personal web page in a university's website.
   8 A website set up by a special interest community group emphasising the dangers of genetically modified foods.
   9 A press release published on a major corporation's website.
   10 An interview with a scientist published in *Nature*.

Business and Technology Journalism

Focus:

- Types of journalism
- Journalistic style
- Feature articles

The ability to develop new products, invent new methods for doing things or discover how the universe works requires also the ability to communicate your results to various groups for support, funding or publicity. In such cases, your audience could comprise people who may not have the same level of technical knowledge as you, but who may have an interest, financial or social, to learn about your findings. This chapter looks at techniques that will assist you to write an appealing and informative article for a specialist magazine or company newsletter. It also describes in more detail the features of journalistic writing, which were introduced in Chapter 2 and will be developed further when discussing writing for the public in Chapter 6.

As opposed to other kinds of journalistic writing that address the wide public or the general consumer, high-level specialist journalism addresses an audience that is more versed in subject-specific terminology and that is more motivated in acquiring the information presented. Business journalists, for example, present more detailed and accurate information than advertisers.

In advertising jargon, the language directed to the general consumer is *marketese*: direct selling in a sensational and highly emotive tone – the language of television commercial scripts and popular consumer magazine advertisements. Because it addresses the wider public, or the consumer in general, marketese lacks specificity and is characterised instead by frequent use of generalities focused on highlighting the benefits of a product for the lowest common denominator of the population. In contrast, high-quality business and technology journalism uses language with a strong informative content, which not only entertains, but also educates. The targeted audience are those who know what their specific needs are, and who can communicate in the jargon of the industry – at least on a basic level.

Another reason for including this chapter is the diversification of the contemporary job market. Professionals may occupy a range of different roles in their careers, some of which may involve communicating with the public. Also, the development of freelance journalism, spurred mainly by the proliferation of online venues, provides opportunities to business professionals and experts in technical and scientific fields to popularise their skills and knowledge to a wider audience – and increase their income sources at the same time!

A journalism primer

Types of articles

Journalists divide news into hard and soft varieties. *Hard news* is the information that readers need to know: the 'breaking' or 'hot off the press' news of events that happen suddenly and affect a great number of people or a whole community. Hard news is ephemeral. Although the information presented may have serious and long lasting consequences, the actual news itself becomes outdated quite rapidly. Examples of hard news are reports of war outbreaks, earthquakes or stock market changes. *Soft news*, on the other hand, is the kind of information that people want to hear and its relevance or popularity does not disappear as rapidly as that of hard news. Examples include technological developments, profiles of leaders and fashion research (see also Hay 1990; Garrison 2004; Batty and Cain 2010).

Below are some major journalistic genres, found in most specialist magazines:

Editorial

This is an opinion article written by the editor(s), dealing with a current news topic, usually one that is covered at more length later in the issue. Depending on the publication, editorials can be provocative and/or strongly opinionated, with a 'call to arms' approach intended to increase awareness of an issue. In more formal journals, editorials introduce the theme of the issue and briefly present each of the contributors' articles.

News stories

These present the facts in current events and developments. News stories are generally not long – a one-page story would be long; most news stories take up a quarter to half a page. They describe the facts in the event by following the five W's and one H questions (what, where, when, who, why and how). News stories follow the 'inverted pyramid' format of organisation, and in business and technology journalism they are largely based on press releases.

Features

These articles elaborate on topics that may have been news stories weeks or months before. They describe the topic in terms of its history, constituent parts, applications, relevant people, possible benefits and/or dangers. They come in different lengths, and are based on secondary research as well as primary research, such as interviews. The cover story of the magazine is a feature, usually located close to the centre of the publication.

Opinion articles

An issue of a magazine may have two or three opinion articles of different lengths, scattered throughout the issue. These present an analysis of a topic in terms of the argument(s) it generates. In some cases, a slot where an opinion article appears (a *column*) becomes associated with a particular writer and his/her style (the *columnist*). In other cases, opinion articles are written by scholars who specialise on the topic, and who can, therefore, present an expert opinion.

Interviews

The usual format for this genre is question and answer. These articles focus on an individual's contribution to a topic, and present this topic through the direct words of that individual, spurred by the writer's questions.

Profiles

These articles balance information on a topic with a personal narrative of a key individual associated with the topic. They are similar to interviews in some ways, since, if the profile is of a living person, they are largely based on an interview with that person, with additional or background information from secondary sources.

Reviews

These articles describe and comment on the quality and innovation of a book, film or game. They often compare their object of analysis with others in the field, showing its advantages and drawbacks. For writers, producers and developers, getting a favourable review in a reputable publication is a much-desired achievement.

Layout considerations and page design

Magazine layout is pivotal in editorial decisions about length and presentation of articles. Magazines have a set layout, which determines content choices – not the other way around. In other words, a magazine will not change its layout and the space it assigns to each type of article to accommodate a particular article, no matter how interesting or how important this article may be. The article will be edited and formatted in the magazine's standard manner. This is analogous to buying furniture. It is unlikely that you would demolish walls and restructure the building to fit particular pieces of furniture. It is much more likely that you would measure the space you have and then buy furniture to fit that space. Printing is costly, and changes to templates make it even costlier.

The following are the main layout considerations:

- **Space**: word limits are required for each article in relation to the space allotted for the article in the magazine template layout.
- **Paragraph length**: magazine articles generally have shorter paragraphs than reports or essays. Paragraphs would need to be even shorter if printed in columns (more on this below).
- **Visuals**: some articles are graphic-intensive and others are more verbal. In general, visuals effectively complement documents written in journalistic style. Visuals are chosen to convey the meaning more accurately to target audiences, and are designed with the target audience's assumed needs and expectations in mind.
- **Sections and headings** (*crossheads* in journalistic jargon): space determines sectioning. Crossheads are used, generally, in longer articles as a form of signposting to direct readers' attention. They are also effective in cutting down on transitional sentences and paragraphs and are used when brevity is required. For example, a sentence or even a paragraph can be deleted if space requires it and its content summarised in a phrase that becomes a section heading. As regards organising content into sections, the general rule for journalistic articles is that they are *top-heavy*, that is, they place important and/or catchy information at the beginning.

Page design is divided into four aspects: proximity, alignment, repetition and contrast.

Proximity

This refers to the spatial layout that displays related objects. For example, you should leave more space before a heading than after it. Headings belong to the text that follows them and should be closer to that text. Also, photos and captions should relate to each other and come close to the relevant text. Different elements should be separated by space to create a hierarchy of information.

Alignment

This refers to the horizontal and vertical elements on the page placed in balanced positions in relation to each other – as opposed to thrown together at random. For example, keep unity on a page by aligning every object with the edge of some other object. In a table, for instance, you could align the objects on the left with the left edge of the page, and the objects on the right with the right edge of the page.

Repetition

This refers to repeating elements that tie different sections together. Bullet points, colours and typefaces can be repeated to provide visual impact and help the reader recognise and scan through the pages quickly and easily. By repeating certain elements, you reinforce the uniqueness, or personality, of a publication, as readers become aware of the characteristic motif of the publication – a bit like a signature.

Contrast

The opposite of repetition, contrast refers to putting together elements that are different and thus creating a visual impression on the reader. The use of contrasting elements acts as an information hierarchy and increases scanning ability. Contrast adds a dimension to the page, introduces an element of surprise and shows that it has depth and variety. Contrast can be used in colours, fonts and direction. To create an effective and impressive publication, balance repetition and contrast.

Here is some terminology that journalists use to talk about layout of articles and pages:

Title is used for all articles except news stories; headline is used for news stories. Titles can be creative and cryptic; headlines are not: they are structured in sentence form, present tense, leaving out articles (a, an, the). For example, a title could be Swept Away (an actual feature article in *New Scientist* on tsunami); a headline could be Largest Tsunami Ever Recorded Hits Country.

Pullquote is text pulled out of the article and used as a highlighting device – the pullquotes of an article should themselves tell a story (i.e. summarise the main points of the article).

Subhead is the text that comes under the title and is used to give more information on the article's topic. Subheads are useful when the title is too enigmatic and needs explanation.

Crosshead is the journalistic term for 'heading' (see above).

Caption is the text that accompanies a visual.

Organisation of content

Paragraphing

The purpose of paragraphs and sections is to divide and prioritise information into meaningful chunks. This helps to highlight points and issues and to encourage a sense of sequence and development. Bear in mind that people assimilate and commit to memory 'chunks' of information that comprise between about five and seven items. This should guide your paragraphing style, especially in journalistic documents where a direct and conversational approach is favoured.

Magazine article paragraphs tend to be short, often running to two or three sentences. Most magazine articles are printed in columns: a short paragraph will look longer in a narrow column format than it would if spread across the page. Even one-sentence paragraphs are acceptable in articles as long as they do not run in succession. Like short sentences, short paragraphs have a more intense effect than long ones because they concentrate meaning in a few words that stand out from the rest of the text. This is why in magazine articles one-sentence paragraphs are often placed at strategic places to provide a striking effect.

Also, magazines tend to work on the assumption that the reader will have a relatively short concentration span and may not necessarily want to follow an item in detail. In many cases, magazines are read at hours of leisure, coffee and lunch breaks, while riding the bus, etc. Writers, therefore, cannot assume that the reader will invest the time and attention necessary to absorb a complex document. Accordingly, the writer has to present the information succinctly and directly without elaboration and in-depth analysis. The tone should have a conversational impact rather than conceptual density. Finally, magazine articles also compete for attention. As opposed to a formally commissioned report, which can assume that the reader has a vested interest to read it closely, a magazine article often needs to grab the reader's wandering eye. In this situation, having long paragraphs would be daunting and discouraging.

Organisation of information

The order in which information is presented in a text is a strategic device providing the writer with the means to craft information so as to produce the most desired effect. In feature articles, the beginning is very important, so put there information that is likely to attract the readers' attention and not put them off. If your readers are non-specialists, avoid densely technical jargon in the beginning of the article. For example, anslysed example 7 on Botox is objectively informative and balanced. However, it avoids emphasising the technical aspects of the drug and discouraging the reader, by describing them towards the end of the article and placing them in an appropriate context.

Journalistic style revisited

Chapter 2 looked at style in terms of sentence structure. Here we revisit it in terms of content. Business and technology journalism makes unfamiliar concepts and developments familiar, by presenting information that is clearly relevant to readers, in a creative and zesty way. This involves skills of analysis and synthesis: of combining innovation and the new in a framework that also contains assumed shared knowledge between writer and readers. When popularising your topic, choose language and techniques that are:

Factual: Give as much factual information as possible, while avoiding a 'dry' tone. Use the five Ws and one H questions to guide you.

Rational: The business reader is usually interested in making an evaluative judgment. Therefore, rational descriptions of an economic, technological or business nature are best. Emotional appeals may fall flat unless they are supported by a rational basis.

Specific: Give specific examples where possible. People love to read about other people, so include quotations, success examples and testimonials. Also, describe experimental data where possible to provide some evidence for your statements.

Technical: While avoiding tediously technical jargon that may alienate the more uninformed readers, use the jargon and dominant metaphors of the industry that you represent. Business and technology journalism is *cult* writing: it should be both innovative and popular. Show that you can speak as an *insider* who knows the concerns, strengths and needs of the industry, and with whom your readers can identify as 'one of us'.

Analysed example 7

In the Quest for Youth: Understanding Botox®

In the battle against aging, Botox® has emerged as the world's favourite weapon to fight wrinkles and fine lines. Botox users are rumoured to include celebrities such as American former presidential candidate John Kerry and pop Diva Madonna – among thousands. But what exactly is this Botox®? How does it work? And are there side effects that need to be considered before selecting this method for regaining a youthful appearance?

Botox® is an easy and affordable treatment. In fact it is nicknamed the 'lunch-hour face-lift,' because it is a simple injection costing on average US$400 and taking 10 minutes – very different from the traditional 'face-lift,' a major and expensive plastic surgery which requires the patient to undergo anesthesia, long-recovery time, and potential scarring. However, unlike plastic surgery, in order to maintain wrinkles at bay with Botox®, treatments need to be repeated every 4–6 months.

Botox® is Allergen Inc.'s trade name for botulism toxin type A, a neurotoxin produced by the bacterium *Clostridium botulinum*. Botulism toxins, of which there are seven distinct types, attach to nerve endings and reduce the release of acetylcholine, the neurotransmitter responsible for generating muscle contractions – and resulting wrinkles. Cosmetic Botox® injections are a diluted form of this neurotoxin, and work by temporarily relaxing the muscles into which they are injected.

In the 1950s, researchers discovered that injections of botulism toxin type A into overactive muscles decreased muscle activity for 4–6 months. However, it was only in the 1980s that ophthalmologist Alan Scott discovered that the toxin could be used to treat blepharospasm, an

Sets the scene

Highlights popularity of product

Introduces the article by indicating its sections in the form of questions to be answered

Description of product showing user benefits. Last sentence acknowledges limitation.

Simple scientific description of the Botox process

eye muscle disorder characterized by uncontrollable contractions. Allergen Inc., then a small pharmaceutical company specializing in eye therapies, bought the rights to the product in 1988. The drug was renamed Botox®. Further clinical trials continued and in April of 2002, Botox® was approved for cosmetic treatments, including temporarily eliminating wrinkles, facial lines caused by excessive muscle contraction.

History of the product, linking it with research and experimentation

Botox® is generally considered safe by medical authorities, and has been approved by several international drug authorities. However, side effects are possible, although all known ones are temporary, and no cases have been documented of systemic complications. Clinical trials reveal that the most statistically significant side effect, observed in 3.2% of patients treated with Botox® versus 0.0% placebo, is blepharoptosis, or 'droopy eyelid,' which results from either injection of too much toxin or injection into the wrong facial area causing paralysis of eyelid muscles. Other common side effects include headache, respiratory infection, nausea, and redness at the injection site. In the US, the Food and Drug Administration (FDA) also recently issued a warning against popular 'Botox® parties,' at which patients combine Botox® with alcohol in a non-medical setting. This may be dangerous for two reasons: 1) alcohol thins the blood, allowing it to more easily pass into the skin, increasing bruising, 2) since, as with all medical interventions, complications are possible, the patient needs to be at a location equipped to handle an emergency.

Introduces side effects; emphasises their low risk.

Objectively lists side effects.

Focuses on one possible problem in using the product and explains it in more depth.

Ends on a high note, suggesting the future looks good for the product.

Today, Botox® is used in over 70 countries, and the popularity of the treatment is growing. Clinical trials continue, and novel uses for Botox® are emerging for controlling side effects.

The following article compares two (fictional) operating systems: the commercial OpenEye and the open source Salter. The first version of the article is a draft where the writer describes plainly the pieces of information that will make up the final. The second version is an example of how a plain listing of facts can be 'spiced up' to produce the creative and energetic style characteristic of 'insider' technology journalism. The target audience is IT enthusiasts.

Version A: Draft

OpenEye vs Salter

For the last few years, OpenEye has been the strongest company in the computer operating system market. This has been because of a lack of real alternatives, but now OpenEye is being challenged by Salter. This system was created by Mark Salter and it is becoming famous. It is based on the source code of an older system, called Marcus. OpenEye beat Marcus, but now Marcus is getting stronger by making another system very similar to it on a basic level. It is cheaper than OpenEye and also has some qualities that OpenEye does not have.

First, Salter costs very little. Its only expenditure is in the side effects of its implementation. It was made this way in order for users to continue developing it as they are using it. On the other hand, OpenEye costs about $700 to start with, and would require much more money if used as an investment.

Second, Salter is faster than OpenEye and it has more functions. Because Salter has been built by engineers all over the world in an open format, it has a variety of functions. For example, it is very easy to network using Salter and this is a serious consideration for IT experts.

The drawback for Salter is that, like Marcus, its predecessor, it is difficult to use. Only specialists with considerable expertise can understand its use, since it uses many of the same commands as Marcus. Also, as Salter was made to run from a command line based shell interface, it is not as visually impressive as OpenEye. OpenEye, on the other hand, uses a graphical user interface, or GUI, as its method of control, which is easy for non-experts to use.

In conclusion, OpenEye is easier and is visually more pleasing than Salter. Salter, on the other hand, is more advanced and gives expert users the satisfaction of control. Increasingly, it is overcoming its weaknesses and becoming more and more competitive for OpenEye.

Version B: Revision

OpenEye vs Salter – The contest

For the last few years, OpenEye has dominated the computer operating system market. This has been because of a lack of real alternatives, but times are changing and the OpenEye empire may be brought to its knees by a man called Mark Salter. Salter has developed an operating system that has gained mention worldwide. And the name of the new heavyweight? You guessed it – Salter.

Salter was developed from the source code of an older system called Marcus. OpenEye has ruled supremely ever since it overthrew Marcus, but now Marcus is making a comeback with a clone of itself. But why would OpenEye have cause to be afraid? After all, it has already defeated Marcus once. What does Salter have to offer that OpenEye does not?

First in most people's minds is the question of price. How much is this going to cost to implement? Salter has the perfect answer to this question - nothing! Well almost nothing. There is always going to be some outlay when implementing a new operating system, but Salter takes a long step forward by offering itself for free. Salter was made so that it would be openly available to everyone, thus making it possible for anyone to help develop the system. With this in mind, most applications and other such software are available for free on the Internet, which is more than can be said for the popular OpenEye system. Not only are you looking at a large outlay for the initial purchase of the product, which starts at around US$700, but you could be looking at thousands of dollars being invested in software titles.

A determining factor in whether or not an operating system will be successful, is likely to be the expertise required to use it. This is where Marcus lost out to OpenEye. While Marcus was and still is a more powerful operating system, it required a highly skilled technician to run it. Like Marcus, Salter was originally made to be run from a command line based shell interface, and so it lacks the lustre of the beautiful graphical interface that OpenEye provides. At first glance, Salter even looks like Marcus as it uses many of the same commands and thus is almost as difficult to use. OpenEye, on the other hand, uses a graphical user interface or GUI, as its method of control. This means that almost anyone can use it, and it provides a great introduction to the world of computers for complete novices.

There is no debate as to which system is faster. Salter is light years ahead of OpenEye as far as speed goes. Functionality? Salter wins the race hands down. Because Salter has been built by engineers all over the world in such an open format, there is almost nothing it cannot do. Networking is a breeze, and anyone in an IT position would have to seriously consider Salter over OpenEye. While OpenEye may be more aesthetically pleasing and simpler to use, it does not have the same degree of mastery that Salter has when it comes to making the computer do what you want it to. The fact remains that until Salter becomes easier to use, OpenEye will still be the juggernaut. But Salter continues to grow in strength, and so the war rages on.

Accuracy in journalism

As a scientist or technical professional, you are faced with a dilemma when popularising a complex concept: how accurate can you be while also avoiding jargon, equations and formulas? How appealing and entertaining can you make your article without betraying the complexity and seriousness of your topic? By creating a light-hearted approach will you not also be sacrificing depth? In short, will you be misleading your readers into thinking there is an absolute truth where in fact there are only conjectures and hypotheses? Such doubts have plagued science writers for a long time. Einstein, for example, described this situation quite neatly in 1948:

> Anyone who has ever tried to present a rather abstract scientific subject in a popular manner knows the great difficulties of such an attempt. Either he succeeds in being intelligible by concealing the core of the problem and by offering to the reader only superficial aspects or vague allusions, thus deceiving the reader by arousing in him the deceptive illusion of comprehension; or else he gives an expert account of the problem, but in such a fashion that the untrained reader is unable to follow the exposition and becomes discouraged from reading any further. If these two categories are omitted from today's popular scientific literature, surprisingly little remains (cited in Barnett 1948: 69).

There is no simple answer to this predicament. Three factors, especially, must be considered. First, as noted earlier, space is a major consideration in journalism and it is impossible to do justice to a complex topic by examining it from different angles and analysing it in depth within such space constraints. In this respect, popular science *books* have an advantage because they have the length necessary to expand and elaborate. Second, audience is another major consideration. People still need and want to be informed about technological developments even if they do not have the same expertise as the initiators of these developments. At the same time, it would be unrealistic to expect them to understand terminology and methods that have taken professionals years to learn. Therefore, an interpretation becomes necessary. Third, the market and general social context should be taken into account. Technology develops in hand with the evolution and diversification of society, in which market forces and commercial interests are major factors. Connecting technology and science with its social relevance, the theory with the application is, therefore, important, as is identifying the links between scientific endeavour and commercial practice.

Within this framework, popularisations of science and technology can be fruitful if the writer:

- understands that s/he cannot be as thorough in a popular document as in a specialist or scientific document and must, therefore, be carefully selective
- has a sense of visualisation and narrative and can explain concepts in terms of images and stories, keeping in mind that being simple does not mean being simplistic
- can resist the temptation to exaggerate, generalise or sensationalise in ways that would mislead the reader into thinking that a debatable and inconclusive topic is certain.

Hedging (using terms that mitigate certainty and absolute constructions) is a major difference between academic/scientific writing aimed at specialist, peer audiences, and journalistic/popular writing aimed at a wider public. One of the reasons that professionals are often suspicious of journalists is the tendency of the latter to simplify and generalise from inconclusive results, and thereby to discourage or raise the hopes of the public inappropriately. Science writing scholar Jeanne Fahnestock (1986 and 2004) gives some interesting examples of this. In the debate about whether the sexes are equally endowed with mathematical ability, she quotes scientists' statements and compares them with their interpretations in popular publications.

Here is the scientists' claim:

> *We favor the hypothesis* that sex differences in achievement in and attitude toward mathematics result from superior male mathematical ability, which *may* in turn be related to greater male mathematical ability in spatial tasks. This male superiority is *probably* an expression of a combination of both endogenous and exogenous variables. *We recognize, however, that our data are consistent with numerous alternative hypotheses.*

> (Benbow and Stanley: 'Sex differences in mathematical ability: Fact or artifact?', *Science* 1980, cited in Fahnestock 1986: 284; my emphasis)

Here is one popularisation of the claim:

> According to its authors, [...] Benbow and [...] Stanley of Johns Hopkins University, males inherently have more mathematical ability than females.
> ('The gender factor in math', *Time Magazine,* cited in Fahnestock 1986: 285)

And here is another:

> The authors' conclusion: ' Sex differences in achievement in and attitude toward mathematics result from superior male mathematical ability.'
> ('Do males have a math gene?', *Newsweek,* cited in Fahnestock 1986: 285)

Table 8 shows some common communicative strategies that characterise the styles and content choices of specialist writing and journalistic writing.

As an example of how these strategies work on the textual level, consider analysed examples 8 and 9 dealing with the topic of movement in humans and robots. Both are introductions to their respective articles: analysed example 8 is taken from *Nature*, a scientific journal for scientists; analysed example 9 is taken from *New Scientist*, a popular science magazine for non-specialist science enthusiasts. As is the norm, the article from which example 8 comes was written before the article from which example 9 comes, with the latter being a popularisation of the findings presented in the former.

Developing a feature article

When writing a feature article you are explaining how something works or how something has developed over time, informing the public of something new and/or important and interpreting complex information in an understandable and appealing way (for more on business and technology feature writing, see Roush 2004; Kaku and Cohen 2012; Starkman et al. 2012). In effect, you may be doing one or more of the following:

- describing the parts of your object and their interrelationships
- tracing the history of the object and describing its changes
- describing the object's qualities and characteristics
- analysing the object's value.

Analysed example 8

Academic/Specialist Style

Although people's legs are capable of a broad range of muscle-use and gait patterns, they generally prefer just two. They walk, swinging their body over a relatively straight leg with each step, or run, bouncing up off a bent leg between aerial phases. Walking feels easiest when going slowly, and running feels easiest when going faster. More unusual gaits seem more tiring. Perhaps this is because walking and running use the least energy. Addressing this classic conjecture with experiments requires comparing walking and running with many other strange and unpractised gaits. As an alternative, a basic understanding of gait choice might be obtained by calculating energy cost by using mechanics-based models. Here we use a minimal model that can describe walking and running as well as an infinite variety of other gaits. We use computer optimization to find which gaits are indeed energetically optimal for this model. At low speeds the optimization discovers the classic inverted-pendulum walk, at high speeds it discovers a bouncing run, even without springs, and at intermediate speeds it finds a new pendular-running gait that includes walking and running as extreme cases.

One way of characterizing gaits is by the motions of the body (Fig. 1a). In these terms, walking seems well caricatured (Fig. 1b) by the hip joint going from one

> First four sentences set the scene, indicating the issue that the article discusses

> Introduces the main topic: mechanics-biased models

> Explains the choice of the minimal model used in the article

To achieve this effectively, use a combination of these strategies:

Define terms and differentiate them from other similar ones. This is very useful when you are writing about a large topic with many subdivisions, aspects and categories. By defining it, you are specifying the parameters in which you will explain it. Consider using sentence or paragraph-length definitions for complicated topics, and *parenthetical definitions* for less complicated ones (see below for examples).

circular arc to the next with push-off and heel-strike impulses in between. Similarly, running could be caricatured by a sequence of parabolic free-flight arcs (Fig. 1c), with impulses from the ground at each bounce.

Why do people not walk or even run with a smooth level gait, like a waiter holding two cups brim-full of boiling coffee? Why do people select walking and running from the other possibilities? We address such questions by modelling a person as a machine describable with the equations of newtonian mechanics. The basic approximations are: first, that humans have compact bodies and light legs; second, that gait choice is based on energy optimization; and third, that energy cost is proportional to muscle work. We use a simplification of previous models, perhaps the simplest mechanical model that is capable of exhibiting a broad range of gaits that includes walking and running. Although the model is a mechanical abstraction that is not physically realizable, it is subject to the laws of physics. Because of its simplicity, the model is amenable to interpretation. It can also be studied with exhaustive and accurate simulation experiments, far beyond what is possible with human subjects.

Adapted from: Srinivasan, M. and Ruina, A. (2006). 'Computer optimisation of a minimal biped model discovers walking and running', Nature 439, 5, pp. 72–75. Reprinted with permission.

Refers to three figures that show in schematic form the information presented verbally in the paragraph.

Describes the types of gait in technical terms.

Questions that draw attention to the significance of the problem. This makes this piece less technical than others, but that is consistent with the style in the Letters section of Nature, which tends to publish work in progress or less formal articles than other sections. Note that the 'you' pronoun is avoided in these questions.

Explains how the questions will be answered in technical terms.

Lists approximations to clarify assumptions and measurement scales.

Gives extensive justification of choice of method

Give an analogy. For example: 'Using the same principle as an overhead projector, an epidiascope projects three dimensional images onto a screen using a magnified beam of light.' This gives the reader the gist of what you are saying and makes complicated terms and processes easier to grasp. In the same light, you can contrast the term to what it is opposite to or different from. This is useful if you think the reader may misunderstand a topic by confusing it with something that looks similar but is actually very different.

Analysed example 9

Journalistic/Popular Style

They're everywhere. From the Imperial Walkers of Star Wars to the alien tripods from War of the Worlds, there's something about walking robots that captures the imagination. Maybe it's that they look alive. Maybe it's that machines with two legs look human. Whatever the reason, they have give engineers a headache for decades: making robots that walk well has been an enormously difficult trick to pull off.

Until now, that is. It seems walking robots are finally up and running. Surprisingly, we may have toy makers to thank for this. In 1938, the American inventor John Wilson filed a patent for a toy that, when placed on a gentle slope, would walk on two pivoted legs with a comical waddling motion that served to lift the swinging feet clear of the ground. Wilson's 'Walkie' waddled its way to success, and its descendants can be found in toyshops to this day. These gizmos don't need batteries or clockwork. Gravity alone is enough to set the legs in motion.

We humans don't waddle like the Walkie because we can bend our knees to ensure our

Annotations:

Begins with creative generalization. The referent of the pronoun 'they' is enigmatic, inducing the reader to read more.

Makes reference to widely known popular texts.

Speculates using examples from everyday life.

Last sentence introduces the topic of the article. Note also the informal phrase 'trick to pull off'.

Sentence fragment acting as transition to the second paragraph. As noted in Chapter 3, fragments are inappropriate for formal writing, but work well in more creative styles.

Play on words – 'up and running' is a literal description of the robots' movement as well as an idiom meaning 'operational'.

Brings in the toy example to ground scientific research in a popular activity.

Give examples that illustrate the functions or properties of the topic you are explaining. This helps the reader to put the topic in context and relate to it better.

Compare the topic with others to show its special features or common attributes. As with analogies, comparisons are useful in helping the reader classify the topic in a category with which s/he is familiar, and/or to understand the innovation or specific nature of the described object.

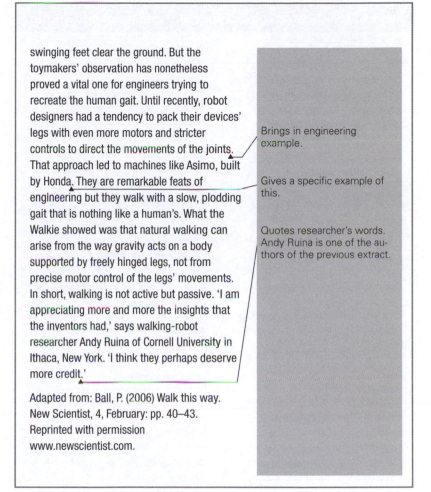

swinging feet clear the ground. But the toymakers' observation has nonetheless proved a vital one for engineers trying to recreate the human gait. Until recently, robot designers had a tendency to pack their devices' legs with even more motors and stricter controls to direct the movements of the joints. That approach led to machines like Asimo, built by Honda. They are remarkable feats of engineering but they walk with a slow, plodding gait that is nothing like a human's. What the Walkie showed was that natural walking can arise from the way gravity acts on a body supported by freely hinged legs, not from precise motor control of the legs' movements. In short, walking is not active but passive. 'I am appreciating more and more the insights that the inventors had,' says walking-robot researcher Andy Ruina of Cornell University in Ithaca, New York. 'I think they perhaps deserve more credit.'

Brings in engineering example.

Gives a specific example of this.

Quotes researcher's words. Andy Ruina is one of the authors of the previous extract.

Adapted from: Ball, P. (2006) Walk this way. New Scientist, 4, February: pp. 40–43. Reprinted with permission www.newscientist.com.

Describe the properties/qualities of an object or situation and detail how it works or how it occurs and under what circumstances.

Suggest reasons for a situation or development. This is useful when you think the reader is likely to ask the question 'why'. It justifies a current state of affairs by explaining what caused it to come into being.

Tell a story that illustrates your discussion. This is useful in making conceptual information more concrete by describing a 'physical' situation

Table 8: Stylistic strategies of specialist and journalist writing

Specialist style	Journalist style
Concentrates on objects, events and outcomes. Credibility comes from showing that a claim stands objectively, independently of personal merits of specific persons.	Concentrates on people, their intentions, thoughts, hopes and reactions. Interest comes from showing the human interest aspect of professional endeavours.
Uses jargon and specialist terminology. Shows that writer is a member of the expert community.	Avoids jargon. Instead 'translates' technical terms into everyday language. May give examples to illustrate the meaning of specialist terminology. In specialist journalism, writer uses 'insider' language to establish peer–audience dynamics.
Uses specific claims or statements that are testable and falsifiable. Supports these claims with specific and detailed evidence, such as facts and figures.	May rely on general observations when explaining a phenomenon. May appeal to imprecise constructs such as 'common sense' and 'people'.
Avoids certainty. Uses 'hedging' to modify the certainty aspect of statements ('might,' 'appears to be,' 'it seems,' 'evidence suggests').	Describes events with more certainty. Does not need to look at different sides of a hypothesis, but may present one view only. Uses imperatives (command type structures).
Avoids emotional evaluation of observations. Instead uses words that specify and quantify. Concentrates on factual information rather than on feelings about this information.	May use evaluative adjectives, such as 'terrible', 'fantastic', etc. Shows relevance of abstract data for personal experience, for example, through examples of everyday life.
Appeals to scientific community and not to individual readers. Avoids excessive use of personal pronouns	Appeals to ideal, personalized readers, using techniques such as direct questions and use of pronouns.

where the ideas you are talking about were at play. Stories are very effective in assisting the reader to visualise, and, therefore, to better understand, your description.

Describe a process. This is a way to show how something is done, a protocol or procedure. Describing processes also comes into play when giving instructions on how to carry out a task.

Describe applications. This emphasises the practical aspects of research, by showing how inventions and discoveries can be used in everyday life.

Use visual aids, such as a diagram or photograph. If you choose this strategy, make sure you explain in your text what the visual is intended to show and how it fits in your written explanation. To avoid digressing from your text to explain a diagram, consider using side-bars that contain visuals and text, and provide self-sufficient information that complements the information presented in the body of the article.

Here are some examples of these strategies in action.

Defining

You can give an extended definition of an object or phenomenon, a sentence definition or a parenthetical definition. An extended definition takes one or more paragraphs and includes explanations of the meaning of terms, as well as a description of the general category in which the defined object belongs.

Be careful that your definition does not contain terms that will themselves be obscure to your target audience. If you have to use such terms, ensure that they too are explained or defined. Lead the audience from the familiar to the unfamiliar. Sentence definitions are condensed versions of this, while parenthetical definitions explain the meaning of a term without disrupting the sentence in which they are found.

Here is a one-paragraph definition of 'presence' in virtual reality. Notice how the writer justifies the choice of 'presence' in a discussion of virtual reality, by pointing out that it is one aspect of virtual reality when seen in terms of human experience rather than of technology. The writer leads gradually to a one-sentence precise definition of 'presence' by first describing some of the attributes of the term.

> The key to defining virtual reality in terms of human experience rather than technological hardware is the concept of presence. Presence can be thought of as the experience of one's physical environment; it refers not to one's surroundings as they exist in the physical world, but

to the perception of those surroundings as mediated by both automatic and controlled mental processes. Presence is defined as the sense of being in an environment (Steuer 1995: 35).

The following is a form of parenthetical definition, using a dash (dashes are generally preferred to parentheses in journalistic articles for layout reasons).

Dating back to Newton's laws of motion, the equations of physics are generally 'time symmetric' – they work as well for processes running backwards through time as forwards (Barry 2006: 36).

Giving an analogy

Analogies are useful when you are presenting a difficult topic or a topic that the reader has little knowledge of. The advantage of analogies is that they can clarify and explain a topic by tracing a parallel pattern with another topic that may be easier to grasp. The disadvantage of analogies is that, if not used carefully, they can confuse the reader by understating or overstating a topic. You use an analogy by juxtaposing two situations and showing their common features and qualities. Rhetorically, an analogy is equivalent to a simile. For example, here is how writer Flannery O'Connor addressed a class in writing:

I understand that this is a course called 'How the Writer Writes', and that each week you are exposed to a different writer who holds forth on the subject. The only parallel I can think of to this is having the zoo come to you, one animal at a time; and I suspect that what you hear one week from the giraffe is contradicted next week by the baboon (cited by Kane 1984: 89).

Giving examples

A paragraph of example/illustration could lead off with a topic sentence that states the general principle or idea. Your second sentence will usually contain the phrase 'for example' or 'for instance', or variations on this. If you have a lot of example paragraphs to write you could introduce variation by employing some substitutes for 'for example' and 'for instance'. You might perhaps write, 'An interesting case of *X* is...'.

Another way to exemplify is to define or describe the example in theoretical terms in one sentence, and then go on to elaborate by means of more visual language or by recounting a story that would make the conceptual description more understandable to non-specialists. The following extract exemplifies these principles. The first sentence states what the example represents. The second sentence describes how it does this and leads into a more vivid story to get the point across. The third sentence provides a link to a second example, created by the linker 'similarly'. The fourth sentence once again describes what the example stands for theoretically; and the last sentence illustrates the concept by creating a more tangible image:

> One notable early example of an attempt to provide great sensory breadth in a mediated presentation is the Sensorama device, developed by Mort Heilig. This arcade game-style simulator utilizes four of the five senses to simulate a motorcycle ride: Users see the Manhattan streets go by, hear the roar of the motorcycle and the sounds of the street, smell the exhaust of other cars and pizza cooking in roadside restaurants, and feel the vibration of the handlebars. Similarly, many park theme attractions, particularly those at Walt Disney World and Disneyland, use a high degree of breadth in order to simulate a sense of presence. The addition of changes in orientation, haptic sensations, smells, and tastes, in combination with auditory and visual sensation, are particularly effective in this regard. For example, the Star Tours and Body Wars simulators combine a motion platform with multi-channel sound and film to simulate space travel and a tour through the human body, respectively (Steuer 1995: 43).

In the following extract, novelist Stephen King explains the importance for writers of reading. To illustrate this, he gives examples of the many occasions available for people to read in the course of a day. Notice that the writer adopts a first-person perspective in presenting his examples. This is effective because the writer is an expert in the field he describes (writing), and so his personal experience is directly relevant.

> Reading is the creative center of a writer's life. I take a book with me everywhere I go, and find there are all sorts of opportunities to dip in. The trick is to teach yourself to read in small sips as well as in long swallows. Waiting rooms were made for books – of course! But so are theatre lobbies before the show, long and boring checkout lines, and everyone's favorite, the john. You can even read while you're driving, thanks to the audiobook revolution (King 2000: 114).

Comparing

When comparing, select some qualities from an object and describe how they compare with qualities of another object. Create a balance between similarities and differences. Two objects that are completely different cannot be compared – it would be like comparing an artichoke and an elephant. Similarly, two objects that are identical do not have enough distance between them to allow comparison – this would be like comparing yourself with your image in a mirror. In such cases, other strategies of description and explanation would probably be more effective.

Adverbs and adjectives of comparison are useful in this strategy. 'More', 'less', 'fewer' and words ending in -er or -est show comparison. In addition, there is a range of signpost words and phrases that express the relation of comparison/contrast, for example, 'similarly', 'conversely', 'also', 'in the same way', 'after all', etc. The following extract compares two cameras. Notice that the writer chooses to base the comparison on user needs and skills.

> Both model *X* and model *Y* are great cameras, containing features for the beginner as well as for the more advanced photographer. However, model *X*'s ease of use and limited extra features mean it is more targeted towards the amateur or novice photographer who occasionally wants to dabble in manual photography, but still needs an automatic camera. Model *Y*, in contrast, with its more powerful system and additional features is more for the serious photographer who occasionally wants to take photos without setting up the scene. Financially, it sets you back a bit more, especially if you purchase all the extra gadgets, but you can take it further – which is great if you get serious about your photography.

The following extract compares science and art.

> The scientist works mainly at the level of very abstract ideas, while his perceptual contact with the world is largely mediated by instruments. On the other hand, the artist works mainly on creating concrete objects that are directly perceptible without instruments. Yet, as one approaches the broadest possible field of science, one discovers closely related criteria of 'truth' and 'beauty'. For what the artist creates must be 'true to itself', just as the broad scientific theory must be 'true to itself'. Thus, neither scientist nor artist is really satisfied to regard beauty as that which 'tickles one's fancy.' Rather, in both fields structures are somehow evaluated, consciously or subconsciously, by whether they are 'true to themselves', and are accepted or rejected on this basis. So the artist really needs a scientific attitude to his work, as the scientist must have an artistic attitude to his (Adapted from D. Bohm 1968: 32–3).

Describing qualities

Here you detail the features or aspects of the object. This is a spatial strategy, so remember to chunk qualities in categories and prioritise information if appropriate. You can list qualities or describe them in paragraph form. The following example lists some aspects that make up the quality of a virtual reality system. The writer first lists the aspects, and then explains each by asking a question from the user/reader's perspective.

> To the layman's eye, the quality of the VR system is based on the following:
>
> 1. The details of the graphic. Does he really look like a relatively believable robot? Is this an aesthetically pleasing and compelling environment?
> 2. The responsiveness of the image. Do objects move in real time to match my gestures? When I reach out, is there a delay before my computer-generated hand reaches out?
> 3. The safety and comfort of the helmet. Does it fit? How dirty is it? Can I get out of it if I get claustrophobic?
> 4. The ease of use of the input device. How coordinated do I have to be to use this thing?
>
> (Adapted from Hawkins 1995: 178–9)

Suggesting reasons

When adopting this strategy, present your topic as something whose existence requires justification or explanation. Then describe one or more possible causes. You can begin by describing the causes leading to a phenomenon and then describe the phenomenon itself, or you can describe the phenomenon and then go to its possible causes. In the following example Bill Gates speculates on the reasons for revolutionary software. He achieves this by listing several possible causes, and leading to his answer.

> What does it take to create revolutionary software? Does it mean being first to come up with a new idea, or being first to turn that idea into a product? Does it mean carrying out pioneering research, or making incremental improvements to what's already there until you get it right? Does it mean becoming a giant, or standing on the shoulders of giants? Usually, the answer is a bit of each. Most software blends innovation, inspiration, and incremental improvement in equal measure (Gates 2000).

The following extract presents a reason why roboticists do not build more life-like robots. Notice how this paragraph also leads to a definition of a phenomenon.

> One reason researchers have shied away from building more sophisticated androids is a theory put forward in 1970 by roboticist Masahiro Mori. He proposed that our feeling of familiarity increases as robots appear more and more human-like, but that our comfort level plummets as slight defects in behaviour and appearance repulse us, as if we are watching a moving corpse. Mori called this the 'uncanny valley'. The term is widely used by roboticists and has spread to the animation industry, where it describes people's reaction to increasingly realistic digital characters (Schaub 2006: 43).

Telling a story

When telling a story, decide how much of your story your target reader is likely to be able to absorb without a break and how much they want to know. Also, make sure that your story clearly relates to the topic that you are attempting to explain, by explicitly making connections between the two. For example, the following extract tells a story to explain why many people find the concept of evolution difficult to understand. Notice how the writer begins the paragraph by stating his main topic. Then he asks two questions constructed from the perspective of 'most people'. He then recounts a story, which becomes a story within a story, giving 'most people's' version of why evolution is difficult to grasp. He ends the paragraph by extrapolating that it is the time element in evolution that 'most people' find difficult to conceptualise.

> Most people find evolution implausible. Why is my spine erect, my thumb opposable? Can evolutionists really explain that? Once I attended a lecture by the writer Isaac Bashevis Singer, and one of the many biologists in the audience asked Singer about evolution – did he believe in it? Singer responded with a story. He said there was an island upon which scientists were certain no human being had ever been. When people landed on the island they found a watch between two rocks – a complete mystery. The scientists when confronted with the evidence of the watch stuck to the view that the island was uninhabited. Instead they explained that although improbable, a little bit of glass, metal, and leather had over thousands of years worked its way into the form of a watch. Singer's view differed from that of the scientists – as he summarized, 'No watch without a Watchmaker.' This story reflects the feeling many people share that random chemical

interactions cannot explain the existence of life on earth. The reason it is hard for such people to grasp the evolutionary viewpoint is the difficulty in grasping the immense time a billion years actually is (Pagels 1983: 196).

Here is the beginning of a story created to describe the development of sun- and wind-operated boats. Notice how the writer dramatises the situation by describing a realistic scene where events took place, and even the thoughts and emotions of the main character.

The solar sailing story began a decade ago when Robert Dane, a doctor in the fishing town and seaside resort of Ulladulla in New South Wales, found himself on the shores of Canberra's Lake Burley Griffin, He was watching the city's annual race for solar powered boats, and, as a keen sailor, was sorely disappointed by the spectacle. As far as he could tell, it was nothing more than a bunch of boffins piloting boats clumsily loaded with banks of solar cells. There was no feel for sailing, no integration of the solar technology with the boats and no understanding of what it takes to push a vessel efficiently through water (Thwaites 2006: 52).

Describing a process

The principle behind presenting a process is quite similar to the principle behind story-telling. When presenting a process, divide it into stages going from the beginning of the process to its intended result. Sentence openers such as 'first', 'next', 'then' and 'finally' are useful in describing processes and so are numbers and lists. If the process includes technical terms, remember to adapt them to the technical level of your target audience. The following paragraph describes a process for extracting titanium.

The process takes place in an electrolytic cell. The cathode is connected to a pellet of titanium dioxide powder, while the anode is made of an inert material such as carbon. The two electrodes are immersed in a bath of molten calcium chloride, which acts as the electrolyte. When the power is switched on, electrons at the cathode decompose the titanium dioxide into titanium metal and oxygen ions. The ions flow through the electrolyte to the anode, where oxygen is released as a gas (Hill 2001: 36).

Describing applications

When describing the applications of a discovery, you are, in effect, listing possible future or present situations where the discovery is put to action.

Applications show different uses of a product or method, so you could describe them by listing ('first', 'second') or adding ('also', 'another application'). Here is an extract from an article describing how science defines the feeling of love as the result of biochemical and genetic processes. The extract outlines some ways in which such research may be useful.

> Is this useful? The scientists think so. For a start, understanding the neurochemical pathways that regulate social attachments may help to deal with defects in people's ability to form relationships. All relationships, whether they are those of parents with their children, spouses with their partners, or workers with their colleagues, rely on an ability to create and maintain social ties. Defects can be disabling, and become apparent as disorders such as autism and schizophrenia – and indeed, as the serious depression that can result from rejection in love. Research is also shedding light on some of the more extreme forms of sexual behaviour. And controversially, some utopian fringe groups see such work as the doorway to a future where love is guaranteed because it will be provided chemically, or even genetically engineered from conception (*The Economist* 2004: 10).

Analysis of example

Read analysed example 10 on the planet Mars and notice how some of the strategies described above are used in its composition.

Integrating quotations

An important difference between specialist and journalistic documents lies in use of quotations. In formal reports, as in academic writing, quotations have a secondary function: they are there to provide credibility or lend support to an idea. In journalistic writing, on the other hand, ideas or facts are often crafted around quotations, foregrounding the immediacy of spoken language. For this reason, specialist documents avoid extensive use of quotations, which give the document a choppy or fragmented appearance. This is not the case for journalistic articles, however, where it is generally expected to attribute opinions, facts and ideas directly to people by reporting their speech.

This difference in emphasis is highlighted in the way quotations are integrated in the text. In specialist documents, lead up to a quotation so that the sentence begins in your own words and ends with the quotation.

Reverse this technique in journalistic writing: begin the sentence with a quotation and end it with your comment. Compare these extracts. The first is appropriate for a report and the second for a magazine article.

> *Extract 1*
> Conservation International, North Motor Company and Nielsen Engineering have agreed to collaborate in three 'walkway projects' in the Amazon Valley and Indonesia. These projects involve creating walkways that allow visitors to traverse densely forested areas without the need of roads. This is an important step in promoting both tourist activity and the safety of the forests. As the Public Relations Manager of Conservation International points out, 'tourism can boost an economy, but it will bust it if it destroys the environment.'

> *Extract 2*
> Conservation International recently joined forces with Motor and Engineering companies for a series of ventures promoting tourism in environmentally safe ways. 'Tourism can boost an economy, but it will bust it if it destroys the environment,' says Tim McIntyre, Public Relations Manager of Conservation International. 'Ecotourism can be as, if not more, profitable as a logging-based tourism industry, especially in our era of environmental awareness', he adds.

Another difference in the integration of quotations and attributed knowledge in specialist and journalistic documents is the kind of referencing to sources. In specialist documents, such as reports and academic articles, references follow one of the formal styles, APA, Chicago, etc. This means that the full source is named either in a footnote, or in an end-of-text reference list. In journalistic articles, on the other hand, the convention is to include the person's name and affiliation within the body of the article, preferably in the sentence that includes the quotation. References to journals where research was initially published are placed in brackets at the end of the sentence or paragraph that describes this research. Notice how this is achieved in the following example.

> *According to Jeremy Gruber, legal director of the National Workrights Institute based in Princeton, New Jersey,* US companies can legally watch everything employees do – and only two states require employers to tell workers they are under surveillance (Newitz 2006: 30, my emphasis).

Analysed example 10

Life on Mars

Can Mars contain life? Is there any possibility that we are not alone in this solar system? Close examination of these questions has led scientists to propose that the following characteristics (rare for any planet) are necessary for Mars to support life:

- The planet must have a strong magnetic field which is created by the spinning of liquid metals deep inside. This magnetic field acts like a force-field to prevent the harsh winds and energies of the Sun from stripping away atmosphere and clouds like a gas-powered leaf blower.
- The area in which life evolves must be relatively stable. Life is delicate and would not survive repeated bombardments by meteors and other objects, which would cook any developing organisms in hot gas and magma.
- Water is necessary for all life. It dissolves almost any compound and allows organisms to produce energy for their own growth and survival.
- Life needs an atmosphere with enough carbon dioxide to allow the surface of the planet to be warmed by trapping the Sun's rays much like the Greenhouse Effect.

Lists qualities necessary for life on a planet.

With the explosive growth of spaceflight technology, examining Mars for these planetary characteristics has finally become a reality. The Mars of today, unfortunately, does not meet these criteria. The planet's core is not spinning anymore leading to the lack of a magnetic field and an atmosphere. All of Mars's water is either deep underground, out of the Sun's reach, or frozen in the ice caps. Finally, Mars is a very cold planet with frozen carbon dioxide that cannot be used by living organisms.

Gives reasons why Mars cannot support life

Leads, hooks and ties

In contrast to reports, scientific and business magazine articles do not develop in a linear fashion. Also, they do not state assumptions and background, or give justifications for assertions. They are subjectively descriptive in that they describe an object from the point of view of the

Thus, for all you ET fans out there, the chance we find any living organisms on Mars is very small. 'What's the point of exploring Mars for life?' you may ask. Mars may be cold and dead now, but it wasn't in the past.

Transitional paragraph leading to a historical report on Mars' atmosphere

About four billion years ago, Mars was a stable planet while Earth was still in its infancy. New data analyzed from the Mars rovers shows that Mars had an active core resulting in a magnetic field comparable to present day Earth – enough to maintain an atmosphere of carbon dioxide, oxygen, and water. Analysis of Martian canal-like structures reveals a cloud system similar to Earth's and vast oceans several kilometers deep. During this time, Mars was also volcanically active, theoretically providing organisms with energy that could be harnessed for life. Four billion years ago, Mars met all the criteria for a living world. In fact, many scientists have a difficult time arguing against life on Mars!

Tells a story about Mars' situation in the past

Why do we care about fossils billions of years old? Evidence of ancient life on Mars has very important consequences for our understanding of how life begins. In 1984, scientists working in Antarctica discovered a meteorite from Mars approximately 4.6 billion years old. This Mars object created controversy, as many scientists suggested the meteorite contained evidence of bacterial life. If such meteorites indeed contained Martians, as could be confirmed by our expeditions on Mars, all living organisms on Earth may have evolved from Martian hitchhikers. We might be, in fact, the last traces of Martian life.

Gives reasons for an interest, and leads to a speculation that further supports the reason.

mental and/or physical state of the reader – they tell the readers what they want them to see.

A report would start by describing the background, overview and assumptions, and then go on to detail different aspects of the topic leading to a set of recommendations. Instead, a magazine article plunges straight into the description of the product or discovery that the article discusses, immediately showing its relevance to the interests or needs of the reader. It then goes on to present different facets of the topic, beginning with the most crucial and continuing in diminishing importance. It may end quite abruptly, or it may end with one or two sentences that tie in a comment, opinion or evaluative remark to the preceding discussion.

A corporate client needs less invitation to read a report, and expects more precision from the outset. A magazine reader, on the other hand, wants to be seduced into reading the article. The *lead* is the opening statement that should attract the reader to the article. Its job is to relate your main topic to what you believe your reader's general interests and experience are. A *hook* is similar to a lead, although it is usually more 'spicy' or provocative. A hook should be well baited, so that your reader is tempted to carry on reading. Avoid abstractions and densely technical language at this point. The following article on 'virtual banking', for example, makes lively use of an opening question:

> How long would you spend queuing in a bank before storming out? The American bank technology company NCR wanted to find out what really goes on in customers' heads when they enter a high-street bank. So it commissioned CyberLife to breed surrogate people that could wander around inside a virtual bank and test the layout of machines and services – without the time and expense of real-life tests (Davidson 1998: 40).

The sentences following the hook in the first paragraph add background to the topic or issue. As with formal report introductions, you may also add a sentence that states what it is that the ensuing article will do, although this is not necessary. The following extract, for example, leads by stating a fact and asking a question about this fact from the reader's point of view. It then goes on to overview the specifics that the article will discuss in more detail, and ends with a statement on the purpose of the article:

> The two market leaders in non-professional cameras are the Canon X and the Pentax Y, but what makes them so good? The X leads the market by being so jam-packed with features. However, the Y holds its own with its ease of use and a slightly better price. Here we set them head to head and pull them apart for our readers.

If you have more space to expand, you may also consider using a short narrative as the lead. As people respond more strongly to narrative information than to any other form, your chances of intriguing and capturing your audience are increased. For example, below is the lead from Richard Branson's (2012) article, 'Why we need more women in the boardroom'. It begins with an example from a personal situation that sets the scene for the paragraph's last sentence, the question that forms the basis of the article. This is also an example of an analogy between trial juries and company executive boards.

> I recently watched *12 Angry Men* – that classic 1957 film about a jury struggling to decide the fate of an 18-year-old man who has been charged with murder. The movie gives you a sense of how the legal system worked in the United States back then, when juries were less diverse. By today's standards, we would find it unsettling if a jury were comprised of 12 middle-aged white men. So why have so many business leaders been slow to take notice when women are absent from the boards of their companies?

The *tie* is an optional device that ends the article with a comment or question summing up the writer's attitude towards the topic. More attention is paid to introductions in articles because of the aim to capture attention, and the fact that most readers look at the opening sentences of an article before deciding whether to invest any more time in it. If space allows, however, a good tie does have the effect of emphasising the main message of the article and making it more memorable for the reader. For example, Richard Branson's article, whose lead is cited above, on the lack of women in executive positions in business, also has an interesting tie, which loops back to the lead:

> So take a look at who's sitting around your boardroom table. If you see 12 angry men, it's time to write a new script! (Branson 2012: n.p.).

Here are three more examples of leads and hooks.

1. What goes ding in the night? Apparently the space shuttle Atlantis, which last month sustained one of the largest debris hits in the history of NASA's shuttle programme (*New Scientist* 14 October 2006: 7).
2. Scientists are finding that, after all, love really is down to a chemical addiction between people (*The Economist* 28 December 2006).
3. There are nine planets in our solar system. Or there are eight. Or there are ten, or maybe even twenty-three. No one knows. A planet

is an arbitrary thing, a notion. In a matter of weeks, however, the International Astronomical Union, meeting in Prague, is likely to issue a definitive description (*The New Yorker* 24 July 2006).

Analysed example 11 shows the magazine layout of the article *Life on Mars* presented earlier in this chapter. Notice the formatting sections, as they would conventionally appear in print publications, and their terminology.

Submitting an article for publication

When you decide to submit an article to a magazine for publication, make sure you are familiar with the topics and styles of your chosen magazine. You have a higher chance of having your article accepted if it fits with the 'culture' of the magazine. All magazines have details of the editor, so if you cannot find submission guidelines, contact the editor to request them – this is the editor's job and, besides, most magazines are looking for fresh ideas and new writers. In most cases, you will be required to submit a proposal summarising your article and noting its significance and the types of readers it is likely to interest (more on proposals to editors in Chapter 7).

In order to familiarise yourself with the stylistic conventions of your chosen magazine, follow these steps:

1 Read carefully each article in recent issues of the magazine. Note the basic question or topic that they deal with and trace the ways that they answer it. How do they use the five Ws and one H? What new knowledge do you learn from the articles? What facts do you learn?
2 Notice the tone of the articles. Are they humorous? Serious? Technical? Chatty? This will give you a hint on what tone to give your own article.
3 Notice the use of research. Have the writers conducted primary research, such as interviewing people, or are most articles based on secondary research – the consultation of written sources? How many quotations do the articles use? How much information is paraphrased, that is written in the writer's own words? List the sources. Check some of them to see how the writer used them in his/her article.
4 Notice the use of pronouns ('I', 'you', 'we', etc.). Are articles written mostly in an impersonal, objective style or do they rely heavily on personal comment? How does the writer refer to him/herself? Does s/he use personal pronouns?

5   Notice the leads and ties. How long and snappy are they? Do the articles rely strongly on leads to 'bait' the reader, or are other elements, such as pictures or quotations of famous speakers more prominent?

6   Underline the first sentence in each paragraph. They should form a step-by-step sequence. Then note the cohesion that the writers have used: the linking words and phrases within paragraphs and the transitions from one paragraph to the next. Often the same words or ideas will be repeated in the last sentence of one paragraph and the first sentence of the next.

7   Notice how the articles develop their theme. Is the article structured chronologically, developmentally, by alternating examples, point by point? How did the writer build the organisational structure to answer the title's question?

8   What techniques does the writer use to make the article both informative and appealing? For example, does s/he use analogies, anecdotal examples, metaphors, personal stories, rhetorical questions, direct questions to the readers, etc.?

9   Notice the title. It may have been changed by the editor; nevertheless, how does it reflect the article? Does it tease, quote, state facts? What technique does the writer use to make the reader want to read the article?

10 Look at *para-textual elements*, such as visuals, pull-quotes, subheads, etc. Although the editor may have produced these, you can still get an idea of the type of 'framing' that the magazine requires, and this will give you some tips on what types of information the editors consider important.

Analysed example 11

Life on Mars

**The potential of the red planet
to sustain living beings**

Can Mars contain life? Is there any
possibility that we are not alone in
this solar system? Close examination
of these questions has led scientists
to propose that the following characteristics (rare for any planet) are
necessary for Mars to support life:

First, the planet must have a strong
magnetic field which is created by the
spinning of liquid metals deep inside.
This magnetic field acts like a force-
field to prevent the harsh winds and
energies of the Sun from stripping
away atmosphere and clouds like a
gas-powered leaf blower.

Second, the area in which life evolves
must be relatively stable. Life is delicate and would not survive repeated
bombardments by meteors and other
objects, which would cook any
developing organisms in hot gas and
magma.

Third, water is necessary for all life. It
dissolves almost any compound and
allows organisms to produce energy
for their own growth and survival.

Fourth, life needs an atmosphere with
enough carbon dioxide to allow the
surface of the planet to be warmed by
trapping the Sun's rays much like the
Greenhouse Effect.

The Exploration of Mars
With the explosive growth of spaceflight technology, examining Mars
for these planetary characteristics has
finally become a reality. The Mars of
today, unfortunately, does not meet

Title – fonts for the title,
subhead and pullquote
are Lucida Bright.

subhead

hook

visual – notice how the
visual is aligned with the
text

caption

pullquote

crosshead

tie

Mars at its 2001 opposition.
Reproduced courtesy of NASA and the Hubble Heritage Team
(STScI/AURA; www.stsci.edu/institute); Acknowledgemnt: J. Bell (Cornell
University).

still in its infancy. New data analyzed from the Mars rovers shows that Mars had an active core resulting in a magnetic field comparable to present day Earth – enough to maintain an atmosphere of carbon dioxide, oxygen, and water.

Analysis of Martian canal-like structures reveals a cloud system similar to Earth's and vast oceans several kilometers deep. During this time, Mars was also volcanically active, theoretically providing organisms with energy that could be harnessed for life. Four billion years ago, Mars met all the criteria for a living world. In fact, many scientists have a difficult time arguing *against* life on Mars!

these criteria. The planet's core is not spinning any more leading to the lack of a magnetic field and an atmosphere. All of Mars's water is either deep underground, out of the Sun's reach, or frozen in the ice caps. Finally, Mars is a very cold planet with frozen carbon dioxide that cannot be used by living organisms.

'Mars had an active core resulting in a magnetic field comparable to present day Earth'

Thus, for all you ET fans out there, the chance we find any living organisms on Mars is very small. 'What's the point of exploring Mars for life?' you may ask. Mars may be cold and dead now, but it wasn't in the past.

About four billion years ago, Mars was a stable planet while Earth was

Why do we care about fossils billions of years old? Evidence of ancient life on Mars has very important consequences for our understanding of how life begins. In 1984, scientists working in Antarctica discovered a meteorite from Mars approximately 4.6 billion years old. This Mars object created controversy, as many scientists suggested the meteorite contained evidence of bacterial life.

If such meteorites indeed contained Martians, as could be confirmed by our expeditions on Mars, all living organisms on Earth may have evolved from Martian hitchhikers. We might be, in fact, the last traces of Martian life.

Activities

1 Research the business or scientific magazines that publish in an area you are interested in. Find out the submission requirements of each magazine and make a style-format analysis of the types of articles each magazine publishes. Then write a memo to your instructor detailing your findings.
2 Analyse a feature following the guidelines presented in this chapter. Bring your analysis to class for discussion. Concentrate on what impressed you about the article and what areas you think could be improved. Did the writer answer the questions you had on the topic? Could s/he have been clearer and more accurate within the space limitations?

Writing for the Public

Focus:

- Press releases
- Web content
- Social media
- Public speeches

This chapter looks at some major business genres targeting a public audience and the situations in which they are used. It begins with an overview of public relations writing, and then focuses on writing press releases, content for business websites and contributions to social media sites.

Public relations texts

Much of a company's success depends on the perception that the public has of it, and on its reputation in dealing with consumers, clients and the general social context in which it operates. The way a company communicates with its public and the ways in which it creates and sustains relationships become paramount in its continued progress and expansion. The two related business fields that focus on the social status of the company are *marketing* and *public relations* (PR). The first is concerned with the design, branding and positioning of products, while the second is dedicated to identifying, maintaining and correcting factors that contribute to the company's reputation and public image (for PR and PR writing, see also Bivins 1999; Davis 2004; Theaker 2008; Kent 2011; Morris and Goldsworthy 2012).

Genres that publicise a company's products and services, as well as the company's contribution to social endeavours include:

- **Press releases:** short documents written for the media, functioning to publicise a new development, product, service or policy. They are sent to media outlets and published on the company's website.

- **Websites:** the company's representative in cyberspace, websites tell the company's story, its mission, organisation and products. Currently, they are the first source of information for a company.
- **Brochures and prospectuses:** booklets that describe the company's products and/or services. A prospectus is a larger document than a brochure and includes more detail. These can be delivered in print or in digital medium, depending on audience and purpose. In many cases, large organisations have both versions available.
- **Flyers and posters:** similar to brochures and prospectuses but smaller, these are one-page advertisements of an event or product. These too can be delivered in print and digital medium.
- **Mission statements:** the company's concept of its main goals, objectives and reason for existing, the mission statement is addressed as much to employees and investors as it is to the wider public. Since the mission statement is posted on a company's websites, however, it is generally perceived as a public relations text.
- **Newsletters:** in-house magazines that report the company's news to various stakeholders, including clients and members. They can be delivered in both print and digital medium, although digital medium is rapidly becoming the favoured form, especially if the recipients are professionals. Newsletters are akin to magazines and the guidelines presented in Chapter 5 are applicable to these.
- **Letters:** short texts that carry messages of different kinds to customers, members and other stakeholders. Letters can be part of welcome packs and membership packages, or they can inform of the formal outcome of a procedure, such as rewards. Letters also accompany other texts such as prospectuses. Chapter 3 discusses letters in more detail.
- **Annual reports:** documents written at the end of a financial year, and detailing the successes and failures of the company during the year. An important document for investors, annual reports combine technical and financial details with motivating articles on how the company fulfilled its mission during the year. Annual reports are public documents, and most large organisations provide access to them on their websites.
- **Social media:** contributions to social networking sites such as *Facebook* and *YouTube*, updating the public of new developments to the minute, and enabling users to respond or comment.
- **Speeches and press conferences:** texts written for oral delivery, speeches can be addressed to the wider public through the media or to employees and stakeholders through the company's internal communication channels.

When deciding on a public communication strategy, it might be useful to think of possible media in terms of *push* and *pull*. Push media are those that transmit information to the public, who are quasi-passive recipients. Broadcast media, such as television and radio, are examples of push media. Pull media, on the other hand, are those in which a company participates in a community and attracts an audience from that community. The digital media, especially social networks, but also, to a lesser extent, websites are examples of pull media. As technology evangelist Guy Kawasaki, says, 'push technology brings your story to people. Pull technology brings people to your story' (Kawasaki 2011: 135). Each type of medium has a different degree of control. In pull technology the company has less control and needs to take a more adaptive approach. From a consumer's perspective, pull media allow users to select and combine information that they receive from organisations. To take an example from music, a CD is a push medium; in contrast a playlist created by downloading selected songs from a site such as iTunes, is a pull medium.

Press releases

Press releases target an audience of news professionals, working either in print or broadcast, and announce new and important work or events. Sometimes press releases are sent to specialty audiences, such as convention organisers. At other times, they are placed on the company's website, on the 'press', 'public relations' or 'journalism' page. Often they are mailed to target press representatives as part of a press kit, which may include testimonials, quotations and product features – anything a journalist would need to know to write an article.

Press releases vary in length from half a page to three or four pages, depending on the significance of the announcement and on the number of people or companies involved. Press releases are known as *uncontrolled* news. That is, the writer and issuing organisation have no control over the final version in which the news will appear. Therefore, clear organisation and adequate facts are important. The first paragraph gives all the information the press wants, structured around the five Ws and one H. It states what the situation or product is, who is involved, where and when it was produced, launched or used, why it is interesting or important and how it is different from others or from its predecessors. The subsequent paragraphs give more background and details in descending order.

Press releases are a kind of news story, and therefore follow the conventional layout and organisation of information used in news reporting. This is known as the *inverted pyramid format*. There are two

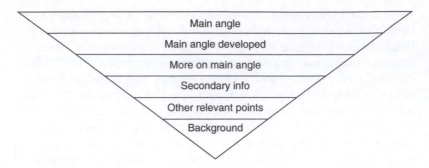

Figure 3   Inverted pyramid

reasons for this format: one is that research has shown readers of news to habitually focus on the beginning of the article and ignore the rest or skip through it, making the beginning more important; the other is that the length of an article is determined not only by its content but, more significantly, by the amount of space available on the page. Conventionally, editors cut down sentences from the end of the article to make it fit. Journalists are therefore required to write in inverted pyramid format: the most important information in the article is placed first. Non-essential information appears in the middle and end of the news item. The inverted pyramid format is shown in Figure 3.

As regards the content of press releases, the focus or angle is very important: depending on your product, event or service, will the most effective means of communicating your message be by detailing qualities, by explaining functionality and application, or by showing its novelty with regard to its predecessors in a historical framework? Press releases can be *promotional* or *informative*.

When writing a *promotional* press release, apply one of these strategies:

Product-centred strategy: This looks at features of the product, event or service, and builds a message around them. This strategy turns the product into a desirable object by using signs of value, such as prestige, ease, ethical standards, high-status, aesthetic appeal or expertise.

Prospect-centred strategy: This focuses on needs and wants of the target audience and turns product attributes into client benefits. It emphasises the functional aspects of the product in relation to their practical results or applications. It usually achieves this by outlining how a product may be used, or the products' effect on people.

Although the two strategies can be used simultaneously, the need to have a clear focus or angle means that effective press releases tend to construct their message around one of the two strategies. Regardless of the selected strategy, a press release is a promotional genre, so where possible emphasise and highlight the product's *unique selling point* (USP), describing the qualities that make it distinctive or unique in relation to predecessors or competitors. Focus on innovations and on the specific attributes and benefits that make the product a novelty.

As an example of a product-focused strategy, study Analysed Example 12, on a new laptop produced by the fictional company Wicked Wisdom.

One way to write a promotional press release is to decide on the image your want to create of the product and on the customer needs that the product satisfies, and then to brainstorm some key words, phrases and metaphors that capture this verbally. Then use these words and phrases at strategic points in the release. For example, example 12 is constructed around the idea of 'light' and 'beautiful', and this is reflected in the use of superlatives (i.e structures that show the highest level of something, such as –est adjectives) *slimmest, lightest, unique, the best, the most, the first, sharpest*. Also, the release repeats words that denote beauty, such as *beautiful, gorgeous, stupendous, magical, wonderful, dazzling, eye-catching* and *attractive* in every paragraph as well as in the title. Such strategic repetitions 'drill' the message and create a memorable impression of the product in the reader's mind. It is also more likely that these words, because of their prominence in the release, will find their way in the articles and news stories written by journalists on the product. In fact, one outcome sought after by press release writers is to encourage journalists to publish as much as possible of the original release (indeed the ideal is to have it published verbatim) in their articles.

When writing an informative press release publicising an event, development or new policy, use a narrative (storytelling) structure that recounts actions in a chronological order, highlighting their implications and importance.

Some important items in both promotional and informative press releases are:

- Clear presentation of names, dates and titles. If you use acronyms, make sure you explain what they stand for. Do not take for granted that readers will understand them, no matter how famous these acronyms may be.
- Easy to find contact details of people that the press can contact for more information. Ideally, include phone numbers, email addresses, fax numbers and physical addresses. These come at the end of the release, like a signature.

Analysed example 12

Wicked Wisdom Presents Vision

Lightest Laptop in the World with 14 inch Screen, Gorgeous Look and Dozens of Unique Features

CHICAGO—June 27, 2013—Wicked Wisdom today announced the release of Vision, the slimmest and lightest laptop in the world, with a new design that features a beautiful 14 inch screen, 15-hour battery, the unique performance and ultra- speed of 7-4500U (1.80 GHz / 3.00 GHz), and the dazzling look of HD Graphics 4400. Vision comes with OpenEye 6 operating system and, unlike other slim laptops in the market, it includes a DVD drive, and three USB drives – all without adding any weight. Loyal to its promise of giving the best vision ever, it even comes with the option of glossy or anti-glare screen.

'Vision is the most beautiful and functional machine that we've ever created,' said Andrew Watson, Wicked Wisdom's Vice President. 'We've created Vision with the best balance of innovation and functionality. Weighing only 1.2 kg, Vision is now the lightest laptop available, a product both stupendous to look at and multi-functional to use, with an attractive, custom-built 14 inch screen to suit all tastes. Its 8 GB of memory and 500 GB hard drive make it also the most powerful laptop of its kind.'

The title provides information on appearance and functionality of product and this focus is sustained throughout the release. Notice the use of superlatives 'lightest' 'gorgeous' and 'unique' to suggest the highest quality.

Consistent with the top-heavy approach of press releases, the first paragraph summarizes all the important features of the product. It also plays on the word 'vision' and the name of the product, Vision.

The second paragraph elaborates on the features listed in the first, in the form of a quotation.

Vision is the lightest laptop in the world, with an all-new carbon fiber construction that is 10 percent thinner and 20 percent lighter than other laptops. The 500 GB powerful hard drive was designed by Wicked Wisdom to increase performance and efficiency, and to support all the wonderful new features of Vision. And of course since fiber construction has no moving parts, Vision tops all others also in durability and long life.

The third paragraph continues the emphasis on superlatives (thinner, lighter). It also introduces the name of the company and positions it as an agent in the events.

The magical 14 inch screen supports millions of colors, and the HD Graphics 4400 make it the best choice for gamers and photographers alike. It is also the only slim laptop in the world to come with the option of glossy and anti-glare display – respecting the uniqueness of its users. Equipped with GMA technology, Vision gives the sharpest image from any viewing angle – perfect for making that eye-catching presentation or watching a favorite movie.

Paragraph four includes the superlatives 'best,' 'the only' and 'sharpest.' It also mentions the uniqueness of the users, which creates an association between products and users through 'uniqueness.'

Vision supports super-fast wireless standards, so you can surf the internet, download and stream content almost faster than you can think. As for battery life, Vision runs up to 15 hours, enabling you to word process, email, give presentations, or watch movies all day long. With the design of Vision, Wicked Wisdom has ushered in a new era in slim and light laptops that are uniquely beautiful in design, can be adapted to different tastes, are ultra-fast and powerful, and have a long life. And all this in just over a kilogram!

Paragraph five combines product qualities with functionality, mentions again the company name and emphasizes the company's role in designing these qualities and functions. Also, it introduces a 'you' angle, which tilts the release towards a prospect-centred approach. The release ends with a reiteration of the 'lightest' message.

- At least one relevant quotation. This makes the release more specific, by focusing on the direct words of responsible parties. It also gives the press an indication of the opinion of key figures and a lead to follow if they want to investigate further. The quotation could also be used directly in news stories and features that media professionals will write following your press release, so you are helping them by including it. Company web pages that contain press releases (and press kits sent to media outlets) also include photos and general information on the company, which journalists can use in their stories.
- A zesty, active and concise style. A press release is still a promotional text targeting publicists (it promotes to the promoters, so to speak). Therefore, follow the guidelines for business journalism given in Chapter 5. Although marketese, or pompous exaggeration, must be avoided, press releases emphasise USPs and can create a memorable image through the use of adjectives and metaphors.

If the press release is broadcast on radio or television timing is very important. The average reader can read about 150 words in a minute. Broadcasts are on average about 30 seconds. So, for a 30-second announcement, you will need about 60–70 words. Practice reading out your announcement to make sure it fits comfortably within this time frame while providing the main information. Also, note that broadcast press releases tend to begin with location. This is an influence from drama, where a scene is described before the dialogue begins. Unless you have reason to improvise, start your announcement by stating the scene. Because broadcast announcements are spoken, avoid abbreviations and acronyms, unless they are well-known (e.g. NASA). Finally, incorporate quotations in your own words (that is, paraphrase them) to fit with the reading voice.

Writing content for websites

An internet primer

High visibility and low cost make websites the most effective and fastest means of publicity. Since the medium of websites is the Internet, an overview of its nature would be useful here. This sub-section is quite basic, so those with more experience in digital media can skip it.

Think of your computer as divided into three parts: the *hardware* (also known as the part that you can kick!), the *operating system* and the *software*. The hardware is the actual electronics and wiring of the computer, and includes memory, hard drive capacity, the presence of different drives (e.g. CD Rom, DVD, etc.) and type of screen. The hardware gives the computer its inherent power, so, for example, if you want to run multimedia applications, you need a computer with a certain size of hard drive and a minimum of megabytes (MB) of memory. Otherwise, the computer will not be able to handle the programs you try to feed it. The next step from hardware is the *operating system* (OS), or platform, that you choose, and this determines general *functionality* (how the computer works) and *interface* (what the design of the screen looks like). It also determines the kind of software you can install and run. Currently, the two most common commercial platforms are Microsoft Windows and Macintosh. There is also a number of free platforms, known as 'Open Source Software'.

Software refers to the programs, or applications, that you install. There is software for different purposes: for example, Microsoft Word is a very widespread word processing program, and Adobe Photoshop an equally popular graphics program. Most software programs come in two formats, for either Windows or Macintosh platforms.

To connect to the Internet, you need a *browser* and an *ISP* (*Internet Service Provider*). The browser is the software that allows your computer to access data on the World Wide Web; for example, Internet Explorer and Firefox are two very popular browsers. The Internet is actually a huge, centreless, network of computers connected through individual *servers* – the part of a company's computer network that connects directly to the Internet. If you are an individual user, you need a provider that has a server in order to connect (usually at a set fee). Companies and institutions have their own servers. What is known as a *web address* (or *URL, Uniform Resource Locator*) is actually a link to a server. If you want to publish any material on the Internet, such as a website, you need a server, which will *host* your site.

Everyday talk often confounds the Internet with the World Wide Web. A distinction is, however, necessary. The Internet includes the Web; in fact, the Internet is the infrastructure level of the medium, and includes such services as email. The Web is the public face of the Internet medium, where users access information on products and services by visiting websites (allowing for the existence of secure pages, of course, which make the Web not so public!).

As noted in Chapter 4, it is important to remember that the Internet is a medium – not a genre. In other words, it provides the means of transmission and exchange of different forms of information presented in different document types. For example, you can send a report via email as an attachment, or post it as a *portable document format* (PDF) on a site. The document would still be report genre, regardless of its medium of transmission. In other words, when composing it, you should still follow the conventions and expectations of report writing. Microsoft Word, for instance, creates documents that are generally intended to be read in printed form or *hard copy*, even though they have been created and maybe sent in a digital medium.

Multimedia

Before anything else, remember that websites are addressed to users rather than readers. This means they must provide information in a way that is consistent with the nature of their medium, and in a way that makes full use of the medium's resources. Digital capabilities are often grouped under the umbrella term *multimedia*, which includes *text, graphics, sound, video* and *animation.* The potential of multimedia is increasingly recognised and used in most areas of communication: in education, entertainment and business. In fact, new fields of communication have emerged through the use of multimedia applications, such as the creative combination of educational, information and entertainment techniques that have come to be known as *edutainment* and *infotainment* (see also Kostelnick and Roberts 1998; Heskett 2005; Bateman 2011).

The fact that the digital medium is actually a collection of different media capabilities gives the web designer a singular task: to coordinate the different media and produce, through their combination, an effective and compelling result. As the technology for graphics, sound, video and animation is constantly changing, the next section focuses on text.

Digital text

Content is still the most important factor in website development. A website is, in most cases, not just an ornamental piece used for decoration. It should provide specific information that will attract and interest readers and motivate them to take some form of action (such as contacting the company, buying a product, etc.) in response to the information presented. This makes text the fundamental element in website development. Surveys of product marketing on the web, for example, generally find that there are more return visits to sites with substantial text content than to those that rely on other multimedia elements. This suggests that most users still expect the graphic elements to complement the text rather than the other way round (Nielsen 2000; Nielsen and Tahir 2001).

The writing strategies outlined throughout this book are valid also for web design. The fundamental principles of clarity, conciseness and accuracy are as important in websites as they are in other types of professional documents. In addition to these, text that is read on a computer monitor requires some other considerations. When writing content for websites follow these guidelines:

Balance text with other media. The visual nature of electronic communication should be acknowledged by blending verbal information with visual or aural components to produce a multi-sensory effect. Sites that rely too much on verbal language exhaust users and are not likely to have a strong appeal. If you have a lot of written information to communicate, it is best to include *portable document format* (PDF) files or printable brochures in your site. These can be printed out as complete, numbered pages, becoming much easier to read.

Begin with the most important information. Although this is valid also for other types of journalistic documents, it is of special significance in websites. Pages load from top to bottom, so the users need to read something compelling in the first eight seconds or they might leave. As graphics take longer to download than text, make sure the users have something substantial to read while waiting – preferably some information on the purpose of the site or on the function of the company hosting it. The most common form of information distribution on the web is the inverted pyramid style, described above. The conclusion or central point of the document goes first, followed by information in descending order of importance.

Organise text into small chunks. Words, sentences and paragraphs should be shorter in electronic format than in print, and they are better presented in columns balanced with other media, rather than across the screen. In all, layout considerations for web writing are more similar to journalism than to other professional writing, such as reports. Visual information is processed faster than verbal information, so try to make electronic text as visual as possible.

Select font, colour and size carefully. Fonts are divided into *serif* and *sans serif*. Sans serif fonts are easier to read in multimedia format, which may include colours and graphics. See the section on typography, which follows, for more tips on fonts.

Restrict the use of upper case to major headings. Experiments have shown that upper case fonts reduce the readability of text and increase reading time by about 10 per cent. Reading from a screen increases reading time by about 25 per cent, so text has to be made as easy as possible to read.

Be aware of the aesthetic that your audience values. Online articles that show an *elitist hipster attitude* (a term coined by the editor of the online magazine *Charged*) tend to be more easily recognisable as a distinctive Internet style, and, therefore, are more appealing. This suggests that there is a trend for online writing to be informal, and playful, although still grammatically correct and well informed ('cool' does not equal 'sloppy'). Comparing this with print formats shows that the electronic text is closer to journalist style than to specialist style. However, the Internet is too diverse to be bound by one aesthetic. There are as many styles in cyberspace as there are cultural communities in the physical world, so audience and purpose analysis techniques are as important here as in other forms of document production.

Cater for international audiences. One thing to remember when choosing words and phrases for your web content is that your audience will be international. This means that many local terms and symbols may be misunderstood by outsiders. For this reason, most multinational corporations employ technical writers and language specialists to *localise* products; that is, to research and recommend appropriate, inoffensive, memorable and pleasant-sounding terminology for international audiences.

Use colour effectively. Colour is useful for emphasising important information, grouping related items, reinforcing site structure and increasing comprehension and recall. When using colour, be aware that it can change the appearance of objects, including text type. For example, warm and bright colours make things look larger than cool and dark colours, so, for example, if you use a black screen use bigger text. Also be aware that people cannot look into bright colours for long, so avoid dense text on a bright screen. *Shape* also affects the appearance of colours. Use blue for large areas and backgrounds, but not for text type, thin lines or small shapes, as it is difficult to focus on blue. To remember the impact of colour on the user, think of the *colour spectrum* (ROYGBIV) running from the front of the screen to the back. For example, red, orange and yellow will stand out the most; blue, indigo and violet will recede into the background. Keep in mind also that colour and shape carry symbolism that varies from culture to culture. This is of particular relevance if you are aiming for an international audience.

Optimise your website for different devices. Don't assume that users will visit the site from a desktop or laptop computer. The internet is also accessed from mobile phones and digital tablets, so keep this in mind when writing text or designing multimedia.

According to usability expert Jakob Nielsen (2000), ineffective web writing is characterised by:

- long blocks of prose, without paragraphing or headings, making it difficult to scan quickly
- overly wordy expositions of concepts, with more than one idea per paragraph
- obscure or confusing headings rather than ones that are immediately understandable and informative
- little or no hypertext or links
- indirect or delayed exposition with main points or conclusions presented near the end of the text (as opposed to inverted pyramid style, which is more effective)
- marketese or exaggerated language
- technically complex elements (such as animations, unnecessary special effects, etc.) that expand file size and slow page loading
- inadequate site search functions that limit navigation.

Besides its use in business websites, digital writing is attracting attention from text and cultural theorists because of its potential to change the cognitive aspects of writing. For example, linguist and philosopher of language Roy Harris (2000) distinguishes three stages in the understanding of writing: *crypto-literacy*, where writing is seen though the lens of magic and secret knowledge, associated with occult or esoteric practices and beliefs; *utilitarian literacy*, where writing is seen as a practical tool for achieving particular ends and being equivalent to speech; and *full literacy*, where writing is considered to be 'a particular mode of operation of the human mind and the key to a new concept of language' (Harris 2000: x–xi). Full literacy has not been achieved by any society yet, although Harris suggests that digital technology could well herald its era because of the extensive experimentation with language that computers encourage and make possible.

Two major factors that contribute to the large scope for experimentation inherent in digital writing are *hypertext* and *collaboration* (see also Landow 2006). Hypertext challenges the linear perception of the printed text by including links to different sites, thereby connecting content from different fields. Hypertext does not only allow for creative associations, but also changes the ways knowledge is defined. Historically, the last time an invention produced a similar result was the creation of the encyclopaedia in the seventeenth century. Collaboration challenges the notion of sole author, since many digital texts are written by various authors. In some situations, such as wikis, collaborative authoring is the norm. This collaborative element of digital writing also enables professionals from different countries to contribute to a project simultaneously, thereby emphasising the importance of 'expert community' rather than 'local community'.

All in the (type) family: fonts

This section looks at typography: the study of writing characters, or fonts. Fonts are arranged in generalised groupings known as 'type families'. Type families are divided into *individual* and *specific*. For example, Arial is a member of the sans serif family, which can include specific groups such as 10 point Arial, 12 point Arial Bold, 8 point Arial Italic and so on. Some of the more common families are:

Serif: Serif fonts have little 'tails' on the end of letterforms. These 'tails' help the eye to quickly define letters and words and are easier to read in print than other families. They have an ancient history: the Romans chiselled serif typefaces on their buildings. One serif font is Century Schoolbook, which was designed in the USA in the early twentieth century for use in primary school textbooks.

Century Schoolbook

Sans serif: The art and literary movements of the early twentieth century, particularly those following World War I, brought sans serif typefaces. As the name implies, the 'tails' are missing, giving a stripped down, unemotional, nihilist typeface reflecting the ideologies of that era. Today, sans serif fonts are the favourites of advertising designers and transportation signage creators. They are the preferred font for electronic writing as they are easy to read on a computer monitor.

Verdana

Script: Originally designed to put feeling back into the mechanical world of printing, scripts are used to imitate handwriting. Never use all uppercase letters in a script typeface. It is incredibly difficult to read.

Lucida Calligraphy

Decorative: Some type is not meant to be read in large text blocks. Decorative faces are great for headlines, signage and other uses, but use them sparingly.

Engraved: Engraved fonts have a classical, sophisticated and elegant look. They are based on the work of John Caxton, the founder of the British printing and typography industry in the seventeenth century.

Colonna MT

Black Letter (also known as Fraktur): In the sixteenth and seventeenth centuries, printing and type design were wrapped up in the political and economic birth of European nation states. A few examples of these 'nationalistic' typefaces remain in Cyrillic (Russian alphabet) and Black Letter. This typefont has a Gothic touch to it and is associated with horror movies, prison tattoos and Nazis! Because of these connotations, use with care. Once again, avoid setting words in all uppercase in this font.

Lucida Blackletter

Dingbats: Dingbats are symbols masquerading as letters. Use very, very sparingly and only for fun. Definitely avoid if precision and clarity are your aims!

✳❂□❉✤✣■✳❂❀▼▲

Website Structure

In developing websites or in evaluating currently existing ones, in addition to content, consider two other factors: *page design* and *navigation*. Design and navigation should be developed at the same time as content. This gives balance and consistency to the website and makes an overall better impression of an integrated product.

Navigation on web pages is equivalent to turning the pages in a book. As the users do not have all the pages in front of them and cannot skip rapidly through them, designers should be careful to create a navigation structure that follows a logical organisation, in accordance with number of pages and amount of information. Navigation takes place through *links*, and in designing links, the considerations are similar to those involved in paragraphing and sectioning written texts. For example, questions to be considered are:

- How many links to make and what to call them.
- What information to put in each linked page.
- How to cross-reference pages so that the user does not have to go back to the Home Page in order to access another link. Appropriate navigation bars at the side and/or top of pages are effective in achieving this.

Navigation involves the *information architecture* of a website. There are three basic architectural designs:

- **Sequential**: this involves simple navigation and is suitable for sites that describe products. This requires scrolling down a page or 'jumping' to a section within the page, usually by means of devices called *anchors*. Sequential navigation is not advisable if there is a lot of information to communicate because it comes across as one big chunk of unprocessed writing and tends to lose the interest of the user.
- **Hierarchical**: commonly used in company websites, this navigates through static taxonomies (i.e. broad categories, equivalent to chapters in a book: 'Company History', 'Recruitment Procedures', etc.). Hierarchical navigation takes the user from one page to another by clicking on links and involves minimum scrolling.
- **Network**: this navigates through associative links and is suitable for research or exploring (search engines are an example of this). Network navigation takes the user from one site to another rather than from one page to another in the same site.

Checklist for evaluating content, aesthetics and usability of websites

How much credibility you give to a website depends, as do all other genres, on *purpose* and *intended audience.* For example, if the site was designed for entertainment purposes, factors such as accuracy of factual information and in-depth analysis of topics would not be suitable criteria for evaluation. Similarly, a promotional site should be evaluated according to advertising, as opposed to scholarly, criteria. For example, does the site attract attention through graphic design and text that is appealing to its target audience? Does it provide information that anticipates the users' questions and concerns?

Table 9 is a checklist of the most important aspects of an effective website. Refer to this checklist both when you design your own site and when you evaluate others' sites:

Table 9: Website Checklist
CONTENT
Relevance
☐ Does the site provide information relevant to its topic?
☐ Does the content reflect the title of the site, and are all headings and sections useful in determining content?

Timely/current information
☐ Does the site include a date for the information it presents?

Purpose
☐ If it is a commercial site, has an exaggerated promotional writing style, or marketese, been avoided?
☐ Is the language and style used appropriate to the content, purpose and audience?

Scannable
☐ Do users have the option to scan table of contents, section of summaries, bullets and boldface, short paragraphs?

Concise
☐ Is the text clear and concise?
☐ Is text organised in small chunks?

Writing
☐ Is spelling and grammar correct?
☐ Is there introductory text where necessary?
☐ Do multimedia elements support the task?

AESTHETICS
Audio
☐ Does the music evoke an appropriate emotion?
☐ Does the audio help to set the scene?

Video
☐ Is it useful?
☐ Is the quality adequate?
☐ Does it load quickly?

Animation
☐ Is it useful?
☐ Is the quantity suitable?

Graphics
☐ Do they complement the text?
☐ Are they stored for maximum compression (in other words, do they take the least space possible for their size and therefore decrease downloading time)?

Colour
☐ Is the choice appropriate for the site?
☐ Is the number of colours suitable?
☐ Are colours used consistently?

Typography
- ☐ Is the font appropriate to the content of the site?
- ☐ Are there sufficient margins?

Layout and design
- ☐ Does the page fit on the screen?
- ☐ Is the layout consistent throughout the site?
- ☐ Does the site appear pleasing?

USABILITY
Download time
- ☐ Does the content download fast enough (up to 10 seconds)?

Ease of use
- ☐ Are options visible without scrolling?
- ☐ Is it possible to compare all options at the same time?

Links/Image map
- ☐ Do link names match page names?
- ☐ Are link headings easy to understand?
- ☐ Do all the links work?
- ☐ Is there a clear link to the Home Page?
- ☐ Are clickable areas obvious in the image map?

Navigation
- ☐ Is the navigation scheme obvious?
- ☐ Does each page include information on the site?
- ☐ Can the user go from one page to another without returning to the Home Page?
- ☐ Is hierarchical and/or sequential navigation used effectively?

Platform and device
- ☐ Does the site work with all major browsers?
- ☐ Does the site work on small and large monitors?
- ☐ Does the site work on mobile phones and tablets?

Social media

As one of the 'new' media (in contrast to the 'older' *print and broadcast media*), the Internet has modelled its design on preceding forms. For example, email, one of the first uses of the medium, is modelled on the memo genre, and website design is modelled on magazine layout. At its inception in the 1990s and early 2000s, the Internet emphasised its visual quality and borrowed cinematic techniques in how it organised and presented information (Manovich 2001). With its growth, however, it is changing focus and form, to a large extent because of the development of interactive features, such as the dramatically rapid expansion of *social networking*.

Social media started with the launch of *wikis* (collaborative writing systems), which allowed different users to contribute to a writing project. *Wikipedia* (launched in 2001) is a prime example of this. The subsequent years saw the development of other social media sites that allowed the interaction of different users: *Facebook* and *Flickr* were launched in 2004, *YouTube* in 2005 and *Twitter* in 2006. These media have come to be known as *Web 2.0*, and are based on *user-generated content* (UGC) – that is, writing produced by users of the Internet regardless of expertise or status (although, of course, access to the Internet and to the particular site, as well as a certain degree of skill, are assumed).

At the same time, the advent of social media saw the development of sub-genres, such as *citizen journalism*, where 'ordinary' citizens create news content, using devices such as mobile phones, and upload it to relevant news sites. Sometimes, as when the news comes from politically restricted areas, such as war zones, news and images delivered by non-specialist bystanders have become the only timely source of information. In fact, this kind of user empowerment in Web 2.0 led *Time* magazine to name as person of the year 2006 'You' (meaning the individual users of the world). This person of the year was imaged by using a reflective surface mounted on a computer screen and carrying the headline 'You. Yes, you. You control the Information Age. Welcome to your world' (Cull 2011: 3).

What is the effect of social media on business, and, in particular, on professional writing? The high popularity of social media (when writing this chapter in January 2013, *Facebook* had about one billion users, which is approximately one out of every seven people on the planet) has made it almost imperative for businesses to incorporate them in their communications strategy. At the time of writing this book, *all* major international corporations had accounts with social media sites, and kept these updated to the minute. In fact, public relations experts advise companies to make the most of social media by joining sites such as *Facebook*, *LinkedIn* and *Twitter*, contributing to *Wikipedia*, adding content to *YouTube*, and blogging.

Social media have allowed companies to very quickly respond to a relevant event, and to direct users' attention to desirable content. For example, the following tweet by IBM, posted on 7 January 2013, aims to raise interest in IBM-related concerns:

IBM @IBM
9 People You Should Meet:
http://asmarterplanet.com/blog/2013/01/22446.html
(Source: https://twitter.com/IBM)

Such entries give writers the opportunity to direct readers to more expansive genres, such as blogs or online articles, and generate more company-controlled data on the Internet. Although they create avenues for discussion and exchange of ideas, they are also means by which to promote the company image.

Social media have also created a new kind of professional, a 'social media expert', with a clearly defined company position. The job of a social media expert is to keep an eye on what users are saying about the company, to respond to users and to advise management on ways to use social media to enhance the company reputation. Similarly, there are consulting companies whose mission is to advise companies on their social media image – known as *reputation management*. These professionals monitor the Internet for potentially damaging information about their client, and assist their client in handling such information if it emerges.

Personal interviews with such professionals have revealed some techniques of reputation management. These include posting positive data to cover the damaging material, and even contacting reviewers and bloggers who have posted negative feedback about the client, to negotiate the removal or amendment of this information. In one example, whose particulars must remain confidential, a company received a negative review by a popular video blogger, whose entry received thousands of views and comments. After research, the company found the blogger's email and contacted him. Following a discussion, the blogger refused to take down his comments, but agreed to post a new entry describing how the company contacted him and showed interest in his opinion. The situation, therefore, was given a different spin, one more favourable to the company. Although the ethical concerns revolving around such matters are complicated, the fact remains that social media have increased peer-to-peer feedback and recommendations, as well as support, and have introduced an era where consumer-to-consumer and consumer-to-company communication has increasing influence on social perceptions of the company. Needless to say, the most ethically constructive way for a company to use customers' reviews and feedback is to learn what people think and to respond to concerns truthfully.

As regards writing style and genre considerations, social media, being informal venues of information, tend to follow journalistic conventions. The speed in which entries are written and the small space they occupy do not allow for elaborations, definitions or extensive analyses. In fact, Twitter modelled its genre on *short message service* (SMS) text-messaging, or *textese*, favouring abbreviated words. It is therefore very important to consider carefully every word written to ensure it has the appropriate impact, as the risks of miscommunication in social media are high.

A trend in the use of social media by companies is to attempt to create a friendly and approachable image in the public mind. This attempt can have both positive and negative results. The positive effects are more clearly seen when the company's tweet or blog entry is about a new product, especially one that is likely to be well-received by the public. The negative effects emerge when the company attempts to use social media to deal with an explosive or controversial situation. In fact, the directness of social media does not create the right atmosphere for the reception of 'bad news'. For example, the tweet below was written by BP on 15 December 2010 while the company was under scrutiny for its oil-spill disaster in the US:

> BP Public Relations @BPGlobalPR
> The bad news – we're being sued by the United States. The good news – they sue in dollars, not pounds. 1.5538
> (Source: https://twitter.com/BPGlobalPR)

Given the nature of the event, and the public's reaction, a humorous tone would not be advisable in any communication about this topic – making the above comment rather inappropriate.

A characteristic example of the misuse of social media is seen in the case of Australian Airline Qantas (see *Qantas Twitter contest draws thousands of angry replies,* 2011). In October 2011, due to an industrial dispute, Qantas grounded its fleet internationally for two days. This resulted in thousands of disgruntled passengers who were left stranded around the world. Instead of using social media to apologise and appease the public, Qantas decided to draw attention away from the strike and on to something more positive. Therefore they started a competition for a luxury holiday and advertised it on Twitter, just one day after the strike ended. This decision backfired on them, however, as they attracted a flood of angry replies. For example, one tweeter wrote, 'Qantas Luxury means sipping champagne on your corporate jet while grounding the entire airline, country, customers and staff'. The tweet obviously antagonised the readers and didn't pay attention to *writer–reader complicity*. Returning to the push–pull media distinction, this tweet 'pulled' unwanted responses. This shows that rhetorical concerns, such as the audience's attitude, should always be taken into account when deciding what to write, when to write it and where to write it.

Example: blogging

Here is the complete blog referred to in IBM's tweet, cited above. Notice how it repeats the word 'smart'. This is a strategic choice since IBM's 'unique selling point' and company image include the category 'smart' (which combines the meanings of intelligence and attractiveness) as a defining feature. To pursue this further, do a search on Google for 'IBM smart' and see how many links you get. Notice also the use of hypertext and tags to connect IBM pages and to ensure recognition by search engines. Regarding style, notice the use of short paragraphs (one to two sentences), and concise but informative sentences – all features characteristic of journalistic style. In all, this blog shows the qualities of business blogging: it raises interest, provides some new information, directs to other company-related material and helps to reinforce the company image by reflecting the company style (in this case centred on the word 'smart').

9 People You Should Meet: A Year of People for a Smarter Planet
By Richard Silberman, Writer/Researcher, IBM Communications

During the past year, we've profiled nine exceptional "People for a Smarter Planet" who exemplify the spirit of change, innovation, creativity and curiosity that lie at the core of building a smarter planet. They are inventors and researchers, academics and executives, thought leaders, dreamers, risk-takers, pioneers.

These individuals come from a wide range of fields and possess an array of interests and expertise. What they all have in common is a passion for their work and a commitment to make the world a better place.

They include Ruhong Zhou, whose avian flu research may help prevent a global pandemic; Dave Bartlett, IBM's smarter buildings guru; Bill Reichert, a Silicon Valley venture capitalist with novel advice for entrepreneurs; and sustainability expert Sarah Slaughter.

If you haven't met them yet, here are nine People for a Smarter Planet you should know.

Technorati Tags: business analytics, cloud, IBM Research, IBM Smarter Planet, innovation, smarter analytics, Smarter Industries, Smarter People

(Source: http://asmarterplanet.com/blog/2013/01/22446.html. Reprint Courtesy of International Business Machines Corporation, © 2013 International Business Machines Corporation.)

Public speeches

A major way in which professionals communicate with the public is through speeches – this is especially true of top management executives. Speeches can be made during press conferences, followed by Question and Answer (Q&A) sessions, or through broadcasts (radio, television), and digital (YouTube, company website) media. In many cases, the speech becomes available in written form for future reference. In all cases, important public speeches are written first, and then memorised or read aloud. Different occasions call for a speech. Also, the speech could have different audiences and would need to be adapted to suit the knowledge and interests of each. For example, speeches to the wider public tend to contain more general information and a zestier style than speeches addressed to investors and shareholders, which include specific details and a more 'bottom-line' approach. Speeches in business contexts generally fall into four broad categories:

Motivation: CEOs and successful entrepreneurs are often invited to give inspirational speeches where they describe their successes and failures and give advice to new professionals.

Promotion: A speech is often an effective medium to promote the qualities of a new product or service because the physical presence of the speaker can enthuse the audience and create interest. This is especially true if the speaker is charismatic and uses appealing and innovative methods of presentation.

Apology: After an accident or mistake caused by a company, the CEO must publicly accept responsibility and apologise. Apology speeches, part of *crisis management* and *image restoration*, are very important in ensuring that the reputation of the company is not damaged irreparably. Apology speeches must be timely (delays have been found to have negative effects on the company reputation) and constructive (the apology itself is not enough – the speaker must show the company is taking measures to effectively repair the situation).

Progress: In large scale projects that have public significance (for example, when tax payers' money is used), it is important to keep the public informed of events and developments. Press releases can play this role, but at pivotal stages of the project a speech can personalise the project and create a favourable impression.

Consider an apology speech as an example. Below is an abridged version of BP CEO Tony Hayward's speech on the oil spill accident in the Gulf Coast of the US in 2010. The speech was delivered by Hayward on 17 June 2010, addressing the congressional committee (the full speech text can be found at http://www.guardian.co.uk/business/2010/jun/17/bp-tony-hayward-oil-spill-statement). Although this is a shortened version it retains the original organisation and sequencing of information.

In terms of content, apology speeches contain the following information in a sequence appropriate to the actual incident addressed. When writing an apology speech consider including these elements:

1 Acknowledge the extent and seriousness of the situation – do not attempt to downplay the importance of what happened.
2 Apologise both on behalf of the company and on behalf of yourself as a fellow human being.
3 Show personal concern by acknowledging the suffering of victims and/or the damage to the environment.
4 Acknowledge the concern of the public: show an understanding of the questions that they are asking.
5 Reassure that the company is taking action and measures to repair the situation and to learn from it so that it is not repeated.
6 Show sincerity and humility: do not claim you know all the answers.
7 Where appropriate (depending on audience and context), give technical and detailed information of causes and/or resources used to fix the problem. Expertise is an important quality in organisational crises in re-establishing trust that the company is using all appropriate resources.
8 Name any collaborating companies or government agencies and explain their role. This is a technique of transparency as well as shared responsibility but it must be handled with great care as it can easily become a scapegoating exercise or appear as a method for displacing blame.

Read the speech and see if and how these elements are present.

Tony Hayward's Speech

The explosion and fire aboard the Deepwater Horizon and the resulting oil spill in the Gulf of Mexico never should have happened and I am deeply sorry that they did. None of us yet knows why it happened. But whatever the cause, we at BP will do what we can to make certain that an incident like this does not happen again.

Since April 20, I have spent a great deal of my time in the Gulf Coast region and in the incident command center in Houston, and let there be no mistake – I understand how serious this situation is. This is a tragedy: people lost their lives; others were injured; and the Gulf Coast environment and communities are suffering. This is unacceptable, I understand that, and let me be very clear: I fully grasp the terrible reality of the situation.

I want to acknowledge the questions that you and the public are rightly asking. How could this happen? How damaging is the spill to the environment? Why is it taking so long to stop the flow of oil and gas into the Gulf?

And questions are being asked about energy policy more broadly: Can we as a society explore for oil and gas in safer and more reliable ways? What is the appropriate regulatory framework for the industry?

We don't yet have answers to all these important questions. But I hear the concerns, fears, frustrations – and anger – being voiced across the country. I understand it, and I know that these sentiments will continue until the leak is stopped, and until we prove through our actions that we will do the right thing. Our actions will mean more than words, and we know that, in the end, we will be judged by the quality of our response. Until this happens, no words will be satisfying.

Among the resources that have been made available:

Drilling and technical experts who are helping determine solutions to stopping the spill and mitigating its impact, including specialists in the areas of subsea wells, environmental science and emergency response; Technical advice on blowout preventers, dispersant application, well construction and containment options;

Additional facilities to serve as staging areas for equipment and responders, more remotely operated vehicles (ROVs) for deep underwater work, barges, support vessels and additional aircraft, as well as training and working space for the Unified Command.

Working under the umbrella of the Unified Command, BP's team of operational and technical experts is coordinating with many federal, state, and local governmental entities and private sector organizations. These include the Departments of Interior, Homeland Security, Energy, and Defense, the National Oceanic and Atmospheric Administration (NOAA), US Fish & Wildlife Service (USFW), National Marine Fisheries Service (NMFS), EPA, OSHA, Gulf Coast state environmental and wildlife agencies, the Marine Spill Response Corporation (MSRC) (an oil spill response organization), as well as numerous state, city, parish and county agencies.

Our efforts in response to this incident are focused on two critical goals:

Successfully stopping the flow of oil; and
Minimizing the environmental and economic impacts from the oil spill.

These are without a doubt complex and challenging tasks. While we have had to overcome hurdles, we are doing everything we can to respond as quickly and effectively as we can.
The investigation team's work thus far suggests that this accident was brought about by the apparent failure of a number of processes, systems and equipment. While the team's work is not done, it appears that there were multiple control mechanisms – procedures and equipment – in place that should have prevented this accident or reduced the impact of the spill. The investigation is focused on the following seven mechanisms:

1. The cement that seals the reservoir from the well;
2. The casing system,which seals the well bore;
3. The pressure tests to confirm the well is sealed;
4. The execution of procedures to detect and control hydrocarbons in the well, including the use of the blowout preventer (BOP) and the maintenance of that BOP;
5. The BOP Emergency Disconnect System, which can be activated by pushing a button at multiple locations on the rig;
6. The automatic closure of the BOP after its connection is lost with the rig; and
7. Features in the BOP to allow ROVs to close the BOP and thereby seal the well at the seabed after a blowout.

I understand people want a simple answer about why this happened and who is to blame. The truth, however, is that this is a complex accident, caused by an unprecedented combination of failures. A number of companies are involved, including BP, and it is simply too early to understand the cause.

In terms of delivery, keep in mind that a speech is a physical performance depending for its effect on tone of voice, volume, body posture, gesture and facial expression. Select words and sentences that would allow the speaker to express his/her physical presence, and avoid long sentences, multi-layered concepts or over-technical terminology.

Interviews

A press interview is an oral communication, similar in many ways to a speech. As successful professionals, you may often be invited to present your work to the public through an interview. Table 10 gives some useful guidelines in preparing for this.

Table 10: Guidelines for media interviews

Before the interview
- Learn as much as possible about the reporter, publication/program interview format, audience.
- Have a clear idea of your goal for the interview.
- Know what you want to say: review your key message points.
- Jot down likely questions and appropriate answers.

Interview tips
- Speak in 'headlines': offer conclusion first, briefly and directly, and back it with facts or 'proof points'.
- Do not 'over answer': short answers are better than long.
- Do not be trapped by a question, 'bridge' it to a related point you want to make.
- When asked about a problem, talk about a solution.
- Do not let false charges, facts or figures offered by a reporter stand uncorrected; interviews are opportunities to correct misconceptions.
- Do not repeat a reporters negative statements: frame your reply as a positive statement.
- Speak clearly: avoid technical jargon.
- If you do not know the answer admit it (positively, if possible) and assure the reporter that you will find and provide the needed facts in a timely manner, or offer to assist the reporter in finding that other source.
- Do not overlap the interviewer's question; begin your answer when the reporter is finished.
- Keep cool – do not be provoked, and never lie to a reporter.

For telephone and radio interviews
- Buy preparation time by asking to call the reporter back if deadline allows.
- Establish an 'interview atmosphere' and mindset.
- Use notes.
- Ask questions in order to gain feedback.
- For radio, speak visually – use words to paint pictures.

For television interviews
- Take care with appearance and clothes: for women, avoid solid black or white or busy patterns; for men, a dark suit works best.
- Do not wear large, shiny or noisy jewellery, unless this reflects the image you want to project.
- Sit upright, but don't be too stiff, slightly forward in the chair.
- Unbutton suit jacket when seated.
- Resist the urge to shout into the microphone; speak and gesture naturally.
- Talk to the reporter/interviewer, not the camera.
- Keep a pleasant expression; smile when appropriate.
- Hold your 'interview attitude' from the moment you are lit until the interview is completely over and the camera is off.

Activities

1 Collect as many public relations documents as you can from two competing companies in the same industry and compare them. What similarities and differences can you find in writing strategy, style and layout? How does the company's image (i.e. the desired way the company wants the public to see it) account for the differences? Can you see any differences between push and pull media?

2 Read Steve Jobs' (CEO and Founder of Apple Computers) famous motivational speech at Stanford University, given in 2005. Analyse its style and structure. Then watch the video and notice how the written speech was 'performed' physically. Listen to the tone of voice and watch the body language. Then discuss your impressions. Both oral and written versions of the speech can be found at http://news.stanford.edu/news/2005/june15/jobs-061505.html.

Reports and Proposals

Focus:

- The report genre
- Types and functions of reports
- Proposals
- Report structure

This chapter looks at longer business documents, in particular proposals, business plans and investigative reports. The guidelines and formats outlined here are based on standard, international conventions where English is the medium of communication. Keep in mind, however, that format and structure of reports vary to a certain extent to suit the needs of the particular company, writing situation and audience. As noted before, many companies have in-house templates that should be used. In all, however, the framework presented here will alert you to the factors that you should take into account when writing reports and creating templates and style guides for others to use.

Essays, research articles and reports

As a professional in business or industry, the longer documents you will need to produce fall into two broad categories: *reports* on various issues to management and/or clients and *articles* for professional associations and journals documenting the data you discovered in your experience. If you decide to develop your writing talents further, you might also publish popular interpretations of your work for non-specialist audiences, such as *essays* for creative non-fiction publications and *journalistic features* for magazines. Therefore, an overview of the differences among these genres would be useful.

Essays

An essay discusses a topic from different angles, synthesises ideas and develops the ramifications of an issue. Essays are generally evaluative and may include a subjective approach, which, when the essay is expertly written, is a deliberate choice. Essays are usually composed of continuous and well-developed (4–7 sentence-long) paragraphs. Cohesion and flow from one point to the next are important for the readability of an essay, especially in the absence of headings, bullet points and other highlighting signals. Essays tend to follow a linear development, building on points indicated in the introduction, and should not be repetitive. Although, to a certain extent, clarity and conciseness are valued in most document types, essays are allowed a more discursive style and idiosyncratic expression to reflect the complexity of the topic with which they deal.

For example, consider the following paragraph, in relation to its essayist patterns, from an essay by David Bohm on creativity in science (Bohm 1998: 1):

Example of Essay Paragraph

Could it be that a scientist deeply wants to discover the laws of nature, so that he can predict natural phenomena, and thus enable man to participate intelligently in nature's processes so as to produce results that he desires? Of course, such prediction and intelligent participation can sometimes be very interesting. But this is only in a context in which these activities are determined by something else that is more deeply significant, such as, for example, a common goal of great importance. Generally speaking, however, there is hardly ever such a common goal. Indeed, in most cases, the content of what the research scientist predicts is in itself actually rather trivial (the precise paths of particles, the precise number of instruments that will register a certain phenomenon, and so forth). Unless there were something beyond this that could give it significance, this activity would be petty, and, indeed, even childish.

The writer reflects on the nature of the scientific process by posing a question and then explaining certain implications of this question. The topic of the text is itself suited to an essay, as opposed to, say, a business report, since it can only be developed by means of speculative reasoning rather than experimental or empirical data. In addition, the answer to the question is not given in this paragraph, suggesting that this paragraph is one 'move' in a spiral of ideas leading to a conclusion that may be open ended. The style is explorative and comprehensive, rather than 'bottom line', direct and concise, as would be the style of a business document.

Research articles

Each topic of research involves different issues, problems and concerns, and requires a methodology suited to its specific qualities. In general, research is classified into two categories. *Qualitative research* is typified by cultural and conceptual studies where findings are more commonly expressed in words and logical reasoning rather than in numbers and statistical frequency. In such cases, a hypothesis is substantiated by consistent argument. *Quantitative research,* on the other hand, is typified by experimental studies in scientific disciplines where findings are usually expressed in numerical, or measurable, form. In such cases, a hypothesis is substantiated by quantifiable evidence, such as statistics.

Qualitative research articles are similar to analytical reports, which are the focus of the next section. Quantitative research articles generally include the following information:

Hypothesis: State hypotheses clearly and describe their relationship to previous research. Often, especially for the purpose of statistical testing, hypotheses are expressed in the *null* form: 'There is no difference between…' or 'There is no relation between…'.

Assumptions: If you make assumptions, state them clearly. Do not take anything for granted.

Limitations: State clearly limitations on time allowed, restrictions on length of document or lack of resources.

Scope: Set the parameters of the study by describing the elements it includes and those it excludes to make the study manageable and coherent. By delimiting the scope you set a focus and establish the big picture that justifies the details.

Definitions: Define all keywords and variables. The interpretation of the findings of a study depends to a large extent on the way major terms are defined. Define variables operationally in terms of how they are measured in quantifiable form.

Research design: Describe and justify the statistical or experimental methods for testing hypotheses. Also indicate if the application of a certain statistical test or experiment will lead to the acceptance or rejection of the stated hypotheses.

Description of population and sample: Describe and justify the population from which a representative or random sample is drawn. Show that you are not biased in your choice of population and/or sample.

Control of error: Show how you control the variables (elements that change in different conditions) that are operating in a given situation. In laboratory work it is usually possible to control major variables. In field studies it is usually only possible to control key variables. In either case, state clearly how variables are controlled.

Reliability and validity: Describe the reliability and validity of test instruments. Ensure that tests provide consistent measurements.

Reports

In business contexts, you may be required to produce three types of reports: *descriptive, technical* and *analytical. Descriptive reports* inform the reader of events that have happened in the past or that are planned for the future, and are detailed and factual. *Technical reports* describe and explain specifications, components of equipment and system applications. *Analytical reports* usually deal with a problem by identifying the issues involved, investigating solutions and recommending action. Whereas descriptive and technical reports may be based entirely on facts, analytical reports include elements of persuasion and logical reasoning. Here we consider analytical reports.

Analytical reports

Here are some major types of analytical reports and their functions (see also Kolin 1998; Bargiela-Chiappini and Nickerson 1999; Bell and Smith 2010):

Proposals and submissions show the highest level of persuasion. A proposal argues for a particular course of action and often takes the form of requests for funding or formal authorisation to pursue a particular project. While an investigative report researches a problem and suggests solutions, a proposal sets out a detailed project and in most cases includes a budget and resource requirements. Submissions argue for or against an issue to be decided by a responsible body. Members of the business community, for example, might make submissions for or against a new taxation bill under consideration by a government select committee.

Problem-solving reports analyse a problem and methodically recommend a specific course of action to solve this problem. They are also known as *investigative reports*. Such reports often require specialist knowledge and are commissioned by a client or management, who requests the writer to expertly judge certain actions and comment in detail on issues and events that relate to a particular situation.

Feasibility studies investigate a possible plan of action and advise on whether the action should be taken. For example, a software company might request a feasibility study to decide whether there is market potential to invest in a new virtual reality game. A feasibility study weighs projected costs against projected income, taking into account such aspects as demographic factors, market demand, the actions of competitors and resource requirements.

To understand better the difference in approach among these types of reports, consider this scenario. Assume you are the Director of Facilities Management in a company, in charge of ensuring security and smooth operation of building facilities. You are confronted with a problem of high electricity costs and inadequate heating. At the moment, the building uses electric heating. You could become aware of the problem in different ways, leading to different forms of communication.

For example, you could become aware of the problem through your own observations, and decide to propose a change in heating from electric to gas. In this case, you would communicate your idea in the form of a *proposal*, which would support the claim that it would be more cost effective to replace the current electric heating with gas. Alternatively, you could be led to believe that the problem is serious and long-ranging, and requires more research to find an appropriate solution. In that case, you would undertake an investigation leading to a *recommendation report* based on the problem that heating costs are high and the building is not warm enough. In your initial stage of research you are aware of the problem, but not the solution: you do not yet know if gas would be more cost effective. Finally, you could begin with the question, 'should we convert to gas heating?' and base your research and analysis accordingly, in order to answer it. Your results would then be presented in a *feasibility analysis*. This would analyse the problem and recommend action but its scope would be more limited than in an investigative report, because you would be considering only one possible solution to the problem.

These alternatives would take the following forms:

Proposal claim: It would be cheaper and more effective to replace the current electric heating with gas.

Trigger for investigation: Heating costs are high but, at the same time, the building is too cold.

Feasibility analysis: Would our heating situation work better if we converted to gas heating?

General guidelines for effective reports

All analytical report share some common compositional and structural characteristics, so these guidelines are relevant:

- Include all the information the readers need. Pay special attention to the problem or situation that triggered the report, the methods used to gather information and the findings of the investigation or data-gathering. In design reports, include information about why you made specific design decisions and justify your choices.
- Structure your report so that readers can easily locate the information they want. For example, some readers will be interested in one or several sections. This is why reports should be divided into titled and numbered sections. The executive summary and the section headings act as signposting showing the readers where to go to get what they want. Also, it is advisable to include a header or footer with identifying information on each page (such as the title of the report and your name or the title of the project). Report sections may be distributed, so readers should know where each section came from.
- Write as clearly and concisely as possible without sacrificing content or detail. Chapter 2 provides guidelines on how to achieve this. Keep in mind that clarity comes not only from style but also from the organisation of information. The pattern you create in sequencing information communicates as much as the data you present. For example, presenting information in chronological order suggests that time and progression or change are important aspects; similarly, prioritising and listing information shows the degree of importance attributed to each item in the list.

Paragraphing in analytical reports

As a researcher and writer, you will find that paragraphing offers a powerful tool for articulating and critiquing your ideas. As a communicator, you will find that paragraphing helps you to keep your reader focused on your topic and line of logic. Paragraphs enable you to divide your material into units that readers can readily cope with and assimilate into their understanding.

Report paragraphs tend to be longer than those in web content or magazine articles, but shorter than in essays. A length of four to six sentences is generally appropriate. By committing yourself to that kind of length you are serving the following objectives:

1 The paragraphs are sufficiently short so that crucial pieces of information catch the reader's eye. Reports generally contain section headings for this reason.
2 But equally, the paragraphs are long enough to allow elaboration and analysis of issues. Enough space must be given so that cause and effect, chronological, comparison/contrast and other relationships between ideas are clearly and fully expressed.

When composing report paragraphs, follow these guidelines:

1 **Avoid a succession of very short (one to two sentences) and very long (eight sentences or more) paragraphs.** The problem with short paragraphs is that they read disjointedly and present the reader with difficulty in linking your ideas together into a main message. With very long paragraphs the reader needs a pause so as to feel that s/he has read and understood a unit of the message. If you rush on without a paragraph break, the reader will soon feel overwhelmed and stop assimilating the ideas and interacting with the text.
2 **Present one main point or idea in each paragraph.** Avoid crowding a paragraph with too much vital information. If you have a large amount of reasoning or supporting examples to give for a point, break them into two paragraphs. Bear in mind that people process and commit to memory chunks of information that comprise between about five and seven items, so structure your paragraphs in a way that reflects this fact.
3 **Make sure there is enough cohesion within the paragraph.** That is, avoid listing a set of disconnected sentences. Similarly, provide adequate transition signals between paragraphs in one section. Show the reader how the idea of one paragraph is connected to the idea of the next paragraph in that section.

There are three main problems writers have when composing paragraphs:

- The paragraph could contain too much information, which can confuse the reader as to what the main point is. This is a bit like a song with discordant rhythm or beat.
- The paragraph could be abrupt, containing incomplete information on the main point. This again loses the reader, who may find it difficult to follow through a point and understand its relevance.
- The paragraph could give enough information on the main topic, but the sentences are disconnected and the paragraph lacks unity. This reads like a list of items with no connection and can be quite dull for the reader who is forced to provide all the links.

Sections and section headings

As opposed to articles and essays, where headings are optional, reports require division of paragraphs into sections, with headings for all sections. Headings summarise the point(s) of each section and make reading under pressure easier. Readers can scan a document and find information without having to read all the text. In reports, this is an important asset because, often, different people read different sections of the report. Also, headings give readers some breathing space, as they indicate where a section has ended. Finally, sections give depth and dimensionality to the report by adding levels. The main sections constitute the main level, sub-sections introduce subordinate levels, etc.

When sectioning:

1 **Balance the sections so that information is distributed effectively across the report.** Avoid short, one paragraph sections; also avoid putting the whole report in one long section. Use sub-sections for details or subordinate points of the idea of the main section. If information is important, do not bury it in a sub-section, but devote a main section to it. On the whole, avoid sub-sub-sections, for simplicity and clarity. Sub-sub-sections add layers and therefore introduce more complexity in what could already be a complex report topic. Reduce the layers by analysing information, and thereby spreading it across fewer levels.

2 **Think carefully of the quantity and quality of the information you want to include in a heading.** If a heading is too vague or general, it defeats the purpose of signalling to the reader the content of its section. Correlatively, if a heading is too long and detailed, it can slow down the flow of reading unnecessarily.

3 **Make sure all your headings of the same level have parallel structure.** When you choose a structure for all your headings, remain consistent throughout the report. For example, if you begin one heading for a main section with a gerund (an –ing form), the rest of the headings in main sections should also begin with a gerund. If you begin a heading with a noun, all headings should begin with nouns, and so on. Parallelism is discussed in more detail in Chapter 2.

The importance of headings becomes clear in the report outline. A report outline lists the sections and sub-sections that you intend to use in your report. A client or project manager often asks for an outline to monitor the progress of the report, to consider extra funding and for similar reasons. It is important, therefore, that your headings are worded and structured in a way that highlights the content and significance of your project.

Numbering of report sections

Headings and subheadings are conventionally numbered according to *alphanumeric* or *decimal numbering* methods.

Alphanumeric numbering:
I. First main idea
   A. First subdivision of main idea
   B. Second subdivision of main idea
      1. First example
      2. Second example
         (a) First detail
         (b) Second detail
   C. Third subdivision of main idea
II. Second main idea

Decimal numbering:
1. First main idea
   1.1 First subdivision of main idea
   1.2 Second subdivision of main idea
      1.2.1 First example
      1.2.2 Second example
         1.2.2.1 First detail
         1.2.2.2 Second detail
   1.3 Third subdivision of main idea
2. Second main idea

The proposal

Proposals are an extremely common type of document in professional settings. Even if your line of work does not put you in a position to write reports – say, if you are a trade journalist or a computer programmer – chances are that the time will come when you will need to submit a proposal in order to get approval and/or funding for a project. The following guidelines give an overview of the standard format and type of information associated with proposals. Many companies and funding agencies have a house-style template to be filled in when submitting a proposal. If that is the case, follow the instructions (they will not be too different from the ones outlined here). If no guidelines are offered, use the model presented here.

Proposals are initiated in two main ways: you either have an innovative idea that you believe will benefit an organisation or company and want to sell it to them, or you respond to a request for ideas that an organisation or company publicise. In the first case the proposal is *unsolicited*. In the second, it is a *request for proposals* (RFP). Unsolicited proposals are investigator initiated, and, therefore, there is often a greater need to sell the concept because it is novel and innovative. On the other hand, an RFP or a program announcement (PA) calls for research in a defined area, or requests an answer to a specific question. Here, it is a matter of matching one's expertise, ideas and plans to the solicitation.

Preliminary work for proposals

To maximise your chances for success, follow these guidelines (see also Johnson-Sheenan 2002; Taylor 2009):

1 **Work on the conceptual framework of your idea** until you really have good control over it.
2 **Articulate your conceptual framework.** Sit down with friends and/or colleagues and practise explaining your idea to them in a brief manner. If it is well conceptualised, you should be able to articulate it in a matter of sentences, over three minutes. Entertain their questions and make notes of the questions that occur. Reoccurring questions are probably indicative of problems in your communication or weaknesses in the concept. Use this feedback to improve your concept.
3 **Investigate the current and previous research.** Make sure that no one has already done the work you have in mind, or if they have, that there is something really different or necessary about your approach. You are going to have to convince the readers that your activities are unique and justified. A major 'howler' is to be informed that your project has already been done, or that you have missed a fundamental piece of work in the research.
4 **Do your homework on the agency or company.** Make sure that your idea falls within the topics they are interested in (especially if writing externally). Also, get as much information as you can on their required document formats. This will determine what attitude and style you should adopt. Familiarise yourself with the culture of the company and choose your words and expression in tune with this culture. If your proposal is unsolicited, find out about the funding capacity of the agency or company. Remember that small agencies cannot afford to fund high budget projects, so it would be a waste of time submitting ambitious proposals to them.
5 **Assess your need for collaborators.** Sometimes having collaborators can substantially strengthen your proposal. However, it is important that, from the project's inception, everyone understands their role. Make sure

that the content of each member's contribution and time allocation is understood and accepted by all.

Proposal components

Most proposals contain the following elements in the body of the document. More or less space is given to each element depending on the nature of the proposal. Therefore, some of these topics would constitute sections in some proposals, and sub-sections in others.

Project description

Identify the problem or question to be addressed and describe its implications. Give some background on the proposed project, including results from prior research. Show a clear connection between the problem, lack or gap that you identified and the role of the proposed project in dealing with it. Visuals that depict the relationship of your work to the current knowledge base or model base are often helpful in getting your message across.

Objectives or specific aims

State concisely and, where possible, in measurable terms the specific aims of the project and the hypotheses that underlie those aims or objectives. Distinguish between short term plans and long term goals. It is always useful to describe how the project can evolve and develop if the expected results are achieved (in other words, what the company or agency is buying in the long run).

Methodology

Describe precisely how you will achieve your objectives. If several outcomes (or result scenarios) are plausible, describe them. Give alternative courses of action in the event that results occurring early lead you away from your original methodology. Anticipate outcomes and have a plan to deal with them.

Evaluation

In certain proposals, especially in those for projects with long term implications, describe plans for evaluating the project. Explain how you will know if the project is producing positive results.

Personnel, qualifications and facilities

Identify who will perform the various activities or procedures described in the plan. Provide justification for each individual appropriate to his/her level of involvement, and include the qualifications of key project personnel. Make clear the reasons that make you or your team the best candidates for the project. Describe the resources that are already available for performance of the project.

Budget and justification

Work out your budget very carefully and give as much detail as possible. Itemise each cost and justify its relevance to the project. The budget is usually presented in cost sheet format. Items commonly included are: salaries and wages; fringe benefits; equipment; travel; supplies; publication charges; postage; telephone; consultants; subcontracts; and indirect costs. A justification section usually accompanies the budget, which explains how you arrived at your totals. Briefly explain how budget items were estimated and why these items are needed, if not obvious.

Sources cited

If applicable, include a list of the sources cited in the proposal, using a method of referencing that is acceptable in the subject area of your topic.

Resume/biographical sketch (optional)

In external proposals, you may need to 'sell' yourself as well as your concept. Include some details about your professional background if you think this will influence the reception of your proposal positively.

Appendices (optional)

Possible items include:

- facilities descriptions
- letters of support, illustrations
- maps
- extensive bibliography
- other material not easily incorporated into the body of the proposal.

Proposal to an editor

If you decide to submit a feature article for publication in a specialist magazine, or have an idea for a book in your area of expertise, you will need to contact an editor for approval. Although similar, in general aspects, to the model outlined above, a book or article proposal differs in some respects.

Publishers' websites include guidelines on how to submit proposals. In most cases, a book proposal is composed according to the following outline.

Description of subject of book and its position in the market

Describe the topic of the book and explain why it is significant or worthwhile in the current market. Position the book in relation to interests, needs and debates in the wider social context. Propose a title.

Distinctive features

Explain the features of the book that distinguish it and give it a unique identity.

Primary and secondary markets

Describe the target readers of the book. Will they be reading it for entertainment, instruction or other purposes? Will the book interest one particular demographic or psychographic group, or will it have different types of readers? How do you know?

Main competitors

This is a very important section, because it shows that you have researched the topic and know what is available in the market. If the book has direct competitors, you must justify why there would still be a market for your proposed book. Select two or three competing books and describe them in some detail.

Comparison of proposed book with competitors

Following from the above, explain how your book differs from the competitors. Describe the distinctive features that would make the book marketable.

Qualifications of applicant

Attach a CV, or give a biographical sketch, highlighting the qualities that enable you to write a book on the proposed topic.

Summary/outline of chapters

Give an outline of the proposed chapters, with a description of each chapter, usually of about half a page. If you have a sample chapter, attach it to the proposal as an example of your approach and style.

If writing to a magazine editor to propose an article, follow this outline.

Description of topic

Describe your topic and its scope, explaining the angle, slant or point of view that you will take. Remember to mention the proposed title (although the editor might change it).

Significance and innovation

Explain why your article will interest the target audience of this *particular* magazine. Why would the magazine benefit by including such an article in its repertoire? Remember that you need to convince the editor that your article will contribute to readers' interest in buying the magazine. Make sure you have investigated the magazine to make sure they have not already published on the topic.

Sources

List and briefly describe about five sources of information that you will use. Justify your choices by explaining the importance of the sources in the relevant field of research. Will you be conducting interviews, or primary research, or will your article be based on secondary sources?

Personal information

Describe your qualifications for writing this article, including any special expertise or knowledge in the subject area. Explain also what has spurred your interest in the topic.

Convincing evidence in proposals

The main function of proposals is to persuade. Selecting the most appropriate evidence or reasoning, therefore, is vital. The best way to achieve this is to analyse the funding agency's mission, values, policies and expectations and to present your project in response to these. A project is acceptable and worthwhile or not depending on particular contexts of reception. Merits of the project are evaluated according to different sets of standards, and knowing these standards and responding to them maximises your chances of being successful. Internal proposals have a different scope and impact than external proposals, which may involve the welfare of the public at large. The range and duration, the project's impact and the cost, are decisive elements in the persuasive force of a proposal, and you should take these into account when planning your strategy.

Argumentation theorist Stephen Toulmin (2003), for example, found that 'logical' arguments are not universal, and different discourse communities have their own expectations of the reasoning process. What is convincing evidence for natural scientists, for instance, may not be convincing for marketing experts, and what is convincing for marketing experts may not be convincing for engineers. This is corroborated by rhetoric specialists. For example, Gerard Hauser points out that:

> When we seek a project extension, argue for a raise, interview for a job [...] we are involved in acts that require good reasons. Good reasons allow our audience and ourselves to find a shared basis for cooperating [...]. You can use marvellous language, tell great stories, provide exciting metaphors, speak in enthralling tones, and even use your reputation to advantage, but what it comes down to is that you must speak to your audience with reasons they understand (Hauser 1986: 71).

In addition to learning as much as possible about the funding organisation, there are two ways to increase your chances of producing a persuasive document. One is to run your proposal by peers and mentors who are knowledgeable on the issues covered, especially if they have been successful in obtaining funding by the organisation to which you are applying. Since many projects in business and industry are collaborative, it should be easy to exchange ideas and get feedback. The second way is to consider your project from the recipient's point of view, and to brainstorm as many possible objections as you can. Play the 'devil's advocate', or get someone to play it for you, and criticise the proposed project from different angles.

Here are some common objections to business proposals:

- The proposed project is not necessary or is not valuable.
- The project is unrealistically ambitious or not well thought-out.
- The requested budget is not well justified so the result doesn't seem to justify the cost.
- The methods are not carefully thought out or are not suited to the objectives.
- The applicant doesn't seem well suited to undertake the project.

Here are some common objections to book proposals:

- The topic is not in the publisher's range of interests.
- There are enough books on the market that deal with this topic (or, the publisher has enough books on this topic).
- The target market is not well defined.
- The topic is too specialised to interest a wide audience.
- The scope (proposed content) is too broad or too narrow.

Table 11 shows the layout of a business proposal.

Table 11: Layout of business proposal

- Title page
- Executive summary (for longer proposals)
- Table of contents (for longer proposals)
- Description of project
- Objectives of project
- Benefits of project
- Proposed method
- Evaluation of project (for projects with long-term goals)
- Facilities and personnel
- Budget
- Proposer's CV (for external proposals)

The business plan

When starting your own business, you need to attract investors, high-quality employees, collaborators and other desired relationships. To achieve this, you must persuade those groups that you are well organised, have a clear, realistic and ambitious vision and are aware of competitors and market needs. The business plan, which many see as a sub-genre of the proposal because of its persuasive approach, articulates these elements and reflects your drive and professional competence. Like other important business documents, a business plan involves identifying the target audience, gathering accurate and convincing data, and carefully sectioning and organising the information in an accessible way (see also Nesheim 2000; Kawasaki 2011). The key sections of the body of a business plan are as follows:

Company and product/service description: This covers the company's mission, history, current situation, strategies and plans for the future. The start-up, or new company, is intrinsically linked with the products and/or services that it offers and which define it. Therefore, discuss the vision of the company in relation to what it produces. Divide this into sub-sections for clarity.

The market and competition: This section defines the company's target market, the industry as a whole, current and potential clients/buyers and competitors. The section should explain how buying decisions are made, how the market is segmented, what your intended market position is and what your defensive strategy will be to deal with competitors. Show that you are aware of your product or services positioning in the local and/or international market, and that you have a clear vision of how it will be distinctive in relation to competitors. Try to formulate your product in terms of a unique selling point (USP), a feature or quality that defines it and distinguishes it from others. Develop a marketing plan and indicate your advertising strategy.

Management and organisation: This section describes members of the management team, their backgrounds and qualifications, as well as needs for new recruits. In this section, discuss also key outside advisors and collaborators. Here you are showing how your Executive Team reflects the vision and mission of the company and the intended stricture of the company. For example, if your product is progressive, it wouldn't help to envision a hierarchical or traditional company structure, as this would conflict with the ideals of the product. Modern, cutting edge companies, such as Facebook and Google, are known for their experimental and informal company structure and work environment.

The future and risk management: Show vision for the future by anticipating possible risks and indicating you have contingency plans and ways to avoid these risks. Include some information on investors' exit strategy, showing that you have thought of the best interests of your investors.

Financial information: This presents the financial forecasts, and is often the most carefully scrutinised section. Here include detailed balance sheets and statements of cash flow and income. Include a funding request that states how much money is needed and for what purposes. The more organised and well thought-out this section is the more likely it is that investors and potential collaborators will develop respect for your foresight and judgment.

Entrepreneurial 'guru' Guy Kawasaki lists the following points in his advice to those starting out in business plan writing:

- **Do not exceed twenty pages in length:** As noted elsewhere in this book, conciseness is attractive in business contexts.
- **Select one person to write the plan:** Although the plan should reflect the spirit of the management team, the writing of the business plan should be coherent and not patchy.
- **Bind the plan with a staple:** Ornamental presentations do not add any value to the plan. Most readers will be looking for content, not window-dressing.

- **Simplify your financial projections to two pages**: Investors and other interested parties want to know your financial plans, but not in extreme detail, nor for more than the first five years.
- **Include the key metrics, such as the number of customers, locations and resellers**: For Kawasaki, this is even more important than actual financial projections because they give a better view of the organisation's plans.
- **Include the assumptions that drive your financial projections**: This gives more substance to the projections, because it explains the rationale on which you based them (adapted from Kawasaki 2004: 70–1).

Table 12 shows the layout of a business plan

Table 12: Layout of business plan

- Title page
- Executive summary
- Table of contents
- List of figures
- Company description
- Market and marketing plan
- Competition and positioning
- Management team
- Risk management and exit strategy
- Financial information
- Appendices (optional)

Example of business plan

Below are extracts from a business plan for a start-up company specialising in body art. The Executive Team's objectives are to establish a high-end tattoo studio targeting a female clientele. The original business plan included considerable financial information and projections, which have been omitted here since the focus of this book is on language. It also included appendices with data from surveys gauging potential client interest, and sketches of the layout of the body art studio. Indication of material that has been omitted is given throughout the extracts. Study these extracts for approach, sectioning and style.

A/T – ART TATTOO

1. Business Description

A/T aims to defragment the tattooing and piercing industry by establishing a chain of upscale body art studios. This is a lucrative business opportunity for two reasons:

- Tattooing and piercing – a $1B industry – is gaining mainstream acceptance. However, existing tattooing and piercing services continue to reflect the 'outlaw' mentality of the older tattoo culture. As a result, there is a large latent demand for body art services geared to the mainstream public. A/T will gain first-mover advantage by capturing this underserved segment.
- Having established its core business – tattooing and piercing – A/T can develop protectable technologies to continue growth and expand into new markets.

A/T's approach is to create body art stores designed to serve the young-to middle aged woman, our target customer. Tattooing, particularly in women has been growing steadily for the past 20 years. Many of these customers seek high-style design, spa-like hygiene and noteworthy service, none of which the current industry provides. Our research has shown that the pent-up demand is from two sources: the 20 percent of women ages 18–40 without a tattoo who are thinking of getting a tattoo and the 65 percent of women with a tattoo who are happy to switch to a provider with the above qualities (see Appendix A for survey data).

In this country, the tattooing and piercing industry currently consists of about 15,000 independent, small scale parlors, with no major players. These establishments are generally thought of as seedy, dirty and unwelcoming. Thus A/T is well-positioned to capture the latent demand by establishing a branded chain with a reputation for quality, hygiene, and service. A/T will price its services at a significant premium.

2. Market

2.1.The Body Art Market: An Overview

Body art's image has evolved over the past few decades. From the tough-guy image of sailors, inmates, and bikers in the 1950's, to the edgy, avant-garde phenomenon of punk rockers of both sexes in the 1970s and 80s, and to glamorous movie stars, musicians and athletes, body art is well on its way to mainstream acceptance today. In 2003 a Harris Poll showed an overall estimate of 16 percent. The primary differentiator is age, for body art appears to be a generational statement. From a low of 7 percent among adults 65 and over, the incidence of tattoos rises to a peak of 36 percent of those between the ages of 25 and 29 (reference to source).

2.2. A/T's Target Customers

A/T is targeting young and middle-aged, middle to upper-middle class women: women between the ages of 18 and 40 with household income of over $60K. Our survey (see Appendix A for details) indicates that 36 percent of this group is already sporting tattoos and this number has been growing steadily over the past two decades. Another 20 percent of women from this group are considering getting a tattoo. Combined with the fact that over 80 percent of body piercings today are done on women, we believe that this is the most valuable underserved customer segment. (See Appendix B for more facts.)

A/T customers are style conscious and have disposable income. They regularly read fashion magazines, frequent spas and visit beauty salons. They can and do spend over $200 on new shoes or a haircut. They are also embracing body art as a form of personal expression. Tattoos and body piercings function as a fashion accessory, a badge of sexual attractiveness, a statement of belief, a commemoration of an important experience, a link to youth culture, or a gesture of rebellion and autonomy.

Our survey indicates that these customers highly value the following services and features not adequately provided by the competition (see discussion on Competitive Analysis below for details):

- Impeccable cleanliness
- Excellent customer service
- Privacy
- Stringent health and safety procedures
- A pleasant, comfortable ambiance
- A good reputation

3. Competitive Analysis

3.1. Today's Tattooing and Piercing Parlors

The following characteristics define the current service providers in the body art sector:

- *Highly Fragmented Industry:* Body art continues to have a back alley structure. Tattoo and body piercing studios are almost invariably small, independently owned establishments. Larger studios are generally run by an owner-operator who provides space for one or more other artists in exchange for a percentage (usually half) of their gross revenue.
- *Uncertainty and Anxiety*: Determining the quality of work at a given studio is difficult for a person who is a newcomer to body art. On a practical basis, friends or acquaintances are almost the only source of information about the skill of an individual artist and a given studio's reputation for safety.
- *Perception of Seediness*: while individual studios may be vigilant about hygiene, employing autoclaves and one-use needles, the common perception is that cleanliness is not a major priority.
- *Rudimentary Facilities*: many tattooists and piercers work in basements, walk-ups, or small store fronts in low rent areas.
- *Lack of Privacy*: Although roughly 40 percent of tattoos done on women are placed on a sensitive area (lower back, hip, chest, etc.), most work is performed in a common area, in full view of other customers, staff, visitors, and passers-by.

4. Marketing and Sales

Initially, A/T will generate customer interest through curb appeal, local advertising, and word of mouth. Distinctive, engaging storefronts (see sketches in Appendix C) in upscale areas with high foot-traffic will entice customers to come in. Once through the door, potential customers can then be subtly wooed by staff members chosen, in part, for their charm, attractiveness, and warmth.

Since many of A/T's target customers will be newcomers to the body art market, customer education is a very important aspect of the business process. The interaction can begin with a customer browsing our website or coming into one of our studios. From there, friendly and knowledgeable staff will answer questions, address concerns, and explain what sets A/T services apart from the competition.

5. Management

A description of the members of the Executive Team members, their qualifications and experience. Emphasis is on what qualifies them to manage a business of this kind.

6. Risk Management

The financial projections discussed in this business plan are subject to the following risks.

6.1. Health Disaster

The sustainability of the business depends on A/T's reputation for health and safety. Being a large company with cash in the bank and assets makes A/T an attractive target for a lawsuit. If one of our customers contracts a disease, such as hepatitis, or has a severe infection from a tattoo or body piercing, A/T may be held liable and could lose many existing and potential customers due to the blow to its reputation.

This risk is mitigated in several ways:

- A/T will uphold the highest health and safety standards in the industry, including safe inks and top-of-the-line equipment. Its procedures will be designed by a dermatologist and their execution will be supervised by registered nurses.
- A/T will investigate the safety of various piercings reputed to be dangerous, such as tongue piercings, before determining whether or not to offer them.

6.2. Entry by a Well-Funded Competitor

Description of this

6.3. Inability to Hire Suitable Tattoo Artists

Description of this

7. Financial Information

In this round, we are seeking an investment of US$750K. This money will be used to open the first store and bring it to profitability. This will validate the A/T business model and put us in a favorable position to seek funding for expansion. The table below shows a breakdown of funds.

Table 1: Requested funds

Amount	Description
US$500,000	Salaries and benefits for employees as business ramps up (including HQ, nurses, tattoo artists, and a receptionist)
US$200,000	Store start-up costs, including furniture, equipment and renovations (see Appendix V for a breakdown)
US$50,000	Unforeseen and miscellaneous expenses, including business travel and advertising

7.1. Use of Funds to date

A/T has secured $55K in seed capital to date from friends and family. The money has been used prudently for conducting market research, commissioning the customer survey, floor plans and sketches, and travel to build our network. We have spoken with artists and piercers in the body art industry, developed contacts with nurses who may become employees, and networked with leaders in the venture capital and entertainment industry.

7.2. Use of Funds from this round

We will use these funds to aggressively pursue the opening of our first store. Note that as the store reaches full capacity, its revenues will offset operating expenses. We expect the store to be operationally profitable in 9 months and will incur the following expenses to get us to that point. Refer to financial tables in Appendix D for our assumptions and revenues and expenses per store.

7.3. Return on investment, exit strategy and risks

The most probable exit strategy is an Initial Public Offering (IPO) in 5 years. While an acquisition is possible, we think it is unlikely due to a lack of synergistic buyers. We expect A/T to grow and expand rapidly, attaining over $50M in revenues by 2017. Assuming a conservative revenue multiple of 3, we expect the company to sell for $150M at IPO.

The problem-solving report

As opposed to a research report, which is usually written to document and publicise research to peers, a problem-solving, or investigative, report may be written by a specialist or group of specialists to a non-expert audience. Situations leading to a problem-solving report include consultancies, where an expert, or team of experts, is recruited by an organisation to identify issues involved in a problem and to recommend solutions, and commissions, where an authority puts together an impartial investigation team to ascertain the reasons for a public disaster. Investigation reports may be written internally, when the investigator(s) is a member of the organisation, or externally, when the investigator(s) is recruited from a 'neutral zone'.

An investigation follows the specifications of a *brief*, or *terms of reference*, and leads to the writing of a report. Like other analytical reports, an investigative report is divided into three main parts, the *front matter*, the *body* and the *end matter*.

Front matter

The front matter includes these components:

Letter/memo of transmittal

The letter or memo of transmittal indicates that the report is being formally delivered to the person or organisation that requested it. Write a letter if the report is for someone outside your organisation and a memo for someone within your organisation. The letter or memo of transmittal identifies the report topic, and scope or extent of the investigation, and communicates key findings.

Title page

This is a single sheet of paper stating the title of the report, the name and organisation of the author and the date of delivery.

Acknowledgments (optional)

This lists the names of people who helped with the investigation of the report and gives a brief description of their contributions.

Executive summary

Most business reports of more than 1,500 words include an executive summary. This summarises the whole report and should be written as a self-contained piece: readers of the executive summary should get a clear idea of the contents of the report. Executive summaries may be written in a block paragraph, but may also include bullet points depending on context.

Executive summaries are one of the most important and widely read sections in a report. It is important not to confuse the executive summary with the introduction, which introduces but does not summarise the report, and is part of the body. Include the following elements in the executive summary of an investigative report:

- A description of the scope and objectives of the report
- A summary of the main results
- An outline of recommendations or solutions.

Table of contents

This lists the sections and sub-sections of the report with their page numbers. The table of contents acts as an outline of the report.

List of figures

This lists the titles of the visuals (tables, figures, charts, etc.) included in the report and the page numbers where the visuals are to be found.

Body of report

The body of the report is divided into these components:

Introduction

This should lead readers from information they already know to information they need to acquire. The introduction may be only a paragraph long, or it may be a major section in itself, depending on the length of the report. Start with an overview statement indicating the general subject matter and context of the report. Then answer the following questions, adapted as necessary for the specific nature of your report:

- Background: why was the report commissioned in the first place? What was the change, problem or issue that led people to believe a report was needed?
- Purpose: what are the specific objectives of the report?
- Scope: what issues are covered in the report? Refer to the brief given when the report was requested. Indicate the criteria used for evaluating the problem.
- Research methods: how were the data in the report obtained? What primary and/or secondary data were used? (If your methods were experimental and complicated, a separate section should be devoted to them, after the introduction).

- Structure: preview the report structure.
- Limitations (optionally): what issues are not covered in the report? What are the limitations of the research methods selected? What assumptions have been made?

Discussion

The middle part of the report is the largest and most time consuming section, and is further subdivided into sub-sections with headings. Use any one of the following methods, or a combination of methods, for organising the discussion section. Make sure that the method you choose is the most appropriate for presenting and explaining information to the target audience, and adheres to the expectations and logical patterns associated with that audience:

- General to specific
- More important to less important
- Comparison and contrast
- Classification and partition
- Problems and solutions
- Cause and effect
- Cost and benefits (advantages and disadvantages)
- Chronological
- Spatial

When discussing aspects of a topic, issues in a debate or possible solutions to problems, you can use a block form or point-by-point presentation. In the block form you combine all aspects, issues or problems together, and then analyse them or propose solutions. In the point-by-point form, you take each aspect, issue or problem and analyse it or propose a solution to it, before proceeding to the next. This is represented as follows:

Block form	Point by point form
Factor A	Factor A
Item 1	*Item 1*
Item 2	Factor B
Item 3	*Item 1*
Factor B	Factor A
Item 1	*Item 2*
Item 2	Factor B
Item 3	*Item 2*

Conclusion

This interprets the facts set out in the discussion. It answers the question 'so what?' Do not introduce new material here; instead, lead straight on to the list of recommendations. In fact, in some reports, conclusion and recommendations are included in one section. In shorter reports, you can omit this section.

Recommendations

Recommendations suggest specific actions. Again, no new material should appear in this section and recommended actions need not be justified (their justification should be clear from the discussion part of the report). Recommendations may be numbered and placed in priority order. Most often they appear in bullet point form. The executive summary and the recommendations are arguably the most important report sections, so extra attention should be paid to them. Recommendations must be realistic, taking into account factors such as cost, location and current policy or practice within the organisation.

Effective recommendations not only state what action ought to be taken, but also specify who should be responsible for implementing it and within what time frame. Recommendations should address *what, where, when, who* and *how* (the *why* having been examined in the discussion section). Make sure all recommendations are grammatically parallel.

End matter

The end matter of the report is divided into these components:

References or bibliography

These list the sources cited in the report. If a source has been influential, but you have not quoted from it or referred to it, list it under the heading 'Bibliography', which should immediately follow the list of references. Use a referencing style suited to your field (APA, MLA, Chicago, etc.).

Glossary (optional)

This defines technical and specialised terms that are not likely to be familiar to readers of the report. Use audience adaptation methods to determine which terms will need to be defined and which will already be known by target readers. Items in the glossary are listed in alphabetical order.

Appendices (optional)

An appendix is a part of your report that is relevant to the main theme of the report, but not essential. An appendix may include material that is too complex, specialised or detailed to be included in the body of the report. Material that supplements or illustrates points made in the body of the report is also suitable for an appendix. Keep in mind that the reader should be able to understand the main points of the report without needing to read the appendices. At the same time, appendices are useful in cases of secondary audiences that may not have the same level of technical knowledge as the primary audience. In such cases you could include in an appendix specifications or explanations targeted to specific groups.

Examples of documents and data printed as appendices include:

- a copy of a questionnaire used in field research
- a list of questions used in interviews
- copies of letters or pamphlets
- maps, particularly if they take up a whole page
- detailed lists of raw data.

Always refer to the appendix in the body of the report and indicate its relevance to the reader. Letter appendices consecutively (Appendix A, Appendix B, Appendix C and so on) and start each one on a separate page.

Table 13 shows the layout of an investigative report.

Table 13: Layout of investigative report

Letter or memo of transmittal
Title page

Front Matter
Acknowledgements (optional)
Executive summary
Table of contents
List of figures

Body
Introduction
Discussion – divided into sections with headings and sub-headings
Recommendations

End Matter
References
Glossary (optional)
Appendices (optional)

Example of brief, executive summary and recommendations

Below is the brief to a problem-solving report. This is followed by the executive summary of the actual report written in response to this brief, and the list of recommendations. Notice how each is connected to the others.

> Law Limited, a legal company, has been having difficulties retaining its junior and intermediate level lawyers. This is an industry wide problem, with law firms generally losing more than half of their junior lawyers before they reach an intermediate level (3–4 years' experience). The Chief Executive of Law Limited has asked you to prepare a report investigating the problem both within the company and inter-company. Write a report that identifies pertinent issues while taking into account the interests of the company as well as the views of the junior lawyers. Outline a few alternative solutions, evaluate them and propose the best solution justifying your recommendation.

EXECUTIVE SUMMARY

This report examines why Law Limited loses approximately 40 per cent of its junior solicitors before their fourth year at the firm. The results are based on an analysis of current employment practice at the firm, a survey carried out on 80 per cent of junior staff, and comparative material that documents a similar situation within the law industry in other English-speaking countries. The report demonstrates that, for purposes of retention, the solicitors can be classified into three classes: those who will leave regardless of the action taken (30 per cent), those who will stay if action is taken (65 per cent), and those who will stay regardless of whether action is taken or not (5 per cent). Based on these findings, the report suggests that retention strategies should be aimed at making the solicitors feel valued and challenged. Methods proposed include a bonus scheme, a mentoring scheme and a professional development programme.

RECOMMENDATIONS

Following the results of the surveys discussed above, this report recommends the following actions:

Implement a bonus scheme rewarding lawyers that surpass a given level of performance. The level of performance and the bonus should be decided by management in consultation with appointed junior lawyer representatives. Both type of bonus and level of performance should be reviewed every three years to ensure their relevance to changing industry standards.

Organise a mentoring scheme where senior lawyers are paired with junior counterparts to discuss problems, aspirations and plans.

Organise formal briefing meetings with management and junior staff to discuss problems of concern. These meetings should take place at least twice a year.

Make changes to the budget to ensure that enough funds are available to maintain a regular orientation/professional development programme. The recommended time allocated to this programme is 15 hours per year for each staff member.

Example of problem-solving report

Analysed example 13 is an extract from a 3,000 word investigative report written by the founder and CEO of a start-up company, called GoDJ, specialising in music sharing on the Internet. The report is written for the Executive Team of the company and is based on research into business communication practices. The writer investigated some case studies of communication practices and problems in business, and is recommending a communications protocol for his company that will assist in preventing such problems. The extract contains the full executive summary, introduction and recommendations, and lists the sections of the report with notes on their content.

Visuals

Visuals include diagrams, charts, tables, figures, graphs, photographs, drawings, clip art and other pictorial or schematic representations. Visuals are alternative methods of presenting information and form a useful non-linear complement to the written word. Information presented diagrammatically or in pictorial form is memorable and can simplify, and thereby make clearer, complicated data. When including a visual in a document, assess it in relation to two factors: *content,* that is how it communicates meaning that is complementary to the meaning presented linguistically, and *design*, that is in terms of its size and positioning on the page.

As regards content, these points are important:

• The visual should be necessary to clarify a point in the document. Do

Analysed example 13

Executive Summary

This report examines the current communication protocol within the new startup venture GoDJ, and suggests improvements. GoDJ is a new music distribution method that allows users to legally share their libraries over the Internet. Since its inception, GoDJ's user base has rapidly increased. With GoDJ's increase in job positions comes an even greater need to maintain effective lines of communication in the company. After investigating communication practices and problems in comparable businesses, such as Google, Yahoo and Microsoft, it has become evident that the current protocol is inefficient and will become increasingly so as company continues to grow. As GoDJ currently only employs a staff of 12, the main forms of communication are through personal emails, phone conversations and in person; however, as the sectors continue to expand, these methods will surely become ineffective. To rectify these issues, a collaborative wiki is recommended that will allow all users to view and participate in company decisions. Additionally, a communication protocol will be established to ensure that communication between different departments is clear. These methods should increase the flow and clarity of communication within GoDJ both now and in the future.

1. Introduction

1.1. Background and objectives

A new and quickly growing business, GoDJ is on track to becoming a large, sustainable and influential company in the music industry. Since its creation in February 2013, with only two founding partners, GoDJ has progressed to employ a staff of 12 and is expecting to add more members to the team in the near future. As this small business continues to grow, it will become ever more important to maintain

The first sentence states the aims of the report.

The second and third sentences give background and context to the problem.

The fourth sentence identifies the problem.

The fifth sentence expands on the problem in relation to the context (the company structure).

The sixth and seventh sentences describe the recommendations.

The last sentence gives a general conclusion on the effects of the recommendations.

Section headings must be parallel on the same level. In this report, main sections use upper case for first letters of all important words in the heading, and sub-sections use upper case only for the first letter of the first word.

Gives background to the report.

effective communication between all sectors to insure GoDJ operates as efficiently as possible; however, as the number of employees and customers increase, this effective communication will increasingly become more difficult to sustain.

Explains problem within this background.

The objectives of this report are to:

- investigate the effectiveness of the company's current communication procedures
- identify areas where miscommunication occurs
- examine the communication practices of comparable businesses in both successful and unsuccessful aspects
- recommend a revised set of policies to improve communication now and in the future

Lists objectives.

1.2. Scope and method

The primary focus of this report is to investigate the reasons for communication failure in business. An important cause of inefficient communication arises when the various company sectors have difficulty exchanging feedback, updates, and other business related information. If this difficulty in communication is present, a business is not operating at its full potential. Using this criterion as a basis, this report will analyse the means of interaction in GoDJ, and determine whether improvements need to be made.

Summarises the main issues discussed in the report

The data in this report were obtained from an employee survey, informal feedback and research into published cases of communication practice in companies, including Google, Yahoo and Microsoft (references to sources).

Explains the method used to investigate the issues.

2. Company Overview

GoDJ is a new music distribution system that allows users from around the world to legally share their music collections online. In its first six months, GoDJ has attracted a community of over 50,000 users and is rapidly adding to that number. There has yet to be a company to imitate our business model, but our indirect competitors in the online music industry are iTunes, Myspace and iMeem. The goal of GoDJ is to surpass these other companies as the most popular and effective means of music distribution on the Internet.

2.1. Company roles
GoDJ currently employs a staff of 12, with four different business sectors. These sectors include teams in programming and development, marketing and sales, public relations and policy and management.

The report then describes the current departments and positions in the company and expectations for future hiring.

3. Current Communication Practices
This section describes how communication takes place both internally and externally.

3.1. Possible problems with current communication practices

This section speculates on what can go wrong with communication-related matters in the company.

4. Case Studies of Business Miscommunication
This section overviews some major ways in which communication is regulated in companies and identifies the factors involved.

not include a visual just for decoration. The visual must be the best way to present the particular information you wish to express. It should convey a message more emphatically, more clearly or more concisely than written sentences, or it should clarify the meaning of the sentences.

4.1. Google
Discusses this case study and links the results to GoDJ concerns

4.2. Yahoo
Discusses this case study and links the results to GoDJ concerns

4.3. Microsoft
Discusses this case study and links the results to GoDJ concerns

5. Recommendations

In light of the above discussion on attested cases of business miscommunication, this report recommends that GoDJ:

- Establish a communication protocol to ensure consistency in the production of documents, both internally and externally. This protocol will include the design of an in-house style manual with instructions to be followed by all employees
- Create a collaborative wiki that will enable all employees to articulate opinions on matters affecting the company, and will facilitate the exchange of feedback among all sectors
- Develop an induction programme for all new staff that will provide training on communication matters, and on the communication principles adhered to by the company
- Employ a communication specialist whose primary short-term responsibility will be to initiate the actioning of the above recommendations

Introduces recommendations and links them with the discussion.

Lists recommendations beginning with action words. Gives as much information as needed to make the recommendations useful without making them too wordy.

- The kind of visual you have chosen (pie chart, image, table, etc.) should be the best for your purpose. For example, a line diagram may be inappropriate for discrete data.
- The visual must be introduced, discussed, interpreted and integrated in the text of the document. Remember that raw data is useless unless its

relevance to the issue at hand is made clear. The reader should not have to work to figure out why the visual is included in the document, or what the significance of the data may be.

- The visual must stand alone in meaning. While it should be interpreted in the text of the document, it should also be self-explanatory and complete, and not obscure or confusing.
- All visuals must be numbered consecutively and given a specific, meaningful title. Include the title of a table above the table, and the title of all other visuals below the visual.
- As with all writing choices, visuals must be designed and formatted in a manner appropriate for the likely audience of the document. Will the visual be clear and appealing from the intended reader's perspective?
- If you have copied the visual from another document or website, remember to write 'Source' under the visual followed by the name of the source.
- If using a table, make all like elements (the factors to be compared) read down not across.

As regards arrangement and design these points are important:

- Make the visual easy for your reader to find; the visual should closely follow the reference to it in the text. Format the document so that visuals do not appear on different pages from where they are mentioned in the text.
- Surround the visual with white space and do not clutter it. This makes it easier for the reader to absorb the information presented.
- Consider whether the visual would be better located in an appendix rather than in the body of the report. If the body of your report is becoming too cluttered, some visuals may be moved to an appendix.
- As a convention, the visual should take up no less than one third of a page, again, for reasons of clarity and visibility.
- Position the visual in alignment with the text, for balance.
- If using colours, note that by ordering colours from light to dark vertically or horizontally, elements will appear to be next to each other. This is because lighter colours tend to stand out and darker colours to recede.

Charts and graphs

Here is a list of different kinds of charts and graphs with guidelines on their uses in documents.

Line graph
Useful for showing trends and fluctuations over time

Column graph
Shows clearly comparisons of amounts. It is presented in vertical form.

Bar chart
Indicates proportions as they are related to each other. It is presented in horizontal form.

Pie chart
Indicates proportion of parts to the whole

Scattergram
Shows correlations between different items

Flow chart
Specifies the relationship between processes

Gannt chart
Combines a process with the amount of time it takes to complete it

Organisational chart
Shows relationships between things and creates a directory

Map
Distributes events or influences over different locations

Exploded diagram
Shows components in a structure

Schematic
Shows relationships between theoretical concepts

Time line
Indicates simple time sequences

Activities

1 You are documentation manager for XXX Software, a growing company, and you supervise preparation and production of all user manuals. The present system for producing manuals is inefficient because three different departments are involved in (1) assembling the material, (2) word processing and designing and (3) publishing the manuals. After studying the problem, you decide that greater efficiency would result if the company started using Cloud computing for the production of manuals. This would enable everyone involved to contribute during all stages. To achieve this, you must write a proposal to be read by the General Manager, as well as by the three Department Managers.

   Brainstorm some reasons that you think these readers would find convincing for your proposal, remembering that they would have different concerns and interests. What would be your persuasive strategy in this proposal?

2 Here is an extract from a report on the development of a computer game, written by one of the developers to the project manager. The writer follows a 'write as you think' approach, which gives the text a muddled and wordy presentation. Also, the style combines specialist techniques (extensive use of technical terminology) with journalistic elements (chatty tone). Revise and edit the text following the guidelines for clear, precise and concise writing

> The game was a drag and drop style board game involving one person directing another person's actions using a set list of verbal commands. The game also recorded moves made during a game for reviewing, either as a textual description or as real-time playback. As well as implementation, documentation of the system was a big part of the project with documents on five major aspects of the system produced. P1, the project plan, described the overall project, what was involved in the current system and our plans to implement a new system. P2, the requirements document, detailed the current system and our proposed solution to the problem presented to us by the client. P3, the architecture document, presented how we intended to develop the system and how it met the requirements determined in the previous document. P4 detailed the user interface of the document and also how it met the requirements of P2. P5, the detailed design document, contained the specifics of the implementation of the system and was intended to be used when coding the system. The documentation was intended to guide the implementation process in order to produce better quality software. I think that the software produced during the project was superior to previous software used for the same reason and I think this can be entirely attributed to following the project software development process.

When I say that the software produced during the project was superior to the software previously used I don't mean that the software produced was a superior piece of software. I think the overall design of our project was a good design that could've been implemented successfully but I do think it was lacking in some areas due to not enough time spend during this phase. It was initially intended that the interfaces would respond to users' commands and pass the responsibility of performing the operations on to various other modules. Little consideration was given to how a textual review would be displayed with regard to getting the information from the storage system to the interface so we ended up with the interface extract the information from a stored round object.

3 Below are some verbal descriptions of actions, relationships, steps and trends. Read the description and decide what kind of visual would present this information graphically. Draw the visual to illustrate. There could be more than one option for each description.

Verbal description	Visual
The budget was divided as follows: supplies 20 per cent, salaries 40 per cent, advertising 25 per cent, shipping 10 per cent and reserve 5 per cent.	
The fuel-mixture container is located on the right top corner of the engine, and the main valve is located below the injector plug.	
Measured values for the X, Y and Z plants were 41.2, 50.8 and 20.5 respectively.	

First, check... Then, open... Next, move...	
The engine is composed of A, B, C and D components.	
The error rate for online help menus was about half of the rate for printed instructions.	
Profits rose continuously in the last five years, even though the number of investors remained constant.	
If X happens, we should do Y; on the other hand, if B happens we should do A.	

Critical Thinking for Management

Focus:

- Principles of critical thinking
- Common fallacies in reasoning
- Uses and misuses of statistics

The ability to reason logically and objectively is considered vital for professional success. In fact, 'objectivity', 'critical thinking' and 'problem solving' are key words in management positions. Together with skills in leadership, teamwork and communication, a demonstrated ability in dispassionate analysis of critical issues is highly sought-after in most professional positions. This chapter addresses this need by describing the main problem areas, especially as they relate to the communication tasks of professional fields.

The terms and ideas presented here form the backbone of all forms of research, investigative writing and objective interpretation of arguments and statements. They also form the basis for professional involvement in corporate policy and public relations. The main value of objective reasoning, as opposed to subjective, or self-focused, opinion, is that it can lead to decisions that benefit a group of people or the wider public. The first part of the chapter describes the cognitive skills related to critical thinking and follows with a review of the thought processes that lead to faulty reasoning in most forms of communication and decision-making. The second part focuses on a major area of manipulative persuasion, statistical data.

Principles of critical thinking

Critical thinking is not an innate gift or talent: it develops with perseverance and dedication. To sharpen your critical thinking skills, try these strategies (see also Sagan 1995; Hirschberg 1996; Cottrell 2011; Burger and Starbird 2012):

1 Think independently

Listen to other points of view, but do not follow any particular viewpoint without examining it first from different angles. Especially be cautious not to blindly accept claims and statements just because they are issued by an authority or expert. Everybody can be wrong, and facts can change as knowledge develops. Therefore, develop your own informed opinion.

2 Think objectively

Try to see from another person's point of view, beyond your own personal concerns. Do not become too attached to a theory or hypothesis because it is yours, or because you have believed it to be correct up to now. Examine why you believe this theory or hypothesis to be accurate, and compare it fairly with alternatives. Play the devil's advocate and find reasons for rejecting it. If the theory survives the test, you will be more prepared to defend it when the occasion arises.

3 Develop intellectual perseverance

Show that you have the persistence to think through all the aspects of a problem. Do not be tempted to give up because a problem is too challenging. Consider more than one hypothesis. If there is something to be explained, think of different ways it could be explained. Then think of how you would test each of the alternatives.

4 Develop observation skills

When you read or listen critically, make sure that you clarify and understand key words, ideas and conclusions. Generate questions about what you read, and remember to place the information you read and hear in context, using audience analysis skills. For example, find out about the audience that the information is directed towards, and identify how the needs of the audience influence the selection of information and the manner in which it is presented. Find out who generated the information, and by what methods. From this, ascertain how credible and reliable the information is. In many contexts, such as science, a hypothesis can be accepted only if it is falsifiable. Something that cannot be disproved can also not be proved.

Also, when reading, try to go beyond merely understanding what the writer has said, by asking yourself questions such as:

- What information is missing from the text?
- If I could meet the writer face to face, what questions would I like to ask?

- What further information do I need to know in order to accurately evaluate the information?

5 Trace analogies

How does what you learn in one context apply to other contexts? For example, if you are a computer engineer, you could notice the similarities between computer code syntax and the rules of sentence construction in English. Pay attention to similarities and differences. Many groundbreaking discoveries were made by tracing an analogy between a phenomenon and an idea, or by serendipity, that is, by recognising connections between seemingly different topics.

6 Establish precision

Precision requires you to be focused and specific in both your ideas and your expression. In your own writing, make a conscious effort to refine generalities and avoid oversimplifications. Distinguish between relevant and irrelevant facts and use technical terminology correctly. If you are considering an argument, remember that all elements must work, not just most of them.

Fallacies of reasoning

One way to study the process of persuasion is to focus on what can go wrong. Many judgements and decisions are based on assumptions made from previous experience and preconceptions that may be irrelevant to the purposes at hand. Although much innovative thinking also makes use of assumptions, guard against constructing arguments that are based totally on unacknowledged claims and weak reasoning. In the final analysis, persuasion and reasoning depend on the *rhetorical conventions* of particular *discourse communities*. What is valid evidence for one group may not be so for another, so you maximise your chances of producing a convincing case if you know what the expectations and conventions of your audience are.

In addition to audience expectations, ethics is another area that should occupy your thoughts. For example, you may have a workable idea for a new form of plastic and you may also have convincing evidence that this development will benefit your organisation, for example, by increasing its competitive advantage and by reducing costs of production. However, this new form of plastic may produce toxic pollution in its manufacturing, and the organisation does not yet have the facilities to recycle such toxic waste. In such a situation, you need to very carefully weigh the organisation's advantages with the negative effects on the wider community, and decide if and how the new product should be developed.

Some of the main tactics that lead to fundamentally illogical arguments are outlined below. In rhetorical theory, these are known as *fallacies of reasoning*. They are extremely common in mass media documents, but also occur in professional and academic contexts:

Appeal to tradition: This occurs when the reason given for following or not following a course of action is that it has always been done this way. This tactic relies on a fundamental psychological trait – the need to trust the legitimacy of a habit. However, as with all forms of persuasion, it can be misused by concealing inherent flaws in the arguments proposed.

Appeal to authority: This occurs when a claim or statement is considered 'true' because its source is an expert in the field or has a respectable and/or popular position in the community. For example, there is an anecdote about a textbook used in a certain country's universities for many years, even though teaching staff were aware it contained some serious errors. The author was a famous professor whom nobody thought they should correct. In this case, the decision to continue on an erroneous path was based on the assumption that respect for authority should override objective evaluation.

Appeal to common sense, 'everybodiness' and universals: This occurs when, instead of providing a methodical argument that develops specific issues systematically, the writer/speaker proposes a course of action because it 'is the right thing to do', or 'everybody knows that it is so'. Sometimes what appears as 'common sense' or 'universally acceptable' is nothing but an entrenched belief that has remained unquestioned for such a long time that it has become tradition. This strategy is based on the human need to belong to a group. Many people would be persuaded to follow a course of action because it appears to fall into established but unquestioned universals, such as 'justice' or 'morality'.

Appeal to opposition: This occurs when, in order to support a point of view, the writer/speaker relies on the fact that the opposite point of view has been disproved or is unsubstantiated. For example, some claim that laws prohibiting the use of drugs should be abolished, because there is no substantial evidence to suggest that such laws actually prevent people from using drugs. Although this claim could be a step in the reasoning process, it cannot be the determining criterion for reaching a definite conclusion. A similar example is that of the existence (or not) of God: arguing that there is a God because attempts to disprove his existence have failed (or vice versa) is a claim based on an appeal to opposition. As Carl Sagan aptly puts it, 'absence of evidence is not evidence of absence' (Sagan 1995: 213).

Appeal to emotion: Very common in consumer advertising, this occurs when a writer/speaker uses an emotive style when presenting an argument, adding evaluative words and phrases or metaphors that are actually irrelevant to the piece of information presented but that have a strong sensory or emotive effect. Usually done to sway opinion on a matter, or to generate a feeling of guilt in the receivers that will induce them to take some form of action, this is what happens when perpetrators of crime are described as 'hideous monsters' and their victims as 'innocent citizens'.

Because of its strong persuasive impact, this is a common device in the mass media. It is also a widespread tactic in some forms of legal reasoning, especially when a lawyer tries to sway the jury's opinion by drawing attention to the defendant's emotional state (traumatic childhood, agitated state, etc.) as a justification of his/her action. This relies on the human capacity for empathy ('what if this happened to you?'), and not on logic.

Appeal to extremes and false dichotomies: This occurs when only two options are offered for a complex issue, undermining a balance. A choice between dictatorship or anarchy would reflect this kind of fallacy. This 'either-or' device often occurs in emergencies where people need to act urgently and do not have the time to analyse an issue in depth. It tends to occur in very simplistic arguments, for example when an element of physical force or immediate urgency overrides the logical aspects of the argument ('give me your money or I'll kill you'). 'Terrorist tactics' are based on this kind of appeal, reflecting a situation where such a state of disarray has been reached that there are not many choices open for action. This is known as the fallacy of the *excluded middle* in classical argumentation.

Appeal to generalities: This occurs when a writer/speaker abstracts certain properties from some specially selected entities and applies them to a larger number of entities. A typical example is stereotyping ('politicians are liars'). Another example is when an argument is based on universal terms ('love', 'progress') that have not been defined in terms of the requirements of the project at hand. The argument is consequently hidden behind abstract notions. The major problem with this pitfall is that it disregards the specifics of particular circumstances and situations.

Appeal to personal aspects: This occurs when a writer/speaker's ideas are rejected because of their status, sex, profession, past record, etc., rather than because of weaknesses inherent to the ideas themselves. Very common in the mass media and in politics, this appeal disregards the issues at hand and, instead, attempts to draw attention away from a claim and onto the personal qualities of the presenter of the claim. This is what happens, for example, when a promising and reasonable idea is rejected by a committee because it was proposed by a junior or inexperienced member. In classical argument, this is known as *ad hominen* (Latin for 'to the man' – attacking the arguer, not the argument).

Appeal to the straw man: Related to the previous, this occurs when a writer/speaker caricatures a position by oversimplifying it or taking it out of context, so that it is easier to attack and demolish. A similar tactic is the use of inappropriate humour. 'Straight' humour is a positive aspect of all communication. However, it can become inappropriate, and even sarcastic, when it is used to encourage laughter or ridicule towards an issue that deserves serious attention. If directed at those holding opposing views, this type of humour may reduce their chances of being heard.

Slippery slope: This occurs when a writer/speaker jumps to a conclusion that is not justified by the premises. Associated with paranoid reasoning, this is illustrated by a statement such as 'If the government imposes restrictions on the petrol used for cars, what stops them from preventing us from driving cars altogether?'.

Special pleading: This occurs when a writer/speaker responds to an objection or observation by claiming that it overlooks some special circumstances. This is usually an evasive or defensive tactic. For example, responding to the observation 'Despite the measures we have in place to prevent accidents, accidents have increased in the last month' by the special plea 'You don't understand people: they don't follow rules' would be such an appeal. A more logical response would be to examine the measures and the claim that accidents have increased.

Begging the question or assuming the answer: This occurs when the writer/speaker bases an argument on premises that should in fact be the conclusion, thus producing a circular reasoning. For example, saying that 'we must institute the death penalty to discourage violent crime' would fall in this category. This is based on the assumption that the death penalty does in fact discourage violent crime.

Card stacking or observational selection: This occurs when the writer/speaker omits what does not support his or her view and concentrates on facts that enhance his or her position.

False extrapolation: This occurs when a writer/speaker extrapolates a claim from observed facts without considering alternative possibilities. An example would be the statement 'We will be successful because we are innovative and law-abiding.' This is known in classical argument as *non sequitur* (Latin for 'it does not follow').

Confusion between causality and correlation: This occurs when a hasty conclusion is drawn from a fact, or when a causal relation is artificially traced between two events that simply co-exist or that follow one another sequentially. This is known in classical argument as *post hoc, ergo propter hoc* (Latin for 'it happened after, so it was caused by'). A major source of misinformation in the use of statistical evidence lies in the frequent confusion between causality and correlation. Two related events that occur simultaneously are said to be in correlation. This does not mean that one event caused the other. For example, consider the high positive correlation between the sale of alcohol and the incidence of crime. This in itself cannot prove that alcohol causes crime. There could be a third factor involved that influences both alcohol sales and crime, for example, population growth.

In a causal relationship, one factor (the cause or reason) produces another (the result or outcome) only if these three factors are present:

1 There is a clear chronological sequence. A must occur before B does.
2 There is a clear pattern of repetition. To establish that A causes B, there must be proof that every time A is present, B occurs – or that B never occurs unless A is present.
3 There are no multiple causes and/or effects. For example, many factors influence reported crime rates: population distribution (age, wealth, race), crime reporting by citizens, changes to laws and regulations and changes to police procedures for gathering and reporting statistics. A seeming drop in crime reporting, therefore, would not mean there is less crime.

This tactic is related to interpretations of quantifiable data, and leads to the next section on statistics.

Statistics and public opinion

Mark Twain (1906) once said that 'there are three kinds of lies: lies, damned lies, and statistics'. This section focuses on a major trouble area of reasoning: the use of statistical or quantitative information in arguing for or against a course of action and for justifying decisions. Interestingly, in the history of science, the study of statistics is a recent phenomenon, with origins in the 'Enlightenment' era of the seventeenth century. Prior to that period, the notion that knowledge could be quantified or counted had no substantial effects. Now, however, virtually every facet of nature and society can be expressed in quantitative terms, that is, in terms of numbers, amounts and percentages.

When discussing an issue, people often give statistics to seal an argument and close off any further debate. Also, managers in business and finance, social policy and education routinely support their policies and decisions with numbers and statistics. Statistics can give the appearance of solidity and 'hard' evidence; numbers are often thought of as irrefutable or undeniable. But actually, the appeal to statistics sets off a whole new set of questions. Where did the statistics come from? What groups in society are excluded from the statistics? If the statistics are accurate, then what decision or action should follow from them? And how can statistical relations and effects be translated into plain English, so that decision makers in business and government can understand them? After all, numbers are meaningless unless they are evaluated or seen within a rhetorical context.

This section overviews and briefly describes six major areas where statistical support to reasoning is abused in order to manipulate attitudes (Freund and Simon 1992; Huff 1993; Sheldon 1994; Paulos 1996).

1 Describing the source of statistics

Statistics are undocumented if the writer does not state their source. Possibly the most common problem with statistical information in the mass media, it makes it very difficult to ascertain whether the conclusions drawn from the statistical analysis are credible, plausible or applicable only to selected cases that cannot lead to general conclusions. Documenting statistics means stating clearly where the statistics came from, where they are published and if they are available to the public.

2 Describing how statistics were generated

Even if the source of statistics is documented, we still need to investigate further to verify that the data are valid. Questions to ask in this regard include: What kind of study was done to establish the statistics? What was the size of the sample? How was the sample selected? Is the sample representative of the general population? Were statistics gathered by interview or questionnaire? If they were gathered by questionnaire, was it filled in face-to-face or by self-reporting? What was the response rate? Who commissioned the study, who financed it and who conducted it? When polling results are compared with results from previous years, have key definitions remained the same? Has the margin of error been specified?

3 Distinguishing between absolute rate and rate of incidence

The *absolute rate* indicates how many items are affected by the issue in question, expressed as a number. By contrast, the *rate of incidence* shows what proportion of the population is affected, expressed as a percentage. The rate of incidence therefore gives some indication of statistical significance. On the other hand, the absolute rate sometimes may sound more impressive, but is not as statistically relevant. For example, consider the effect of the statement that 100,000 people died from a kind of cancer in a specific country last year. What if you now learn that this number accounts for 0.05 per cent of the whole population of the country? Which rate would alarm readers and which would reassure them?

4 Making sure that trends are real

Sometimes very slight correlations or changes in occurrence of an event can be blown up to misleadingly huge dimensions. This is sufficient to set off fears or hopes of a trend, particularly in emotional or volatile aspects of human behaviour. In some cases, a typical example being that of financial markets, the perceived trend can become a self-fulfilling prophecy: if small declines in the market are taken to be evidence of a larger trend, panic selling will indeed cause the market to slump or crash.

5 Distinguishing between quantities given in length or in volume

Expressing quantities in terms of length often sounds more impressive than using volume as a measure. The example given by Paulos (1996: 79) is that of a tower and a box: Which contains more five-cent coins, a tower the diameter of a coin rising from sea level to the height of Mount Everest, or a six-foot cubical box? The answer is the box.

6 Specifying the measure of central tendency

When noting the average of a series of numbers, the writer must indicate whether he/she has used the *mean, median* or *mode*. For data that falls into a normal distribution, such as human height, these three methods of averaging will produce similar results. However, for other kinds of data spread, mean, median and mode vary markedly. For example, assume a country's average income is $40,000. Does this sound like an affluent and fair-to-all society? What if the range occurs between a high of $200,000 and a low of $10,000?

Argument in management

It is often believed that business writing favours the 'bottom line' rather than complicated argument structure. However, although practical outcomes are indeed a major concern in many management decisions, business ventures are also at the forefront of innovation, cultural change and social justice (see also Toulmin 2003). Careful consideration of decision implications and ethical consequences of actions is pivotal in the success and social acceptance of business projects. In fact, successful proposals and business plans (documents with a high degree of persuasive impact) demonstrate evidence of what is known as the three Cs of management communication: *credibility,* the writer's foresight, integrity and judgement; *creativity,* the novelty of ideas; and *compliance,* the willingness to follow industry or company regulations and procedures. All three are expressed in writing through stylistic factors, such as choice of words, sentence structure and forms of cohesion.

Therefore, resist the temptation to bring in emotional appeals, personal attacks or indeed any of the fallacies listed above, as sophisticated readers are likely to scrutinise your writing through the lens of critical thinking. Even if you disagree with your opponent's main idea, you should also concede, or accept, that s/he makes some valid points. Conceding a point shows your audience that you are thorough, thoughtful and fair. A useful rhetorical strategy for constructing an argument in a management context, at both paragraph and text levels, is this:

1 Summarise objectively the opposing argument to show that you have understood it.
2 Acknowledge ways in which the opposing viewpoint is correct.
3 Use a transitional word, phrase, sentence or paragraph indicating contrast or a shift in point of view.
4 State your claim or the different point of view as an alternative to the opponent's proposition.
5 Give evidence supporting your claim, remembering that the value of evidence should be assessed from the audience's perspective.

For example, look at analysed example 14 extracted from a government feasibility report. The writer was asked to investigate whether it would be advisable for Australia to implement compulsory military service because of political upheavals in its neighbouring nations. Notice how the writer uses a model of argumentation similar to the above in supporting his claim.

Analysed example 14

The main premise of the argument in the proposal for compulsory military service is that political turmoil in Australia's neighbours presents a threat to national security. East Timor is barely recovering from war, the Solomon Islands and Fiji have been shaken with military coups, and the Indonesian political scene has had massive changes in the last two years. However, there is no evidence to suggest that this fear be anything but paranoia. Australia has no history as a military instigator nor has this nation faced direct threats in the past. Additionally, Australia's diminutive position in the economic and military world suggests that there is no incentive for any neighbour to attack Australia. Australia's military position has traditionally been one of support for its allies and there are no signs to suggest that this will change in the foreseeable future.

States premise of opposing argument.

Gives reasons that support the premise of the opposing argument.

States own claim after contrastive transition.

Gives reasons to support own claim.

Example of reasoning

A current area of debate, where emotions, vested interests and objective evidence meet, is legislation over gun and weapon control. Although this is prevalent in the United States, where the growing number of mass shootings in recent years has exacerbated the situation, the debate has international relevance. Therefore, it provides a fertile ground for the analysis of reasoning strategies and the use of statistics.

In most Western societies, it is illegal to purchase a gun without first obtaining a licence from the police. The police may deny a licence on certain grounds such as age, previous criminal convictions or mental instability. *Gun control* refers to the legislation regulating gun ownership. The United States is an exception to this, because the Second Amendment in the US Constitution safeguards citizens' right to own weapons, making the purchase of guns not only legally easier, but also, in certain instances, culturally valued.

One reason for the controversy over the effects of strict regulations on the availability of guns is that no conclusive evidence exists which directly links high crime rates with gun possession. Researchers who study the relation between gun control and homicide rates have not, as yet, come up with any convincing proof that strict gun control laws actually lessen the number of gun killings.

Analysed example 15 is an article by John R. Lott Jr, a well-known proponent of liberal gun laws in the United States. It is written in the demagogic end of journalistic style (the tone of the public speaker inciting the audience to take up arms over a topic – quite literally in this case). A belief held by Lott, and other pro-gun lobbyists, is that access to guns can actually lower the crime rate, because law-abiding citizens can use their weapons to stop perpetrators from committing a violent crime. For example, if someone at Sandy Hook Elementary School in Connecticut had a gun when Adam Lanza started his killing spree in December 2012, s/he could have shot Lanza before he had time to kill all his victims.

Using the criteria for objective reasoning and statistical evidence outlined in this chapter, we can use the following questions to guide a critical analysis:

1 How convincing is the reasoning presented here?
2 How credible is the use of statistics?
3 What more information would you need to reach more conclusive results?

Analysed example 15

The Big Lie of the Assault Weapons Ban: The death of the law hasn't brought a rise in crime – just the opposite.

By John R. Lott, Jr.

This wasn't supposed to happen. When the federal assault weapons ban ended on Sept. 13, 2004, gun crimes and police killings were predicted to surge. Instead, they have declined.

For a decade, the ban was a cornerstone of the gun control movement. Sarah Brady, one of the nation's leading gun control advocates, warned that 'our streets are going to be filled with AK-47s and Uzis.' Life without the ban would mean rampant murder and bloodshed.

The title contains a generalisation, 'lie', and an exaggeration, 'opposite'.

The writer accuses the anti-gun lobby of false extrapolation and slippery slope argument.

Well, more than nine months have passed and the first crime numbers are in. Last week, the FBI announced that the number of murders nationwide fell by 3.6% last year, the first drop since 1999. The trend was consistent; murders kept on declining after the assault weapons ban ended.

> This implies an unjustified causality between freer gun control laws and a decline in murders. Significantly, murders by other means than guns are not considered.

Even more interesting, the seven states that have their own assault weapons bans saw a smaller drop in murders than the 43 states without such laws, suggesting that doing away with the ban actually reduced crime. (States with bans averaged a 2.4% decline in murders; in three states with bans, the number of murders rose. States without bans saw murders fall by more than 4%.)

> The confusion between causality and correlation continues here. There could be other factors in those states that encouraged a decline in crime, such as education or economic prosperity. The nature of these states needs to be described in terms of economy, demographics, size, etc.

And the drop was not just limited to murder. Overall, violent crime also declined last year, according to the FBI, and the complete statistics carry another surprise for gun control advocates. Guns are used in murder and robbery more frequently than in rapes and aggravated assaults, but after the assault weapons ban ended, the number of murders and robberies fell more than the number of rapes and aggravated assaults.

> This is an important claim that requires sources, documented statistics and definitions.

It's instructive to remember just how passionately the media hyped the dangers of 'sunsetting' the ban. Associated Press headlines warned 'Gun shops and police officers brace for end of assault weapons ban.' It was even part of the presidential campaign: 'Kerry blasts lapse of assault weapons ban.' An Internet search turned up more than 560 news stories in the first two weeks of September that expressed fear about ending the ban. Yet the news that murder and other violent crime declined last year produced just one very brief paragraph in an insider political newsletter, the Hotline.

> 'the media' is a generalisation that groups different sources in one category. It is also ironic, since this article is also a media document.

The fact that the end of the assault weapons ban didn't create a crime wave should not have surprised anyone.

After all, there is not a single published academic study showing that these bans have reduced any type of violent crime.

This claim is phrased in absolute terms ('not a single… any type'), making it an exaggeration. It would need to be re-phrased to make it more credible.

Research funded by the Justice Department under the Clinton administration concluded only that the effect of the assault weapons ban on gun violence 'has been uncertain.' The authors of that report released their updated findings last August, looking at crime data from 1982 through 2000 (which covered the first six years of the federal law). The latest version stated: 'We cannot clearly credit the ban with any of the nation's recent drop in gun violence.'

Such a finding was only logical. Though the words 'assault weapons' conjure up rapid-fire military machine guns, in fact the weapons outlawed by the ban function the same as any semiautomatic – and legal – hunting rifle. They fire the same bullets at the same speed and produce the same damage. They are simply regular deer rifles that look on the outside like AK-47s.

This is a misleading and inaccurate comparison because hunting rifles and automatic handguns are completely different weapons.

For gun control advocates, even a meaningless ban counts. These are the same folks who have never been bashful about scare tactics, predicting doom and gloom when they don't get what they want. They hysterically claimed that blood would flow in the streets after states passed right-to-carry laws letting citizens carry concealed handguns, but that never occurred. Thirty-seven states now have right-to-carry laws – and no one is seriously talking about rescinding them or citing statistics about the laws causing crime.

This is another generalisation and exaggeration, phrased in emotive and judgmental terms – e.g. 'doom and gloom' and 'hysterically'.

Gun controllers' fears that the end of the assault weapons ban would mean the sky would fall were simply not true. How much longer can the media take such hysteria seriously when it is so at odds with the facts?

Published 28 June 2005, in *Los Angeles Times*. Reprinted with permission of the author.

We are now ready to answer the questions listed above.

1 How convincing is the reasoning presented here?
The article comes from what we called a 'public' source – a newspaper (see Chapter 4). Therefore, it is constrained by limited space and audience considerations. It can only give a perfunctory overview of the situation. At the same time, the style of the article is polemic and emotional, containing serious generalisations, which detract from the objectivity necessary in dealing with a 'hot' topic such as gun control. These factors mean we need more sources, such as scholarly articles, to form an informed opinion. The reasoning is not convincing if seen through the lens of critical thinking.

2 How credible is the use of statistics?
The article does not describe how the statistics were generated. Also, important terms, such as 'murder', 'crime' and 'states' need clear definitions to give context to the statistics.

3 What more information would you need to reach more conclusive results?
We need more information on the methods used to produce the statistics and a clearer and impartial explanation of the opposite view.

Activities

1 Decide which types of fallacy the following statements would fall under. Some of these are borderline and some contain more than one fallacy.

   1 I suggest that we buy Adidas products, as we have been a loyal customer since they produced their first sports shoes.

   2 As it cannot be proven that our new work policy in X country caused the resignations, it should be implemented by other countries.

   3 Intelligent shareholders are against the take-over as it is obvious that such mining results in disastrous problems.

   4 Given that he is the President of Amnesty International, his opinions on capital punishment should not be published.

   5 He enjoys travelling, cooking and mountain climbing. Therefore, he would be suitable for work in public relations.

   6 Because you expect to be looked up to by others, you are likely to be preferred in work situations.

   7 During World War II, about 375,000 civilians died in country X and about 408,000 members of the armed forces died overseas. On the basis of those figures, it can be concluded that it was not much more dangerous to be overseas in the armed forces during that time than it was to stay at home as a civilian.

2 Bring an example of fallacious reasoning to class and be prepared to discuss it. This could be a newspaper article as well as a situation from a movie, novel or television programme. Analyse the thinking implied in your example, paying attention to its genre and rhetorical situation.

Working in Teams

Focus:

- Teamwork in business
- Project management
- Cooperation and conflict

Many projects in business and industry require collaboration for their completion. In fact, teamwork is rapidly becoming the norm in many business projects, especially those that entail the cooperation of specialists in different fields. Therefore, a discussion of the concepts and terms that underlie teamwork and collaboration has an important role in a guide to business communication.

As regards the writing component of team projects, two trends are common. One trend, generally the most successful one, is for the team to have a writer, usually the team member with the best communication skills. This person gathers information from other team members and produces the documents that record and report on the project. The other trend, a more problematic option, is for all team members to contribute to the writing component of projects. This trend tends to be effective if all team members have equal communication skills. Even in those cases, however, it is difficult to build coherence in a document that is made up of styles of different writers. Where possible, select a writer in a team project to avoid a 'cut and paste' appearance. To share accountability, however, ensure that all team members read the document and agree on its content and organisation before submission.

This chapter overviews major elements of teamwork, especially *team dynamics,* the *allocation of team tasks, project management* and *conflict management*. The chapter ends with some real-life testimonials of members of team projects, evaluating the strengths and weaknesses of their teamwork.

Team dynamics

At their best, teams can produce excellent results by combining the specialised skills that individual team members bring. At their worst, teams produce delays, misunderstandings and conflicts. For this reason, the ability to deal productively with other people, peers, juniors and superiors, is a highly valued skill that contributes greatly to the smooth and successful management of an organisation. The success of a team project is largely due to such skilled procedures as effective negotiation, duty allocation and conflict management.

In business, as in other contexts, teams can be effective problem solvers for many reasons, including:

- Teams bring together experts from different specialisations and skill sets.
- More extensive information is available in a team than an individual may have alone.
- Individuals bring different approaches to a problem within the team. This allows for a wide range of options to be considered.
- Improved understanding of the problem and possible solutions is possible, because team members are aware of the reasoning used in problem analysis.
- Risks can often be managed more effectively in teams. What can be a high-risk decision for an individual could actually be a moderate-risk decision for a team, because different team members bring new knowledge to the issue and because risk is often mitigated by increased knowledge.
- Motivation and confidence are likely to increase in decisions made in team situations because individual team members feel supported by others.

Major disadvantages of reaching important decisions as part of a team include:

- Decisions can be made too soon: teams that feel uncomfortable with conflict may decide on the first option which meets with some support from the team members, regardless of whether this would be the best option.
- On the other hand, decisions can take too long if the team cannot agree on a topic.
- If the team structure has no hierarchy or leader there may be a lack of initiative and responsibility.
- Teams may be influenced by one person, whose charismatic or persuasive strengths may induce members to overlook pertinent factors in the problem involved.

- If there is too much conflict in a team, the team may become inoperable or ineffective.
- Teams may displace responsibility so that it may be difficult to hold a team or an individual member accountable for a negative outcome.

Good team dynamics are generally achieved in three main ways:

1 Members are attracted to the team's purpose.
2 Members share similar values, needs and interests.
3 Members fulfil for each other important interpersonal needs, such as *affection* (acknowledging each other's point of view), *inclusion* (allowing each member to play a role in activities) and *control* (allowing each member to determine certain actions pertinent to the member's role).

Task allocation

In order for team work to be productive more is needed than just faith in the goodwill and competence of individual members. What is more essential is a formally implemented system for duty allocation, negotiation, delegation of duties, monitoring of progress and feedback. Ensure that you divide the project into tasks, and allocate the tasks to each team member. Also, ensure that everyone knows and agrees to his/her allocated tasks at the beginning of the project. Three common and effective models for organising team projects are *the sequential, the functional* and *the mix-and-match*. These are broad categories that can be adapted and modified for particular situations.

The sequential model

In this type, each department/section in a company, or person in a group for smaller projects, is assigned a specific, non-overlapping, responsibility in the project. For example, in a software company, three departments are sometimes involved in producing the user documentation:

1 Software specialists assemble the material.
2 Communication specialists are in charge of putting it together and designing it.
3 The art and printing department is responsible for publishing the documentation.

In this case, each department must finish its job before passing the material to another department for the next stage.

The sequential type of collaboration can be effective at times, especially when the work of each segment is specialised and each stage is self-sufficient. However, projects completed sequentially take longer than when other methods are employed, and a project manager is often necessary to coordinate the project and to ensure that deadlines are kept, all parties understand requirements and transitions from one stage to the next are smooth.

The functional model

This type is organised according to the skills or job function of the members. All stages of a project are undertaken concurrently and all parties can monitor procedures at each stage. For example, a four-person team carrying out a user documentation project for software might be organised as follows:

- A manager schedules and conducts meetings, assists team members, issues progress reports to management, solves problems by proposing alternatives and generally coordinates efforts to keep the project on schedule.
- A researcher collects data, conducts interviews, searches the literature, administers tests, gathers and classifies information and then prepares notes on the work.
- A writer/editor receives the researcher's notes, prepares outlines and drafts and circulates them for corrections and revisions.
- A graphics expert obtains and prepares all visuals, specifying why, how and where visuals should be placed and designing the document layout. He or she might even suggest that visuals replace certain sections of text.

All parties work on the project at the same time, and interact regularly through meetings and email communication.

The mix and match model

In this type of collaboration, team members agree on shared objectives and then work independently on separate sections of the project by undertaking all tasks. The team members meet at specified times to compare their work and choose the best samples from each other's work. This approach is constructive in smaller scale projects, when team members have similar skills but cannot meet regularly.

A different version of this approach occurs when all members share the same interactive software and can work on the same project concurrently, each contributing according to their own skills which may or may not overlap. Continuing our software documentation example, a mix and match type of collaboration could mean that members from the engineering, communication and art departments use the same software programs or versions of Cloud computing, and work on the same documentation project at the same time. This would most likely cut costs and reduce time, compared with the sequential model, but it would necessitate that all members work cooperatively, and that project milestones and outcomes are very clearly set out and agreed by all in advance (to reduce the risk of 'you're treading on my toes' syndrome).

The leader

In any kind of collaboration model, the role of a leader is vital. Even in cases where, seemingly, the team works on egalitarian principles and all team members know their duties, liberties and constraints, the presence of a leader can act as a unifying force that helps to maintain cohesion and stability. It is a good idea to select a team leader to avoid the situation where the most dominant personality takes over unofficially. Regardless of whether their focus is to maintain cohesion or to initiate tasks, effective team leaders share certain characteristics. According to Qubein (1986: 96), these common characteristics are:

- They value people: they acknowledge the importance and contribution of others.
- They listen actively: they make an effort to understand the needs and desires of others.
- They are tactful: they criticise sparingly, constructively and diplomatically.
- They give credit: they praise others and their contributions publicly.
- They are consistent: they control their personal moods and are fair in their exchanges with others.
- They admit mistakes: they take the blame for errors they committed.
- They have a sense of humour: they maintain a pleasant disposition and pleasant manner.
- They set a good example: they follow their own regulations.

Effective leaders are not only personally ambitious and well-organised, but should also be people-oriented, willing to assist and direct subordinates and able to improvise and innovate in their field within ethical parameters.

Project management

A project in business and industry consists of a series of activities leading to one major goal or purpose. *Project management* refers to the planning necessary to complete a major project on time, within budget, according to specifications and with the consultation and consent of all relevant parties. Projects tend to be undertaken by a *project team*, a group of people responsible for managing a project. Projects usually begin with a proposal and end with a completed outcome and a final report showing how the initial goals were reached or not. During the progress of a project, the team is generally required to submit progress reports at specified times (such as monthly or bi-monthly), in order to keep management informed of what has been achieved and what still remains to be done.

The components of effective project management are *definition, planning* and *direction*. Briefly, *project definition* involves describing the envisioned final product and its place in the market; *planning* involves identifying and prioritising the tasks necessary for the completion of the product; and *direction* involves allocating roles to team members and setting a timeline for the execution of tasks. Consider each component more carefully.

Definition: As the first step, a project is carefully defined. Aspects of project definition include:

- Project overview: is the project attempting to solve a problem? If so, for whom is this a problem? How is the problem defined? Is the project creating a new product? What are the characteristics of this product? What types of markets will it target?
- Scope: what issues, topics or features will the project cover? How much detail will it provide? What are the parameters that project team members have to work within?
- Outcome: what will the result of the project be? For example, if a mechanical product is being developed, what functions should it perform and to what standard?

Planning: Each step in the process is planned before further action is taken. Tasks undertaken in the planning stage include:

1 Identifying the steps required to complete the project
2 Listing the priorities: What should be done first, second, third?
3 Identifying dependent and independent tasks: Which tasks need to be put aside while other tasks are being completed? Which tasks are urgent and which may be delayed without damaging the project?
4 Creating a timeline for task completion and allocating roles to project team members

Project Managers usually divide tasks into three categories:

1 **A critical task** must be completed on time for the entire project to be completed on time.

2 **A milestone** is an event that signifies the accomplishment of a series of tasks during a project. A milestone often signals the ending of a stage or section in the development of the project.
3 **A deliverable** is a concrete object produced at specific stages in the project (and usually delivered to a manager or client). Deliverables are used in some types of project management, like, for instance, software design and engineering. For example, the systems requirements report, produced near the beginning of the project and describing what the projected software will achieve, is a deliverable.

Direction: Each project is directed according to a line of responsibility. Project managers are responsible for monitoring and controlling progress and activities. Members of the project team report to managers, who in turn report to upper level management and clients. Team members who are able to meet all the requirements of the project at a minimum cost and on time are highly valued.

The direction of a project also involves issues of resources, constraints and risks, which may propel the project forward or inhibit its development:

- Resources: what advantages do the team have in undertaking the project? Are they highly skilled? Do they have a large budget? Do they have adequate time to complete all the tasks? Is up-to-date technology available to them?
- Constraints: is the budget modest? Is the staff limited, in numbers or in knowledge? Are there tight deadlines? Is there a lack of appropriate technology?
- Risks: what are the possible dangers of the project and what can be done to minimise them?

Two particular dangers that often arise in project management are known as *scope creep* and *feature creep*. Both of these can lead to delays, incomplete projects and conflicts within the project team.

Scope creep is exemplified by the tendency of stakeholders and project participants to expect increasingly more from the outcome of the project as it progresses. For example, businesses and users might expect increasing functionality and performance from a product as the process of developing it unfolds.

Feature creep refers to the tendency to add more features and details to the expected product of the project without bearing in mind that the incorporation of these features will take extra time and money. The type of project determines what kind of feature creep may exist. In product design, for example, feature creep leads to the uncontrolled addition of features or functions to the product.

One way to keep the project under control and monitor progress is to have a clear plan at the beginning, agreed upon by all members, to implement a feedback process where any conflicts or miscommunication can be aired and resolved and to discuss progress at regularly organised meetings.

Conflict management

Conflict is embedded in human relations. It arises when there is incompatibility of orientation between individuals or groups, and it can form in such situations as when people have incompatible goals and behaviours, when resources have to be allocated and when decisions have to be made. Conflict is associated with:

- Value: underlying values are different. This is arguably the most important and serious type of conflict because values are entrenched in social interaction and behaviour, and are very difficult to change.
- Interests: what promotes one's self-interest opposes another's. For example, when two colleagues compete for the same promotion inevitably some degree of conflict will arise.
- Policy: existing regulations do not reflect current needs. This often manifests in cases where conflict leads to employees' strikes or group protests. This is what happens, for example, when prices increase but salaries remain static, leading to a strike, or when women have achieved breakthroughs in social equality but legislation regulating gender issues remains at a primitive level, leading to demonstrations or ground breaking legal proceedings. Policy is very closely aligned with value.
- Goals: there is controversy or disagreement about where a project is going. In a project, for example, some members may think the goal is to produce routine results, whereas others may want to produce a radical breakthrough.
- Method: there is controversy or disagreement about how to arrive at the desired outcome. Such conflict may arise when one side is more optimistic about the future, while the other side wants more control over a situation, leading them to choose high-risk methods (such as war over negotiation, for instance).

Managed properly, conflict can result in growth because it allows for different points of view to be aired and considered. Managed badly, it can be destructive and costly – in resources and relationships. Groups can suffer from two opposite evils: too little conflict and too much conflict. A little conflict can be a good thing for change and rejuvenation of outmoded structures and beliefs. A lot of conflict, however, can destroy a project and in serious cases even lead to costly lawsuits and official investigations.

When teams are not working well, it can be a very serious matter, costing the organisation money and time. While the reasons that make a team unproductive are not fixed or universal, there are some guidelines regarding what could not be working right that can be used to clarify the situation:

- The team may lack a leader, or be burdened by an incompetent leader, making it disorganised and dysfunctional as a result.
- The team may be lacking the required specialist skills to tackle a project expertly and confidently.
- Members may feel their personal skills are not appreciated and they may lose motivation (often the result of weak leadership or bad management).
- The team may feel their efforts will not be supported by authorities and funding agencies, especially if they are working under budget constraints and/or on obscure or unpopular projects.
- A conflict of values or expectations may exist where some team members may expect different results from the project or the team may be expecting different results from the management.
- The objectives and scope of a project may be unclear, leading to confusion.
- Personal conflicts may hinder the achievement of goals. This is especially true of competitive environments where people are not accustomed to working cooperatively.

Managing conflict

As it probably has become clear from the preceding discussion, managing conflict is no easy matter. In most aspects of interpersonal communication, contextual factors, such as the setting of the interaction, the background of the participants and the nature of the interaction, are important in pointing to the most appropriate reactions, and conflict management is no exception to this. However, as regards teamwork, a general process for managing conflict could take this form:

1 **Define the problem:** The definition of the problem is the most important step in finding a solution. In many cases there is low morale and a lack of commitment by team members because there is a problem

that has not been voiced or made conscious within the group dynamics. An effective method of discussing the problem that caused this conflict is to describe it in writing. Each conflicting side should describe their perspective on the matter as clearly and as objectively as possible, avoiding 'I said / he said' type criticism. It is also important to avoid generalisations, such as 'they', 'always', 'never', etc., and to determine if the reaction is proportional to the situation. In describing the issue, consider if it had objective grounds to escalate into conflict, or if it is likely to have been caused by misunderstanding.

2 **Analyse the problem:** Once the group agrees on the nature of the problem, the next step is to analyse it in terms of size, causes and criteria of evaluation. At this stage, it is important not to succumb to the temptation of listing possible solutions before having analysed the problem thoroughly. Before answering the question 'what can be done to solve the conflict', team members should answer 'why is this a conflict?' and 'for whom is it a conflict?'

3 **Generate possible solutions:** Brainstorming is usually an effective way to generate ideas that could lead to the resolution of the conflict. At this stage, evaluation or nitpicking criticism of ideas should be avoided and team members should produce as many possible solutions as they can.

4 **Evaluate and test the various solutions:** After the brainstorming stage, each possible resolution should be examined to ascertain its merits and drawbacks. Factors to consider carefully include if the solutions are likely to work, if they are fair to all, and if they can be implemented easily. This should eliminate the solutions that are not worthwhile and leave a reduced number of options.

5 **Choose a mutually acceptable solution**: From the reduced number of possible solutions the one that seems to be the most effective can be chosen for a trial period. The best way to articulate this would be, once again, in writing. At times choosing an option is a risky act, with no guarantees that the selected solution will work. However, if the decision was reached by (relative) consensus, all the parties involved will be responsible for testing it and providing feedback.

One way to maximise your chances for keeping conflict under control is to institute a feedback process, through which all team members air complaints, express satisfaction and propose changes to the team structure at specified intervals. During such feedback sessions, consider evaluating your own and others' contributions and participation following the criteria in Table 14:

Table 14: Criteria for Evaluating Team Member Contribution

- Team members are available when needed and are punctual and reliable.
- Team members communicate clearly and constructively – they provide feedback.
- Team members contribute equally to the project and carry out their tasks as assigned.
- Team members help each other to manage conflict and act as intermediaries in negotiations with other team members.
- Team members are serious about deadlines, protocols and constraints of the project.

Effective listening

Effective listening contributes enormously to group dynamics and conflict resolution. In interpersonal communication, poor listening skills are at fault in many, if not most, cases of misunderstanding. Being a good listener makes one not only an effective communicator but also a strong leader.

Listening involves the whole physical presence. When working with others, much of the communication that takes place when suggesting, instructing, requesting, criticising, praising and negotiating is non-verbal. Listening actively by making a physical and mental effort to understand what someone else is saying engages the whole body, not just ears. It is a way of communicating that signifies that you understand the feelings of the speaker and are interested in their position, and that you are available and willing to consider the situation impartially without judging or laying blame.

Here are six tips for active listening:

1 **Stop talking**: Many people talk too much because they feel uncomfortable with silence. However, you cannot listen if you are talking.

2 **Remove noise as much possible.** 'Noise' is used in the communications sense of *distractions to the unhindered transmission of the message*. Therefore, it refers not only to external factors such as street noise, but also other factors, such as excessive heat or cold and distracting mannerisms. Common distracting mannerisms include clicking pens, shuffling papers, checking clothing or fingernails and gazing around the room. If you need to talk to a team member or colleague about something serious, it is advisable to arrange a meeting in pleasant and relaxed surroundings.

3 **Ask open questions** which begin with the 5Ws and 1H: what, when, why, where, who and how. This helps to keep the conversation on the topic and to obtain as much information as possible on it. When people answer W and H questions they have to reply in full sentences, and so their replies are more factual than they would be if the questions were of the 'Do you…' type, which elicits, simpler 'yes-no' answers.

4 **Be supportive.** Let the other person know that you *want* to know what s/he is talking about. It is well attested that most people will talk if they get attention and interest from the listener. Sensing indifference or impatience discourages a constructive response.

5 **Respond to feelings.** If the situation at hand has an emotional investment by one or all the participants, it is best to acknowledge this. Hidden or 'bottled' feelings may cloud or sabotage the information you require.

6 **Summarise to check mutual understanding.** A summary ensures that both parties have the same understanding of what has been said and helps to create closure to an issue or topic of discussion. In business, for example, a summary is formalised in a Statement (or Memorandum) of Understanding, which lists the points that have been agreed upon in a previous discussion.

Testimonials on teamwork

Below are extracts from the recommendations sections of reports on engineering team projects. These extracts describe problems in unclear task allocation, leading to delays; inadequate structure of meetings, leading to confusion on what needed to be done and who was to do it; lack of leadership, leading to lack of disciplined progress toward goals, and, often, low morale; and inadequate planning, leading to time wasting and miscommunication.

Skills, tasks and roles

One good rule in forming a team is to select members who have a nice distribution of skills. A group whose members all specialise in the same field may be very strong in that one area but lacking in many others.

Considering the allocation of roles, it took us some time to organize ourselves. Our roles were overlapping and after some time we decided to attribute ourselves some more precise functions. We realize that a better way to do this would have been to have a clear definition of our roles from the start, which would have optimized the time spent during meetings by preventing significant overlap. For future teams, we would recommend that the attribution of roles be done with common accord and discussion between team members as early as possible.

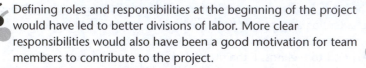

Defining roles and responsibilities at the beginning of the project would have led to better divisions of labor. More clear responsibilities would also have been a good motivation for team members to contribute to the project.

Agendas and structure of meetings

Agendas and schedules are helpful. Project groups cover many issues in a meeting, and it is difficult to keep track of them all. Making a list ensures that all points will be addressed and not forgotten. Schedules help in time management. The large task of tackling a big design project is much more manageable when broken down into smaller tasks that can be carried out one by one.

Our meetings were first planned electronically through e-mail and initiated by any member. During this preliminary organization stage, an agenda could have been delivered, which would have added structure and routine to our meetings.

Another way to enhance team efficiency is better routine. If we always had the same meeting time on the same day, it would prevent confusion and wasted time. The meetings would have more value since people would always be conveniently prepared.

The lack of agendas and minutes also led to inefficiencies during team meetings. This problem combined with the lack of clearly defined roles, led to uncertainties during meetings as to what work needs to be done. Without the project brief, which set milestones and deliverable dates, little progress would have been made during meetings.

Intra-group communication

A group should be flexible. It should be able to account for mistakes and accidents, and be able to change plans in case of emergencies or failures. A team should not be so set on one solution that the whole group dissolves when something goes wrong.

Problems that one member encounters should be brought to the entire team, to make everyone aware of the issues that need resolution and possibly to allow the team to resolve the problem during a meeting.

Leadership

We recommend having a leader. Leaders help organize a group which could otherwise be chaotic from miscommunication or personal conflict. It is good to have someone who can mediate when there is a problem or make executive decisions when the group cannot decide together. The leader can also impose schedules to continue pushing the project towards its goal in a timely manner.

Planning

Planning ahead and not procrastinating is key. Although teams can complete a divided workload more quickly than an individual, gathering and organizing the completed work takes extra time. Procrastination is always bad, but with a group it can be even worse. It is more difficult to gather a group, and not everyone may be available at the same time. Planning ahead allows more flexibility in schedules and allows for unexpected conflicts. It also prevents the whole burden of the project from being dumped on one responsible individual at the last minute.

Teamwork guide

Below is a template you can use or adapt to help you organise team projects in their initial stage.

1 Project Name and Main Objective (Mission)

2 Team Member Tasks

List the main responsibilities assigned to each team member:

Name:

1

2

3

4

3 Planning and Coordinating Issues

1 Decide how you will communicate (e-mail, meetings, etc.), and arrange regular times for this.
2 Write agendas for meetings, and keep a written record of important decisions. In your record, remember to include action items, *who does what and when*. Assign roles to team members for each meeting. These should include: a *leader*, a *scribe* and a *process monitor*.
3 Decide how you will resolve conflict, before it arises. The best way to do this is to formalise a procedure for feedback. For example, allocate some time at the end of each meeting to discuss collaboration issues. Ask: 'is everyone carrying out their assigned tasks effectively?' and 'how could we have improved this meeting?'

Below is a completed template as an example:

1 Project Name and Mission:

Single Biological and Chemical Species Detector

We want to investigate potential markets, devise a business plan and propose a strategy to create a product using ultra-high-Q resonators that has increased functionality over existing products at a viable cost. We would also like to find a market where we would be the first company to resolve problems with our product that cannot be resolved with existing technology.

2 Team Member Tasks

List the main responsibilities assigned to each team member:

Name: Jens Larsen, Team Leader

1 Find potential markets and estimate size

2 Find all competitors in our market and see how much market share each has and why

3 Analyse competitors' costs

4 Identify which market would be most benefited by new technology

Name: Ryan Sing

1 Contact patent holder and read papers

2 Explore alternative markets and applications

3 Look at prices/advantages of similar products/technology

4 Analyse product lifetime

5 Analyse costs of new technology over previously existing technology

Name: Adam Bedford

1 Financial planning – business plan and finding potential investors

2 Analyse feasibility of bringing product to market from concept through production to finished product

3 Find potential customers in the early phase

4 Patent rights and intellectual property. How solid is the patent?

5 Find empirical data and/or prototypes

Activities

1 Assume you are the founder and CEO of a new business. You have an executive team of five people and are now preparing to write a business plan to gain investments and funding. Organise the tasks leading to the business plan following the project management model, and allocate roles and responsibilities to all team members. Set your project out using the templates and guidelines proposed in this chapter.

2 What would you say are the organisational problems that the following statements signify? Some statements may indicate more than one communication problem.

'Our team could tell you how to achieve this in half the time and cost, but if this became public, they'd probably dismantle the team'

'I could have told management this would happen, but I didn't think they would listen, and I wasn't asked anyway'

'There's a better way to do this, but I doubt the project manager would want to learn about it'

'The design team originally made this suggestion, and it eventually made millions for the company. But the design team got nothing out of it'

'I didn't know this was the correct procedure'

Revising and Editing

Focus:

- Revision and editing
- Sentence structure
- Overview of grammar

This chapter gives guidelines on revising and editing a document and on sentence structure. It aims to give an awareness of the communicative effects of grammatical structures and enable you to gain control over the 'mechanics' of writing. It complements Chapter 2 in focusing on language as an important component of writing and communication. The chapter begins with an overview of sentence structure, and proceeds by explaining some common language troublespots: *active and passive voice*; *participial phrases*; *subject–verb–pronoun agreement*; *punctuation*; and *relative clauses*. It ends with a discussion of revising and editing considerations.

The guidelines presented here should help you to produce grammatically correct prose, whatever the context and purpose of the document. Knowing rules and conventions of writing confers confidence and credibility, even in cases where a writer decides to deliberately ignore these rules and conventions. In the famous words of T. S. Eliot, 'it is not wise to violate the rules until you know how to observe them'.

Sentence structure

Sentences and phrases

The minimal definition of a sentence is a word group that contains a *subject* (someone or something that carries out an action – the agent of an action) and a *verb* (the action carried out). This minimal word group is called a *clause*. Many sentences also contain an *object* (the recipient of the action or the thing or person acted upon). For example:

The report	recommended	changes
subject	verb	object

If the word group has no subject or no verb, but still makes some basic sense by evoking an image, it is a *phrase*. This is not a complete sentence; it is a fragment. Fragments do have their place in writing: they create colourful and imagistic effects. However, although their use is justified and often even expected in creative writing and many kinds of journalism, fragments are basically ungrammatical and should be avoided in formal or specialist style.

Phrase: Trying to come to a decision
Sentence: Trying to come to a decision, the project members considered all options

To write complete sentences, make sure you have these elements:

1 **A verb that shows time ('finite' verb):** something happens or is described in the past, present or future. If the word group has no verb at all, it is a fragment, because nothing happens. Make sure your verb has a *tense* (time element). Even if a word group contains a verb, it fails as a complete sentence if the verb has no tense. Remember that gerunds (-ing words) and infinitives (-to do words) have no tense (are 'infinite') and can function as nouns or participles.

   Phrase: The committee considering the proposal
   Sentence: The committee considered the proposal
   Sentence: The committee considers the proposal
   Sentence: The committee will consider the proposal

2 **The absence of a subordinating word:** a word group is not a complete sentence if one of the following words or phrases is placed in front of it:

after	if	until
although	in case	when
as	provided that	whenever
as if	since	whereas
as though	so that	whether
because	that	which
before	unless	while

Consider, for example, this:

While common law has long implied that there is a requirement for mutual respect and fair dealings in the employment relationship.

The word 'while' at the beginning of the sentence implies that there is a second part to this sentence, which contrasts the information given in the first. Without this second part, the sentence is not complete. To correct this problem, either put a comma after 'relationship' and add another clause, or take away 'while'.

Words ending in -ing

A word form ending in -ing can be:

1 **A participial form of a verb**: Having agreed to collaborate on the project, the engineers formed their teams. This is actually a reduced subordinate clause: After they had agreed to collaborate on the project, the engineers formed their teams.
2 **A verb in a continuous tense:** *The excavation continued while it was raining.* In this case, the -ing word is preceded by the verb *be* (was, were, am, will be, etc.).
3 **A gerund:** *Walking is good exercise.* A gerund can be the subject of a sentence and functions as a noun.
4 **An adjective:** *It is tedious to attend boring meetings.* In this case, the -ing word qualifies a noun by describing its attributes (interesting, exciting, frustrating, amusing, etc.).

Types of sentences

Sentences are classified into four categories:

Simple sentences contain one main clause.

The report recommended changes.

Compound sentences contain two or more main clauses connected with conjunctions.

The report recommended changes, and established deadlines.

Complex sentences contain one main clause and one or more subordinate clauses (clauses that would be fragments if disconnected from the main clause).

a) The report, which will form the basis of our decision, recommended changes.
b) The report recommended changes because these are the only way to solve the problem.

Compound-complex sentences contain two or more main clauses and one or more subordinate clauses.

The report recommended changes and established deadlines, because that is the only way to solve the problem.

Note that sentence types are more about the prioritisation of information than about length. In fact, a simple sentence can be much longer than a complex one, as seen in these examples:

Complex sentence: The applicants who were rejected were permitted to apply for the other position.

Simple sentence: After much deliberation and a lot of debate over several meetings, the project members decided reluctantly to accept the committee's proposal to re-design the bridge.

The first stage where you begin your crafting of style is the sentence. Therefore, the more practice you give yourself in constructing different types of sentences and observing their effects the better.

Active and passive voice

The active and passive voices are a major concern for writers, as they can colour a text profoundly by disclosing or revealing information and by highlighting different elements of the sentence. The active voice emphasises the agent and the action of a sentence. The passive voice, on the other hand, emphasises the object, person or thing acted upon. Therefore, using one or the other is a strategic choice. For example:

Active: The manager signed the contract.
Passive: The contract was signed by the manager.
Word order of active voice: subject + verb + object.
Word order of passive voice: object + be + past participle [optionally + by + subject].

Using active or passive voice is not just a matter of variety. As happens also with other forms of sentence manipulation, it orders and prioritises information and, therefore, has an evaluative function. Some people (and grammar checkers) harbour deep suspicions about the passive voice. They will tell you to use the active where possible. There are three reasons for this:

1 The passive emphasises the object, which does not carry out any action (it is acted upon). Therefore, the verb of the sentence becomes weaker. The information content of the sentence appears to be static rather than dynamic. This may be required in some cases (as discussed below).

However, if it is not a deliberate choice, the passive may better be avoided to prevent weakening the sentence.

2 Often, the passive conceals the agent of the action, or at least subordinates it. This may be unacceptable in certain cases where stated responsibility for an action is required for clarity or ethics.

3 As has been emphasised throughout the book, conciseness is valued in many contexts, especially in business and public writing, and the passive adds words to sentences.

However, the passive voice has a definite role for these purposes:

1 The agent is unimportant and, in fact, mentioning the agent may make the sentence awkward:

> **Awkward active**: I/we use the passive voice to move components around in a sentence.
> **Preferred passive:** The passive voice is used to move components around in a sentence.
> **Awkward active**: Trucks take the logs to the factory for processing.
> **Preferred passive**: The logs are taken to the factory for processing.

This purpose of the passive is most evident in scientific writing, where processes and procedures are important because of the results and observations they lead to, rather than because of the personal role of the scientist him/herself in carrying out the process. Notice also that, in this case, the agent is not mentioned at all in the sentence.

2 The agent is unknown:

> **Awkward active**: Someone stole the computer from the lab.
> **Preferred passive**: The computer was stolen from the lab.

In this case, the agent is unknown and emphasis falls on the event. In fact, in some cases, such as in police reports, it would be misleading to include an agent as perpetrator of a deed, if the identity of this agent is unknown or uncertain.

3 The agent is collective:

> **Awkward active**: People/Farmers grow tea in India.
> **Preferred passive**: Tea is grown in India.

In this case, the subject is not individual, and the result or process is more important.

However, there are occasions where using the active voice is a far more advisable choice. As noted above, one occasion is when you want to produce a sharp, energetic and concise piece: the active voice is certainly more direct, succinct and snappy. Another occasion is when your writing involves assuming or attributing responsibility for decisions and making these decisions more personal. In many occasions the passive voice is used to conceal the agents responsible for certain actions, and this can give a harsh and impersonal impression. For example, the impersonal nature of the following sentence gives it bad audience dynamics:

> **Awkward passive:** Your proposal has been considered and it has been decided to reject it.
> **Preferred active:** The Housing Board considered your proposal and the executive committee decided to reject it.

In important writing, such as proposals, formal business reports and official documents, the readers want to know who they are dealing with in order to ascertain who is responsible for different actions. In such cases, use the passive voice with the utmost care to avoid misunderstandings and conflict. The same situation occurs when you write about plans, decisions and reactions to events. Using the passive in such cases mystifies the topic, since the agents remain unknown, and produces a generalised and vague effect unsuited to professional writing.

Consider this extract. The first sentence is acceptable because it sets the scene and focuses on a process. Notice, however, how the use of the passive in the other two sentences puts the writer in a distant and detached position that leaves the reader with a general impression of the situation but with no specific, factual, information. Who raised questions? Who questioned the ethical viability of GMF procedures?

> Genetically Modified Foods (GMF) have been used commercially in food products available to the general public since 1996. This was met with general outcry and many questions were raised about the safety of the products. The ethical viability of such procedures and the impact that GMF would have on the environment were also questioned.

Active and passive voice activities

1 Convert these sentences into the passive, if possible, and discuss their effects.

   a The experts that the CEO invited confirmed the gravity of the situation.
   b The terrorist squad disarmed the bomb that threatened to destroy the building.
   c The project team leader could not organise the meeting because he broke his leg.
   d The manager decided to extend the deadline by a week to allow the team to finish the first part of the project.

   Now convert these sentences into the active and discuss their effects.

   a The chemicals are sealed in containers and taken to the laboratory for tests.
   b The analyst felt sure that the files had been tampered with.
   c The plan was approved and permission has been granted to begin implementing it.
   d Your report should be revised carefully before it is submitted for consideration.

2 This extract is written mostly in the passive. Rewrite it using active structures, and making any other necessary changes. Then observe and discuss the effect of the two versions.

   The Employment Contracts Act 1991 has been controversial since it came into force. Generally, it has been opposed by trade unions and supported by employer's organisations, although different views might have been held by individual unions and employers. In this Act, the machinery of Industrial Conciliation as the primary means of wage fixing was abolished. Also, state sponsorship of the trade union was ended, and protected status taken away from employees. Trade Unionism has been affected substantially by the 1991 Act, and the power in industrial relations was tilted towards employers.

   In contrast, in the Employment Relations Act 2000 unions are given the right to represent their members in bargaining for collective employment agreement with employers. This is particularly significant because only union members can be covered by collective agreement. Collective bargaining may be undertaken by non-union members, but any agreement that is reached will be individual.

Participial phrases

Participial phrases contain the past participle of a verb (verbs ending in -ing, -en and -ed) and no subject. Participials reduce clauses that show a temporal (before, after) or a causal (because, so) relationship. They add variety and, often, formality to your writing and are useful stylistic choices. Study these sentences and their participial alternatives, and notice how using this construction can introduce variety in your writing:

Compound sentence: The CEO agreed to support the proposal, so she attended this month's meeting.
Sentence beginning with participial phrase: Having agreed to support the proposal, the CEO attended this month's meeting.
Sentence with subordinate clause: Many investors are turning to mutual funds this year, because they think that interest rates will fall even further.
Sentence beginning with a participial: Thinking interest rates will fall even further, many investors are turning to mutual funds this year.

Participial constructions generally serve the following functions:

1 They help keep your writing concise by reducing words.
2 They provide you with a tool to give your writing more variety.
3 They make your writing more formal.

Frequent error with participials

Using participial phrases incorrectly may lead to the common error known as *misrelation* or *dangling modifier*. This occurs when the verb of the participial does not agree with the noun it is identified with, which would be the noun immediately following the participial phrase:

Misrelation: While inspecting the nuclear reactor, a loud crash alarmed the supervision team.

– was the loud crash inspecting the nuclear reactor?

Corrected: While inspecting the nuclear reactor, the supervision team was alarmed by a loud crash.

– note that to correct the relation while keeping the participial, the sentence has to change active to passive voice.

Corrected: The loud crash alarmed the supervision team, while they were inspecting the nuclear reactor

– this removes the participial and adds a subordinate clause.

Misrelation: Having solved the problem, it was easy for him to get any job he wanted.
Corrected: Having solved the problem, he could get any job he wanted.

Participial phrases activity

Combine the following sentences by turning one of them into a participial.

1 The managing director allocated an extra $2 million to our department. He was pleasantly disposed towards our supervisor's project.
2 The General Manger was faced with numerous accusations of misconduct. He was forced to resign in June.
3 Small business owners can give too little attention to choosing a good location for their business. This results in lower profits or even bankruptcy.
4 She attained a good reputation and the admiration of her colleagues in the corporation. Because of this status, she had no problem finding a new job.
5 The Employment Relations Act is based largely on the presumption that the employment relationship is a human relationship. With this attitude, it has been possible to solve successfully many disputes.
6 The unexpected settlement money that the company won in the court case gave them the opportunity to expand their business internationally. This resulted in a surge in confidence and increased optimism among all company members.

Subject–verb–pronoun agreement

A common troublespot in writing is misusing a singular verb with a plural subject and vice versa, or a plural verb with a singular pronoun and vice versa. This sentence, for example, comes from a professional document:

> **Incorrect:** The facts in the case and all the evidence provided has been considered in the final decision.
> **Correct:** The facts in the case and all the evidence provided have been considered in the final decision.

In the incorrect version of the sentence, the verb 'has been' does not agree with the subject, which is 'the facts in the case and all the evidence provided'. The writer wrongly assumed that the word closest to the verb, 'evidence', is the subject.

Some general guidelines for correct subject–verb–pronoun agreement are:

1 Collective nouns (such as *police, family, government, team, audience,* etc.) can take a singular or a plural verb. Your choice depends on whether you want to emphasise their collective nature or the fact that they are composed of individuals. However, ensure that if you use a pronoun to refer to a collective noun, it has the same number as the verb:

Incorrect: The audience showed its appreciation. They gave the speaker a standing ovation.
Correct: The audience showed their appreciation. They gave the speaker a standing ovation.

2 Correlatives (*either–or, neither–nor, not only–but also*) have two subjects. In this case, the verb must agree with the subject closest to it:

Incorrect: Not only the workers but also the supervisor were affected by the fumes.
Correct: Not only the workers but also the supervisor was affected by the fumes.
Incorrect: Not only the supervisor but also the workers was affected by the fumes.
Correct: Not only the supervisor but also the workers were affected by the fumes.

3 Phrases separating the subject and the verb do not affect the number of the verb or pronoun:

Incorrect: The scientist, together with his troupe of devoted followers and supporters, have occupied the second floor of the building.
Correct: The scientist, together with his troupe of devoted followers and supporters, has occupied the second floor of the building.

However, subjects joined by 'and' or 'both–and' are plural and take a plural verb and pronoun:

Incorrect: The scientist and his troupe of devoted followers has occupied the second floor of the building.
Correct: The scientist and his troupe of devoted followers have occupied the second floor of the building.

4 The pronouns 'each', 'every', 'anyone', 'everyone' and 'no one' are singular and should take singular verbs and pronouns.

Incorrect: He stated that anybody is welcome to apply for membership; as for applications, each is to be assessed according to their own merit.
Correct: He stated that anybody is welcome to apply for membership; as for applications, each is to be assessed according to its own merit.

In informal writing, as in speaking, this rule is by-passed to avoid cumbersome sentences.

Informal: Everyone brought their books
Formal: Everyone brought his/her books

Subject–verb–pronoun agreement activity

Select the correct verbs in the following sentences:

1 The mob (was, were) mindless of the consequences of their actions.
2 Neither the general nor his men (was, were) prepared for the sudden attack; not only the men but also their leader (were, was) ready to retreat.
3 Assessments of essays and the exam (is, are) expected to be completed tomorrow.
4 An estimation of profits and losses (are, is) advisable before deciding.
5 The lecturer, together with her tutors, (are, is) going to attend the meeting.
6 Confidence and initiative and courage to take risks (lead, leads) to promotion in that field.
7 The issue most on his mind (are, is) efforts to negotiate a settlement.
8 The audience (were, was) conscious of its power to influence the course of the performance.
9 The decision to install the new computers and to update the software programs (have/has) been finalised by the executive committee.
10 Sharks, because of their secretive nature, and potentially aggressive behaviour, (has/have) always been a difficult topic of study.

Punctuation

Punctuation marks are a device that introduces rhythm and pace to the written text. Although they do serve to reflect in written form the dynamic aspects of speech, it would be misleading to equate them with the breathing patterns of speaking, because punctuation follows syntactic (i.e. grammatical), and not phonetic or physical, aspects of language. Therefore, reading a text aloud is not an accurate means of deciding where to insert a punctuation mark and what this mark should be. There are some grammatical rules that writers should know. This section overviews these rules.

A comma is the weakest pause mark. Others, in order of increasing duration or suddenness of the pause, include:

semicolon – ;
colon – :
ellipsis – ...
dash – –
quotation marks – '...'

full stop (or period) – .
exclamation mark – !
question mark – ?

Correct use of punctuation has changed over the years. Older texts often use punctuation quite differently from modern texts. The following guide gives you an overview of punctuation usage that is the current international standard.

Comma

Three main categories cover most of the cases when a comma is required:

1 Inserting words, phrases or clauses into a sentence.

We often add extra information to the basic core of sentences by adding phrases that give more detail, help to keep the reader on track or just generally add more variety to sentence structure. When adding phrases to a sentence, or moving phrases out of place to add variety, set off these additions and interjections with commas. These changes are made in three places:

a) Sentence openers:

> **Transition signposts**: However, I...
> **Interjections**: Well, I...
> **Adverbs:** Often, I...
> **Prepositional phrases:** In board meetings, I...
> **Participial phrases:** Having completed the project, I...
> **Adverbial clauses:** Whenever I try to think, I......
> **Appositives:** A successful entrepreneur, Steve Jobs...

b) Sentence insertions:

These have the same function as the openers, but produce a less emphatic effect. For example:

> **Inserted participial phrase**: The executive, having completed the project, decided to take a break.

Note: If you use insertions, remember to use commas at both ends.

c) Sentence enders:

Inserting a phrase or clause at the end of a sentence gives the least emphasis to the information contained in that phrase or clause. For example:

Participial ending the sentence: Give this to the presiding officer, the woman sitting next to the door.

2 Joining two clauses with and, or, but, nor, yet, so, for (coordinating conjunctions).

Two sentences can be joined with a comma and a coordinating conjunction (or, in case of a short sentence, with a conjunction alone):

Simple sentences: I took part in the competition. I came first.
Compound sentence: I took part in the competition, and I came first.

3 Listing items in a series.

A comma is used to list items in the same category in one sentence.

Listing items: The position requires writing annual reports, internal memoranda, newsletters and online documentation.

Frequent questions on the comma

A frequent question is if a comma is always needed before a coordinating conjunction. Opinions vary on this: some insist that a comma is necessary, while others suggest it is optional. Although it will not be considered wrong to include a comma in this case, it is acceptable to omit it in shorter sentences. This is especially justified when space limitations count, as in magazine and web publishing. The space taken by the comma is typographically significant, and this should be considered.

A similar question is if a comma is always needed after a prepositional phrase that begins the sentence. Again, the ideal answer is yes: you cannot go wrong by including a comma after a phrase, to set it off from the sentence that it modifies. However, if the sentence is easily read and understood without the comma and there are typographical space limitations, omit it. This occurs more often with prepositional phrases than participial ones.

Easily understood sentence: At present(,) the company does not have a financial manager.
Confusing sentence: After moving the tenants, who inherited one million dollars, bought their own mansion.
Corrected: After moving, the tenants, who inherited one million dollars, bought their own mansion.

Frequent errors with the comma

Comma Splice: this occurs when you join two full sentences with a comma. This is corrected by inserting a period, a semicolon or a coordinating conjunction in the place of the comma.

> **Comma Splice**: The committee contributed to the project by sending delegates to the meeting, however, these delegates were not adequately informed of recent developments in software design.
>
> **Corrected using period:** The committee contributed to the project by sending delegates to the meeting. However, these delegates were not adequately informed of recent developments in software design.
>
> **Corrected using semicolon**: The committee contributed to the project by sending delegates to the meeting; however, these delegates were not adequately informed of recent developments in software design.
>
> **Corrected using coordinating conjunction**: The committee contributed to the project by sending delegates to the meeting, but these delegates were not adequately informed of recent developments in software design.

Subject–verb disjunction: this occurs when the subject is separated from its verb with a comma. Subjects may be separated from verbs with prepositional and participial phrases as well as with subordinate clauses. In these cases, commas are inserted at either end of the phrase or clause. This way, the phrase or clause is set off the rest of the sentence.

> **Incorrect**: Authorised to seal the agreement, the company representatives, will meet with each board member individually during their visit.
>
> **Correct:** The company representatives, who are authorised to seal the agreement, will meet with each board member individually during their visit.
>
> **Incorrect**: Designers, play a pivotal role in the success of marketing products, through their sills in attractive presentation.
>
> **Correct**: Designers play a pivotal role in the success of marketing products, through their skills in attractive presentation.
>
> **Correct**: Designers, through their skills in attractive presentation, play a pivotal role in the success of marketing products.

Semicolon

The semicolon is used in the following cases:

1 It joins together two independent sentences. It indicates a stronger pause than a comma, but a shorter one than the period, and shows that there is a close relationship between the two joined sentences. For

instance, the first example below consists of two sentences that distribute information equally. The second example below consists of one sentence with two clauses joined with a semicolon. This suggests that the second clause is directly related to the first as an explanation or result.

> **Two sentences:** Branding is a major stage in the marketing process. It determines how consumers will visualise and relate to the product through its name.
>
> **Two clauses joined with semicolon**: Branding is a major stage in the marketing process; it determines how consumers will visualise and relate to the product through its name.

2 It separates items in a list, when one item or more in the list already contains a comma.

> **Listing with semicolons**: Attendees from overseas should submit a copy of their passport, showing the photo page; a certified check or money order, payable in local currency; and a stamped, self-addressed envelope.

Frequent errors with the semi-colon

Connecting a phrase to a sentence: this occurs when a semicolon is used to connect a participial or prepositional phrase to a clause. The correct punctuation mark for this case is the comma.

> **Incorrect**: The project team could not continue with the intended plan; having encountered unexpected opposition from major stockholders.
>
> **Correct**: Having encountered unexpected opposition from major stockholders, the project team could not continue with the intended plan.
>
> **Correct:** The project team could not continue with the intended plan, having encountered unexpected opposition from major stockholders.
>
> **Correct**: The project team, having encountered unexpected opposition from major stockholders, could not continue with the intended plan.

Introducing a list: this occurs when a semicolon is used to introduce a list of items or bullet points. The correct punctuation mark for this case is the colon.

> **Incorrect:** With your application include the following;

- A complete CV with contact details of three referees
- Transcripts of academic qualifications
- A completed application cover form.

Correct: With your application, include the following:

- A complete CV with contact details of three referees
- Transcripts of academic qualifications
- A completed application cover form.

Colon

The colon has the following uses:

1 It introduces quotations a sentence or longer in length. If the quotation consists of a few words, a comma will suffice. Each case is illustrated by the example below.

> **No use of colon before quotation**: The CEO made it clear that 'only under exceptional circumstances' will the plan change.
> **Use of colon before quotation**: The CEO made it clear that 'only under exceptional circumstances' will the plan change. He said: 'The situation is pretty clear-cut. The majority of stockholders have voted for the new system to be implemented on an experimental basis for three months. Until this trial period passes, there is nothing more to be done.'

2 It introduces a list of things, whether the list is written in-line or vertically. The example below illustrates this.

> Three groups may attend the meeting:
> - Members of the executive committee
> - Press representatives
> - Stockholders.

3 It shows the outcome or effect of an action. In this case, the colon plays a similar role to a semicolon. However, it has a more visual, and, therefore, more dramatic effect than a semicolon.

> He looked at an amazing sight: the house had totally collapsed.

Ellipsis

Ellipsis marks are much rarer in business writing than in creative or informal writing, because they reflect an incompleteness that is inconsistent with the purposes of professional documents. Ellipsis marks are mainly used for the following purposes:

1 To show hesitation or interruption. This is the most conversational use of the ellipsis, very rare in business writing. The extract below, from one of Ian Rankin's Inspector Rebus novels, exemplifies this in the representation of Rebus' meandering train of thought:

> Rebus commiserated for a couple of minutes, thinking of his own doctor's appointment, the one he was missing yet again by making this call. When he put the phone down, he scribbled the name Marr on to his pad and circled it. Ranald Marr, with his Maserati and toy soldiers. You'd almost have thought he'd lost a daughter ... Rebus was beginning to revise that opinion. He wondered if Marr knew how precarious his job was, knew that the mere thought of their savings catching a cold might spur the small investors on, demanding a sacrifice ... (Rankin 2001: 352)

2 In quotations, to show that a part of the speaker's statement has been omitted, usually because it was irrelevant to the writer's main concern. This is the most common use of ellipsis in business and academic writing. To show that the ellipsis is not part of the quotation, enclose it in square brackets. For example, in the quotation below I have included the introductory sentence to a section, then omitted the remainder of that paragraph going straight on the next paragraph, from where I have also omitted a few words that refer to a diagram that is irrelevant to my discussion:

> 'All researchers must support contestable claims with evidence, but they must then explain that evidence, treating each major bit of evidence as a claim in a secondary argument that needs its own evidence. [...] If you like doing things visually, put this on a wall-sized chart. Pin-up index cards [...], then try different combinations of secondary arguments.'

Dash

Dashes (hyphens) have the following uses:

1 They enclose information that is secondary to the main point of the sentence and that can be omitted or skipped – similar to brackets (parentheses). In this case, a dash goes at each end of the additional information. Avoid this in sentences that contain important information or when you want the readers' undivided attention, because, like brackets, dashes show a divergence from the main issue and can be distracting. Also, keep in mind that they can make a sentence unnecessarily long, so, where conciseness or directness is your aim, avoid them. The following examples illustrate this.

Example 1: She would have liked to see those letters. Chances were, they couldn't be recovered, either because they'd perished – been disposed of with Lovell's effects when he'd died – or had gone overseas. An awful lot of historical documentation had found its way into collections overseas – mostly Canada and the US – and many of these collections were private, which meant few details of their contents were available (Rankin 2001: 228).

Example 2: Both developers were away from the meeting – one at home sick, the other attending a trade fair – so no major decisions were made that would affect the outcome of the project.

2 They have a similar function to the colon in introducing a set of things, and to the comma in setting off a comment on the information presented in the main clause. As opposed to the colon or comma, however, the dash makes the information it sets off more emphatic.

In this case, the dash can actually make the sentence more concise by enabling the omission of introductory phrases or subordinate clauses. Place the dash before the additional information at the end of the sentence. The examples below illustrate this.

The CEO's decision to support the proposal was welcomed by stockholders – an unusual reception given the specialised nature of the proposal.

An unprecedented number of professionals attended the meeting – most of them engineers.

Apostrophe

Apostrophes are used for two purposes:

1 They show possession or ownership. In this case, they come before the possessive *s*. If the word already ends with an *s*, such as in plurals (pen – pens), in some names (Mars, Ross) or in some nouns (boss, albatross), the apostrophe comes after the *s*. For example:

- the dog's tail (one dog)
- the dogs' tails (more than one dog)
- the student's grade (one student)
- the students' grades (more than one student)
- the boss' plan (one boss)
- the bosses' plans (more than one boss)

2 They make contractions (combine two words into one). In this case, the apostrophe shows that there is a word, like *is, has* or *not*, missing. This is not a frequent use of apostrophes in professional writing, because contractions are avoided in formal documents. For example:

- isn't it a nice day!
- don't say it!
- it's important
- they've arrived

Frequent errors with the apostrophe

Apostrophe in plurals: this occurs when an apostrophe is inserted before a plural s, like it would be before a possessive s. Distinguish between the possessive s (which requires an apostrophe) and the plural s (which does not).

Incorrect: The information is in two video's
Correct: The information is in two videos
Incorrect: The presidents move was foreseen by many
Correct: The president's move was foreseen by many

Quotation marks

Quotation marks are used when reporting the exact words of a speaker or writer. If the quotation takes up more than three lines, indent it in a block paragraph and set it off the rest of the text. In this case, do not use quotation marks – the indentation signals that the text is a quotation.
Other guidelines for quotation marks are:

1 Use double quotation marks for the beginning and ending of quotations, and single quotation marks for words or phrases that are quoted within a quotation.
2 Use double quotation marks when you want to show that a word or phrase should be taken figuratively or is out of context.
3 Place periods, commas, semicolons, colons, exclamation marks and question marks outside quotation marks, unless the quotation itself contains them. This, however, is a controversial point. In American publications, for example, periods and commas are placed inside quotation marks, whereas colons and semicolons are placed outside. Question marks and exclamation points are placed, according to American convention, inside quotation marks unless they apply to the whole sentence.

Besides spelling, quotation marks are one of the contestable points in stylistic convention. Currently, there are no international standards in quotation mark usage. The best advice is to select a method and be consistent, and, if your organisation has a style guide to adhere to it. If there is an in-house style guide it will most likely include guidelines on quotation marks.

Punctuation activities

1 Insert suitable punctuation marks in the following sentences, if necessary:

   a Proposals a common business document are a major problem for writers.
   b The hotel chain provides its customers with affordable reliable and comfortable service.
   c Travel is educational it broadens your horizons.
   d The operator ran the program the disk drive was faulty.

2 Discuss and correct the punctuation errors in these sentences.

   a In addition to cleaning the assistant janitor must safeguard building keys.
   b In some cases students have doubled their reading speed; effectively halving their time spent in researching for assignments.
   c Everything seemed so different, the buildings were all made of red brick and were all very new.
   d The government 'red tape' has hindered business operations therefore it is important to assist these businesses in such issues.
   e The majority of young shareholders voiced opposition to the proposed plan, this shows that what older generations took for granted is unacceptable for the younger generations who are better informed on alternative options.
   f If you are tired of three-dimensional reality of the laws of physics and of cause, and effect; then virtual reality games will be congenial for you. As here you can: continually defy the odds, encounter firsts, and lasts, and perform miracles.
   g Martial arts training brings many benefits to stressed professionals; it is good for self-rehabilitation in the health of body mind and spirit. An excellent method for the ailing to energise themselves in the search for well-being, vitality is enhanced and can lead to the confidence required for professional success; in any field.

Relative clauses: which and that

Grammatically, both *which* and *that* are subordinating conjunctions, signalling a subordinate clause. However, as grammar checkers often indicate, they are not used interchangeably.

The clause that begins with *which* gives information about the noun that directly precedes it. If the *which* clause in a sentence is necessary to define the identity of the noun that precedes it, do not separate the noun from the *which* clause by putting a comma. In such cases, the *which* clause is called a *defining* or *restrictive* clause. The sentences below illustrate this.

1 The committee accepted the proposal which the project team had been working on for months.
2 The committee accepted the proposal, which the project team had been working on for months.

In the first sentence, the word *proposal* is relative. That is, the sentence literally means that the project team submitted several proposals and the committee accepted the one that the team had been working on for months. In this case, the *which* clause is *defining* and does not require a comma preceding it. It defines which of the proposals was accepted. In a defining clause, *which* could be replaced with *that*.

In the second sentence, on the other hand, the word *proposal* is absolute. That is, the sentence literally means that there is just one proposal in question here. In this case, the *which* clause is *non-defining*, meaning that it is not necessary in order to determine the identity of the noun that precedes it. In a non-defining clause, it could not be replaced with *that*, and always requires a comma to set it off from the main clause.

Because of this double use of *which*, it has become common practice in professional contexts to avoid it in defining clauses. Use *that* in defining clauses and *which* in non-defining clauses.

1 Entrepreneurs, who have an adventurous spirit, need to be resilient and adaptable.
   – All entrepreneurs have an adventurous spirit
2 Entrepreneurs who have an adventurous spirit need to be resilient and adaptable.
   – Only some entrepreneurs have an adventurous spirit, and it is these who need to be resilient and adaptable, not the rest.

Global *which*

You can also use a *which* clause to refer to the whole statement that precedes it. In such cases, do not use *that*. Always put a comma before the clause that begins with *which*. The sentences below illustrate this function of *which*.

1 The troops surrendered their weapons, which surprised the army command.

2 The candidate did not get the position, which was a mistake.

However, because a global *which* is often ambiguous, it is best to avoid it where possible in formal writing. For example, the above sentences would be more precise as below.

1 The army command was surprised that the troops surrendered their weapons.
2 Not giving the candidate the position was a mistake.

Relative clauses activity

Rewrite these sentences to avoid ambiguity.

1 The interest rates fell by 5 per cent, that is interesting.
2 The equipment which we ordered arrived on time which was a great relief.
3 There is only one solution to the problem, which is the course of action, which we must take.
4 Here is a program which eliminates many of the problems which the team has had had with previous models.
5 Methodologies which are a formalised approach to implementing the system vary in their approach which involves both analysis and design.
6 One major problem in science is that no matter how extensively a subject is researched, there will still remain the unknown variable of 'time', which often reveals something which was not considered.

Spelling

Unfortunately, English has no specific rules that you can learn to improve your spelling. The best way to improve your spelling is to read, read, read. A more systematic method is to focus on words that you repeatedly misspell, memorise their spelling and practise writing sentences with these words. For example, set yourself a weekly limit of about 30 words and give yourself 15 minutes a day every day for a specific period (from three to six months, or even a year depending on how bad your spelling is). Every couple of weeks or so test your learning to see if your programme is working. There are no quick-fix schemes for spelling.

As a writer, it is important not to underestimate spelling. Bad spelling is not a minor problem for writers. It shows that you are, at best, sloppy, at worst, illiterate. Also, relying on spell checkers is not a good idea, as they do not identify the context a word is used in. For example, they do not distinguish between *homophones* (words that sound the same but are spelled differently and have a different meaning). *Sun* and *son*, *I* and *eye*, *there* and *their*, *so* and *sew*, *weather* and *whether* are all pairs containing homophones with radically different meanings – indistinguishable by spell checkers.

The following is a list of commonly confused words to practise.

accept	receive (verb)
except	with the exclusion of (preposition)
absent	not present (adjective)
absence	being away (noun)
advice	recommendation (noun)
advise	to recommend (verb)
affect	to produce an influence on (verb)
effect	consequence of an action (noun)
already	by this time
all ready	fully prepared
altogether	thoroughly
all together	everyone or everything in one place
brake	device for stopping
break	destroy, make into pieces
canvas	material (noun)
canvass	solicit, ascertain, survey (verb)
choose	to pick
chose	past tense of choose
complement	round out, add to, complete
compliment	praise, flatter
council	administrative body (noun)
counsel	advise, consult (verb)
device	a plan, an implement
devise	to create

eminent	distinguished, notable
imminent	impending, about to happen
ensure	make certain of
insure	take out an insurance policy
envelop	to surround (verb)
envelope	container for a letter (noun)
formally	conventionally, with ceremony
formerly	previously
lead	heavy metal; to guide
led	past tense of lead
loose	unbound, not tightly fastened (adjective)
lose	to misplace (verb)
passed	past tense of pass
past	at a previous time
personal	intimate
personnel	employees
precede	to come before
proceed	to continue
principal	foremost; chief, leader
principle	moral conviction, basic truth
quiet	silent, calm
quite	very
stationary	standing still
stationery	writing paper
wave	surf
waive	to relinquish, give up
weather	climatic condition
whether	if
which	one of a group
witch	female sorcerer

The following is a list of commonly misspelt words for your reference.

absence	conscientious	license
academic	conscious	lightning
accidentally	criticism	loneliness
accommodate	criticise	maintenance
achievement	decision	manoeuvre
acknowledge	definitely	marriage
acquaintance	eighth	mischievous
acquire	eligible	necessary
address	embarrass	noticeable
aesthetics	emphasise	occasion
amateur	entirely	occurrence
answer	environment	pastime
apparently	exaggerated	permanent
appearance	exercise	perseverance
arctic	exhaust	phenomenon
argument	existence	playwright
arithmetic	extraordinary	preference
ascend	extremely	preferred
athlete	fascinate	pronunciation
attendance	foreign	publicly
basically	forty	receive
beautiful	fourth	referred
beginning	government	rhythm
believe	grammar	schedule
benefited	guard	seize
bureau	harass	sergeant
business	height	strictly
cemetery	humorous	succeed
changeable	incidentally	surgeon
column	incredible	thorough
commitment	independence	tomorrow
committed	indispensable	transferred
committee	inevitable	unnecessarily
competitive	intelligence	vacuum
completely	irrelevant	vengeance
conceivable	irresistible	villain
conscience	knowledge	weird

General proofreading activity

These sentences contain errors in grammar, style, accuracy, clarity, spelling or punctuation. Test yourself to see how well you learned the guidelines given in the book.

1 Having approved the project, the necessary staff was recruited.
2 The basic principal of good writing is clarity.
3 Today pneumatic tyres are fitted to almost all road vehicles, originally they were developed for use on bicycles.
4 One has to be aware of all the facts before you reach an opinion.
5 The decision to introduce computers have already been made.
6 It is estimated that more than a thousand people were effected by the radiation leak.
7 In advertising the brand information includes not only information about the product but also the image related to the product.
8 Although the situation required expert advice, however they attempted to solve it on their own.
9 The refinement process has already started when the minerals will be sealed in the special containers.
10 The report was logical, short, and reading it was easy.
11 In the last couple of years, a pattern has emerged on campus that shows an increase in student enrolments.
12 Everybody must agree for the recommendations to be implemented. This being the standard course of action for implementing recommendations.
13 Through public education, controlling manipulation techniques by making all testing of Genetically Modified Food (GMF) products compulsory, and increasing government funding, safety and acceptance of GMF can be established.
14 The objectives of this report are to establish and strengthen the relationship between small business and government organisations.
15 Judging from the growth rate in small business at 1.4 per cent, it shows that the country's economy is in good shape.
16 The government 'red tape' has hindered business operations therefore it is important to assist these businesses in such issues.
17 With the change in government policy there represents many potential problems that translate to higher costs for employers and a less flexible work force.
18 Having an information system that is not integrated and cohesive could result in X company's inability to effectively capture business information about its operations and customer base, which will in turn affect its competitiveness in the market and have a negative effect on its reputation as a company that produces cutting edge products valued by international business world-wide.

19 The Museum offers people a general range of activities, whether as members of the audience, attending events, being part of a guided tour group, retail therapy, enjoying the restaurants and bars or simply taking a stroll.
20 The using of function keys by a user allows the user to carry out some specific functions within the program.

Revising and editing

For many writers, revising is the most important stage of the writing process. Although some creative writers, for example science fiction novelist Isaac Asimov (1991), claim that they spend minimal to no time revising, many others emphasise the value of revision in taking a draft to its final stage. In fact, many of the problems associated with written communication are due to a lack of revision: inexperienced writers often jump straight from writing to proofreading without going through the revising process – with unfortunate results.

Revision is the process of seeing the text anew (which is, in fact, the literal meaning of 'revise'), so that you gain some distance from it and are able to make extensive changes, if necessary. Revision is not correcting errors in spelling and grammar – the task of proofreading – but rather, a reconsideration of the whole text, its meaning, flow and significance, from the readers' perspective. When revising you must decide, honestly, whether the writing is really effective in relation to audience and purpose. If it is not, it takes creativity and vision to figure out what needs to be changed and how. Revising can also be brutal; sometimes the best way forward is to delete material that may have taken hours or days to draft.

An important part of revision is making sure you have a sustained focus and purpose throughout the document. Focusing encourages you to establish what the main point of your document will be. Every document, from the shortest memo to the most intricate report, must contain one overriding point – the main message of the text. Make sure this point stands out, by stating it in a complete sentence at several different stages of the writing process.

Editing is the process of ensuring that a text complies with company house style and that it follows the conventions of its genre. Editing can involve deleting and reorganising sections (known as *substantive editing*) and checking for style consistency and genre formatting (known as *mechanical editing*). Editing can be done by the writer or by another person. In collaborative writing in business contexts, for example, one team member acts as an editor to the team's reports, compiling and synthesising material from different members' work. Also, the publishing industry has professional editors, who ensure consistency and appropriate formatting of all texts published by a particular company.

Proofreading is the final stage of revision and editing, which looks at the document in terms of grammatical rules (i.e. seeing language as a *system*, made up of grammatical sentences, instead of as *text*). Proofreading also checks for unintentional errors, such as 'typos'.

The following guidelines are relevant for both revising and editing:

When you have a complete document, start revising from the big picture or conceptual content to the details: have you included all necessary information? Did you respond to the brief appropriately and effectively? Never begin by proofreading because this would draw your attention away from logic, meaning and clarity.

After checking for overall meaning, look at the organisation of the document: is this the most appropriate ordering of information, or should you reorganise paragraphs? Remember that, in addition to a 'logical' sequencing of information, there is also a 'conventional' sequencing that depends on the genre of your document. Some journalist genres, for example, would begin with the most important information first, inverted-pyramid style, and would have a catchy lead instead of a formal introduction.

Then re-think the audience: is the style appropriate? Do you need to define terms or give more information? Have you given too many details on a subject your audience is expected to be fluent in? Look at examples and explanations: are they specific, clear and interesting, and not exaggerated, vague, repetitive or contradictory?

Then move to paragraphs and check for unity and cohesion: is each paragraph about one main point? Is all information included in the paragraph relevant to this main point? Does each paragraph flow from the previous, so that the reader can understand the transition between one point and another?

Finally, proofread the text for grammar, word-choice, punctuation and spelling: do your sentences and words provide the appropriate 'rhythm' for the type of document and audience? Are all sentences grammatically correct, clear and concise? Have you avoided unnecessary repetition or wordiness?

Table 15 is a revision chart to guide you in asking the right questions, which will lead to the delivery of a polished and professional final copy.

Table 15: Revision Chart

Context
- Am I writing to the right person?
- Have I learnt as much as I can about my readers?
- Will there be immediate and secondary audience and have I catered to them?

Content
- Is all the information I intended to convey there?
- Do I need to reformulate my argument or main message?
- Do I need to deepen or extend my analysis?
- Do I have irrelevant information? Should I narrow the scope?
- Do I need to re-organise information?
- Do I need to add information to strengthen a point?

Organisation
- Do I need to re-proportion the amount of space given to particular topics to reflect their importance or complexity?
- Have I used informative headings that reflect the content of the sections?
- Have I used sectioning and point-listing so as to highlight important points?

Style
- Do I need to simplify or make more complex?
- Is my degree of formality appropriate?
- Is my tone acceptable for the purpose and content?
- Are my sentences active and concise?
- Have I used enough sentence variety to make the writing less monotonous and more compelling?
- Have I used enough flow and transitions to make the writing coherent?
- Have I ensured that my expression is gender-neutral?

Layout
- Have I formatted paragraphs correctly and consistently?
- Do I need to add, delete or adjust graphics (tables, graphs, charts, drawings, photos)?
- Do I need to adjust the visual aspects (font size, style and consistency, white space, formatting)?
- Is my referencing appropriate and correct? Have I cited sources for all information?

Style guides

Many corporations, large organisations and government agencies have style guides or manuals that describe the stylistic and formatting conventions followed. A style guide is a very useful item, since it directs writers on how to structure their documents. If your company does not follow the conventions set out in a style manual, consider creating such a manual, proposing that one be created or suggesting that an available manual be adopted. Existing manuals include the APA (American Psychological Association), MLA (Modern Languages Association) and Chicago Style Manual.

Even in cases where you only need to produce one document, it is useful to create a style sheet documenting the spelling, formatting and other choices that you made. This not only helps you when revising the document, it also helps others who may take over writing the document, or who may wish to write a parallel document.

Style guides and style sheets help to maintain consistency within a document and in a set of documents produced by the same source. They also answer writers' questions about how they should present their writing. When designing a style guide, include information on the following aspects. Make sure that your choices are justified in relation to the communication situation and the mission of the organisation:

Spelling: do you use American or British spelling? Or are both acceptable as long as consistency is maintained?

Fonts: what regulations will you create about size and type of font?

Formatting: how much space will you allow between lines? How much margin? How will you section and how will you number sections?

Numbers: when do you use figures and when words? The standard convention is to use words up to ten and figures after that, returning to words when you reach thousands, millions and billions. Will you keep this standard or use another?

Abbreviations: what will you abbreviate and how? For example, will you write Mr or Mister? Dr or Doctor?

Punctuation: how will you punctuate? Will you use any punctuation at the end of bullet points? Will you include punctuation marks inside quotation marks or outside?

Visuals: what rules will you have for visuals? Will you have any restrictions on size of visuals in a document? How will you title visuals?

A final note...

The chapter ends with an overview of some major reasons for difficulties or failures in communication in professional contexts. These are taken from specific cases where miscommunication led to disasters or serious damage. Having worked your way through this book, you are now equipped to handle such situations expertly.

Major reasons for faulty communication, on both conceptual (thinking and planning) and mechanical (drafting and revising) levels, are:

Ignoring the company or project's role distribution: in many cases, time is wasted because of documents being exchanged between parties that will not be the final decision makers. When dealing with important projects, involve the right people in the chain of communication and speak (or write) to them in ways they can understand. For example, in engineering projects, administrators, and possibly even marketing managers, are most often involved in the lifecycle of a product. They may not be engineers themselves, so they would require technical concepts to be interpreted.

Not following the rule of 'one document – one message': if you have many pieces of information to communicate, write different documents. Do not attempt to cut corners by cramming as much data as possible in one document. Documents that lack a main message, or 'bottom line', fade in significance, and the important issues they may contain are lost if they are buried in a maze of facts presented indiscriminately. For example, when delivering slide presentations, do not clutter slides with all the information that you want the audience to know. Use the slides to complement, not contain, your oral explanations and supplement the talk with written documents, such as technical and progress reports.

Adopting an unsuitable style: readers are offended if their 'attitude' (the frame of mind in which they receive the document) is not respected. Do not be overly friendly and casual with readers who may expect more respect and formality, and do not adopt a lighthearted approach with topics that the reader treats with gravity. Remember that your sentence structures emphasise different elements and construct them deliberately and with a clear intent. Remember that, after having lost a client, or alienated a manager, it will be near-impossible to regain their trust.

Not being clear, accurate and concise: if you are vague, confusing and inaccurate you come across as unprofessional and untrustworthy. Plan your writing carefully so that you can collect appropriate and adequate data to make it informative for your readers. Revise well to avoid repetitions and what may come across as self indulgent verbosity. Remember that time is precious for business readers.

Not having enough signposting, highlighting and closure: readers are not in your mind, so direct their reading by signalling changes in direction (such as contrast, exemplification, additional point, etc.), distinguishing data according to their order of importance and indicating where one chunk of information ends and another begins. Business readers do not have the disposition to work laboriously through stream of consciousness-type writing, trying to trace the important points. Preview the structure and purpose of your documents in a clear executive summary and introduction, sum up points in appropriate positions and make sure you make clear what action you require the reader to take.

Being unconvincing or irrelevant: people respond more positively to those who communicate on their 'wavelength'. Also, they pay more attention to information that is relevant to their needs, desires and expectations. If you want your advice or warning to be heeded, make sure it is pertinent to the values and goals of your audience. To achieve this, do your 'homework' by learning as much as you can about your readers, and relate your descriptions and explanations to situations that are familiar to them.

Not acknowledging the 'big picture': documents concerning projects with a public relevance may become public at any time. Even if you are an engineer working on technical equipment, your correspondence and notes could come under public scrutiny, if, say, the users of your equipment are harmed because of malfunctions. Therefore, always write documents about professional projects with the idea that more than just your intended readers may end up reading them. Another example is email. If a message you send to a particular person includes information that is pertinent to others, your recipient may distribute the email. Be careful how you phrase email that may be distributed. Have you insulted someone who may receive it? Have you written something that may be misunderstood by some readers? Use foresight when writing.

Not paying enough attention to deadlines: this is a very common problem in all types of writing tasks. The best advice is to not be over-optimistic about how much time you have to complete a task. Plan your time carefully and at different times during the task. Have contingency plans: if you get stuck when doing one task move to something else that you can do more easily. Train yourself to multi-task. And always remember to leave some time for revision and for unexpected delays.

Job Applications

Focus:

- Career values
- Curriculum Vitae formats
- Cover letters

The shape of the workforce and the idea of a 'career' have changed dramatically over the last three decades world-wide. Since the 1990s, rapid changes in technology, the globalisation of the workforce, competitive international markets and the growth of short-term contract work have made the contemporary workplace anxious and fast-paced.

In some instances, people setting out in the workforce today are likely to change careers several times over the span of their working life. Accordingly, employers now look for graduates who can demonstrate transferable skills, particularly in communication, leadership and teamwork. Such skills are transferred from one job to another, indicating a willingness and ability to adapt to new business procedures and new technology.

To survive in this quickly-changing environment, you must be flexible and ready. This chapter will prepare you to 'market yourself' in the workforce by illustrating successful methods of compiling a job application consisting of a resume and a cover letter. Although many of the tips given here will interest all job seekers, the main target readers are those starting out in the workplace.

Knowing your values

Your chances of being good at what you do increase if you actually enjoy what you do. If your job is just a set of gruelling tasks, it is highly unlikely you will excel or stand out in any way. And you can only really be successful in what you value. In fact, successful professionals are unanimous on this. Advice given to new generation professionals by both corporate CEOs and adventurous entrepreneurs emphasises the importance of enjoyment at work for success. Here is a list of questions to guide you on your career quest:

Career Values

What do you want to achieve in your life?
Determine your goals and ambitious. Do you value wealth? Fame? Spirituality? Independence? Do you want a centre stage position in life or would you prefer to work behind the scenes?

What are your skills and talents, and can you make best use of them in your career?
Think of all your talents, interests and abilities. How can you adapt them so that they will be functional in your work? Break down all the work you have done into constituent skills and re-shuffle them. For example, if you have been successful in sports, this could indicate endurance, high energy, collaborative skill, fast thinking, etc. There are plenty of other contexts where these skills would be useful.

How good a communicator are you?
Are you good at writing? Speaking in public? Explaining? Have you ever taught? Do you prefer one-to-one communication or would you rather address a large number of people?

Are you project or process oriented?
Do you like doing short-term projects that you can finalise quickly and move on to something else, or do you prefer being part of a chain, contributing to an on-going process?

Do you prefer to lead or to follow?
Do you prefer following others' instructions, or would you rather instruct others? Do you work best in a corporate, hierarchical, environment, or does self-employment appeal to you more?

What sort of culture would you prefer to work in?
Do you like strict guidelines or a more liberal way of achieving goals? Do you want to be given specific goals or would you rather work with broad parameters? How closely do you want to be managed? Would you rather be left alone to find solutions your own way? Do you want strict hours of work or more autonomy to choose your timetable?

What drives you?
Do you want status? Recognition? Money? Independence? A combination?

What location suits you?
Are you happy in a high-rise building in the centre of town, or would you prefer a suburb, or a specialised location like Silicon Valley? Do you want to have the option of working at home? Travelling? Working in two or more different places?

Adapted from Morgan and Banks 1999, pp. 28–30.

CVs and cover letters

A *curriculum vitae* (CV – also known as a resume) lists your education, work skills and work experience. A CV is often glanced at or skimmed rather than carefully read. In many cases, potential employers spend about 30 seconds on a first viewing of a CV, before deciding whether the candidate is worthy of further consideration. Thus, you should structure your CV in such a way that the potential employer can tell at a glance if you are suitable for a job.

A *cover letter* addressed to the prospective employer accompanies the CV. In the letter, introduce yourself and draw attention to your achievements relevant to the position. The cover letter gives you the opportunity to 'showcase' your talents, including your ability to write convincingly and correctly. A cover letter is also called a 'letter of application'.

Job searching

When looking for a job, make an action plan using this four-step framework to guide you.

1 Assess yourself

Examine your goals, and make sure you understand what motivates you, your values, your strengths and your priorities. Ask yourself the questions listed earlier in the *Knowing Your Values* section. Think about where you would like to be in five years, and what you would like to have achieved. What are your lifestyle preferences and what role does work and professionalism play in these preferences?

2 Research your career goals

After the first, introspective, stage, open up to the world and see what is available to assist you in reaching your goals and achieving your desired lifestyle. The obvious way to look for a job is to peruse the classifieds in major newspapers and visit employment websites. In addition, major recruitment consultants have their own databases where you can access information on professional job vacancies.

Another major way to find out what your options are and what opportunities are available is through *networking*. Tips for networking are:

- Get to know people at courses and through business, trade and professional associations.

- Subscribe to business, trade or professional magazines or newsletters or join online discussion groups and forums.
- Join online social networking sites devoted to professionals, such as www.LinkedIn.com and participate in the blogs and activities posted.
- Establish mentors. A mentor is a senior colleague whose work and personal character you respect. A mentor takes an interest in your career and is willing to advise you. If you leave a company or a programme, keep in touch with your mentor. For example, if you know your mentor is working on a particular project or has a special interest, send announcements or other relevant information.
- Contact career professionals, such as recruitment consultants and 'head-hunters', and discuss your options with them.
- Do volunteer work in a related field. This can help you to meet people in the field and achievements performed as a volunteer can go in your CV.

When networking, take care to:

- Send a thank you note to people who give you helpful leads, and stay in touch.
- Never ask directly for a job! Asking directly puts people on the spot and can make you seem desperate or pushy.

3 Develop a self-marketing strategy

Market yourself as if you were a product (which, in fact, you are, in relation to the employment market). Use the five Ps of marketing:

Product: what do you have to offer? What key skills and qualities can you offer to potential employers?

Price: what is your value in the marketplace? What value do your educational background, experience and professional strengths give you?

Promotion: what themes, signs, phrases or messages can you use to communicate what you have to offer?

Place (distribution): How will you 'circulate' yourself? For example, will you focus on advertised positions, rely on your networking, send your CV to a senior member of a targeted company (known as *cold contact* or *speculative job searching*) or post your CV online? Start a blog?

Positioning: what distinguishes you from other candidates? Do you have a unique selling point (USP)?

4 Prepare some versions of your CV for different purposes

Have two or three versions of your CV ready. Each version should highlight different qualities, but they should also be relevant to the job profile that you will have created using the previous three steps.

Finding information about a company

Before applying to a company – and particularly before attending an interview – find out details such as share price, company structure, annual turnover and product lines. Take advantage of the following resources:

- Visit the company website. Many companies recruit through their websites.
- Browse through publications relevant to the industry in which you hope to work and to which the company belongs.
- Browse through company literature, such as brochures, newsletters and annual reports.
- If possible, visit the company itself and get a feel for its culture and atmosphere.

Find out as much as possible about the industry of a company, by asking these questions:

- What products or services does this industry offer?
- Who are the major players and up-and-comers?
- What are the critical success factors for a company in this industry?
- What is the outlook and hiring potential for this industry?
- What type of talent does this industry attract, hire and need?

Find out as much as possible about the particular company you are interested in applying to, by asking these questions:

- What distinguishes this company from others in the industry?
- What are the company's culture, values and priorities?
- Who are its leaders and what do they stand for?
- How does this company treat its employees?
- What is the company's reputation?
- What would it be like to work there?

CV formats

CVs tend to be classified into three main categories: *chronological*, *functional* and *targeted*. All types of CVs should satisfy certain general standards. They should:

- Provide information that is relevant, clear and concise
- Highlight and provide evidence for your strengths and achievements
- Inspire confidence
- Form an agenda for the interview

Chronological CVs

The chronological format lists education and work experience in reverse chronological order (most recent items listed first). Chronological CVs are useful if you have a steady work history, and/or all or most of your recent work experience is relevant to the position.

Do not use a chronological CV if only one or two jobs in your work history are relevant to the position sought, or you have a complicated or diverse work history that may raise doubts as to your reliability, or you have many gaps in your work history that are difficult to explain, or you are pursuing a career change and wish to highlight transferable knowledge and skills.

Functional CVs

Functional CVs focus on knowledge and skills, rather than on dates or places of employment. They are useful if you are changing careers and some of your previous experience is not relevant to your target job or if you want to highlight specific skills rather than list your employment history.

In a functional CV, the most marketable information is presented at the front of the document. The functional format allows for selective organisation of information and enhances your ability to customise the CV for the particular position.

To become aware of all the knowledge you have gained in your experience, list all the responsibilities you had for each job. Think of everything that you did each day at work, including all the small tasks or the tasks that were so routine that you hardly noticed them. If your list gets too long, edit it by deleting activities that may not be directly relevant to the job you are applying for. The following verbs may help you compile your list:

Action Words to Describe Skills

accomplish	define	inform	provide
act	delegate	initiate	publicise
adapt	demonstrate	innovate	publish
adjust	design	inspect	recommend
administer	detail	install	record
advertise	determine	institute	rectify
advise	develop	integrate	relate
affect	devise	interview	report
analyse	direct	invent	represent
anticipate	distribute	investigate	research
approach	draft	lead	resolve
approve	edit	maintain	review
arrange	educate	manipulate	revise
assemble	enlarge	market	scan
assess	establish	mediate	schedule
assign	evaluate	moderate	select
assist	examine	modify	serve
budget	exchange	monitor	speak
build	execute	motivate	staff
calculate	expand	negotiate	standardise
catalogue	facilitate	obtain	stimulate
chair	formulate	operate	summarise
clarify	fund-raise	order	supervise
collaborate	generate	organise	survey
communicate	govern	originate	synthesise
conceive	guide	participate	systemise
conceptualise	handle	perform	teach
conciliate	hire	persuade	team-build
consult	identify	plan	train
contract	implement	present	transmit
control	improve	preside	utilise
cooperate	increase	produce	write
coordinate	index	promote	
counsel	influence	propose	

Always use verbs in the active voice to describe the activities you perform or performed in your work experience. Use the present tense for positions currently held and the past tense for positions previously held. Omit 'I'.

Where possible, use the *STAR (situation, task, achievement, result)* method to highlight your successes, either in the CV itself or in the cover letter. First state the situation where you had to perform a task, second describe the task, third go to the outcome of your effort and fourth state how your employer, or profession as a whole, benefited from the way you carried out the task.

Targeted CVs

Targeted CVs follow the specifications or templates given in an application package or job advertisement. They are often similar to functional CVs, but concentrate on skills that are directly relevant to the requirements listed in the position description. When writing a targeted CV, answer the question or follow the formatting directions given by the recruiting company.

Optional features

These features are not necessary. Analyse your audience, context and professional culture and decide whether or not you wish to include them. If in doubt, leave them out.

Personal information. In most Western societies, gender, religious beliefs, age, ethnicity and marital status are irrelevant to many kinds of employment, and, in fact, are considered confidential by law. You are not obliged to state any of these in your CV when applying for a job. In practice, however, job seekers include personal details in their CVs if they feel that their personal circumstances are advantageous. Examples include: if you are a Catholic and you are applying for a position in a Catholic organisation it would be wise to mention your religion, and if you are young but have achieved a remarkable amount it would be wise to mention your age.

Photograph. Employers in certain countries and in certain sectors of the economy, may favour photographs on CVs. Others find them irrelevant or even misleading, because they de-focus objective skills and capabilities. For example, in the information technology sector or in education, a photograph is generally not necessary.

Hobbies/Interests. Include a brief list of hobbies and interests if they indicate knowledge or skills relevant to the job, such as leadership, teamwork, resilience or determination. You can also set your CV apart from others if you specify unusual hobbies, or if you demonstrate excellence in a particular pursuit. If your hobbies are humdrum or irrelevant leave this section out altogether.

Career objective. A career objective states the applicant's goals and ambitions within a specific industry. If you are unsure or undecided about your long-term goals, or if you want to project versatility and resilience, leave this section out (unless, of course, it is specifically requested in a targeted CV). If you do decide to include an objective, make it short but focused. It should inform the employer that you are moving in a certain direction, specify your work preferences and serve as a focal point from which to review your CV.

Referees. You do not need to include names of referees or references unless they are specifically requested. However, since referees will play a role if you are shortlisted, it is wise to include a statement such as 'Referees are available on request', either at the end of the CV or in the cover letter.

Nationality or residential status. This is only relevant if it affects your availability for employment – for example, if you are on a working visa. Include this if you have an international background and the potential employer may wonder if you are eligible to work in the particular country.

Presentation of CV

How the CV is set out depends on the medium of communication. For example, if posting the CV on a website, where it might be read off a screen, use more highlighting, such as bullet points and headings, and minimise the information on each page. If sending out a hard copy where you were specified to limit the CV to one page, obviously you need to set it out differently to maximise the limited space. Adapt the following guidelines in relation to the specific circumstances of each application:

- Ensure readability by leaving as much white space as specifications allow, and by using a clear font, size 11–12.
- Align points down the page and preferably indent them.
- Do not use more than two fonts, perhaps one type for the main text and another for headings. Consider using only one font unless creativity is required by the job and you have flair for design.
- Do not use more than one highlighting technique: bold or underline or italics – not all three.
- Use a clip to attach all pages: this makes it easier for the CV to be photocopied.
- Do not use coloured paper that will hinder photocopying.
- As with other business documents, include a header or footer on each page, and page numbers, in case pages get mixed up.

CV templates

It is not wise to copy a standard CV format from a book to which countless others also have access. Instead, by making your CV as individual as a signature, you increase your chances of attracting the attention of those that can further your career. So use these templates of a full CV as a guide or inspiration, but tailor them to suit your individual aspirations and strengths.

Template for chronological CV

Name	Your full name
Address	Your current residential or business address (where you want your correspondence sent).
Phone numbers	Home and or business numbers (you may include a cell-phone number, but not just that).
Email address	Your business or personal email address (if you are applying for many jobs while still working, it's best to get a personal address to avoid too much traffic in your business address).
Education	List your educational qualifications with most recent first.
Employment history	Name of employer, position (job title), period of employment, duties, achievements. Begin with current or most recent position and work backwards.
Professional Memberships	Briefly list them, if relevant.
Computer skills	List your skills of operating systems (e.g. PC, Mac), and software packages (e.g. Microsoft Word, Adobe PageMaker).
Languages	State the languages that you know and degree of fluency.
Interests	List, only if relevant.

Template for functional CV

Name	Your full name.
Address	Your current residential or business address (where you want your correspondence sent).
Phone numbers	Home and or business numbers (you may include a cell-phone number, but not just that).
Email address	Your business or personal email address (if you are applying for many jobs while still working, it's best to get a personal address to avoid too much traffic in your business address).
Skills and abilities	List the major skills you have acquired from your experience. List only those skills that you can demonstrate, but be creative in highlighting their relevance for the job you seek.
Education	List your educational qualifications with most relevant first. Include all professional development and short courses that you attended.
Computer skills	Depending on the kind of job you seek and the kinds of skills you have, you could list your computer skills separately to highlight them. Include operating systems (e.g. PC, Mac), and software packages (e.g. Microsoft Word, Adobe PageMaker).
Languages	State the languages you know and degree of fluency.
Professional memberships	Again, briefly list them, if relevant.
Awards and Achievements	List, only if relevant to the new job.
Employment history	Name of employer, Position (job title), Period of employment.
Interests	List, only if relevant.

Here are some commonly used phrases to summarise and highlight skills.

Skill Phrases

General
works well under pressure
able to adapt to new situations
able to learn quickly
capable of accepting responsibility
works well without supervision

People skills
able to work as a team member
good sense of humour
able to deal effectively with clients
handles people with patience and understanding
works well with people from different cultures

Communication skills
able to communicate effectively with clients
capable of initiating and completing projects
trained and supervised new staff
able to communicate effectively with others
excellent communicator

Organisation skills
excellent organisation skills
able to plan, organise and supervise projects
capable of working on different projects
completes projects accurately and on schedule
punctual
dependable in all situations

Leadership
excellent leadership skills
accepts responsibility
dealt efficiently with emergencies
comfortable with taking the initiative
supervised activities of team members
successful project manager
successfully organised staff/team members to attain goals

Look at the following chronological CV, and notice how the writer summarises his skills at the beginning and then demonstrates how he used these skills in particular work situations.

Lee B. Wilson

Address, Phone number, E-mail address

Summary

Accounting Professional / Payroll Administrator combining cross-functional competencies in all phases of accounting, information systems, and staff supervision and management. Proficient in managing and developing financial reports and controls using staffing and technology efficiencies. Ability to contribute as a team player and interface with professionals on all levels. Expertise includes:

* Payroll administration
* Quarterly & Year-End Reporting
* Automated Accounting Information Systems
* Inventory Control & Purchasing
* Financial Reporting
* Corporate Tax Compliance
* Corporate Accounting
* Job Costing

EDUCATION

1997: Masters in Business Administration, Y University
1995: Bachelor in Business Management, X University

PROFESSIONAL EXPERIENCE

2002–present: **Controller,** Platinum Choice Corporation, City, Country

Plan, manage, and provide leadership for accounting department including payroll, budgeting, cost accounting, managerial accounting, financial reporting, financial analysis, and purchasing. Scope of responsibility spans both the corporate and divisional level. Provide financial expertise to outside firms, including banks, auditors, and government authorities.

• Managed $4 million in annual operating budgets allocated for personnel, facilities, and administrative expenses.
• Established improved accounts receivable that reduced outstanding receivables by 25% during the first quarter.

- Implemented automated cost accounting systems to analyze profit improvement opportunities.
- Worked in cooperation with management teams to restructure corporate pricing on all major product lines, resulting in a 14% profit improvement.
- Successfully guided the company through annual outside audits.

1998–2002: **Accounting Consultant**, Merrill Lynch Consultants, City, Country

Recruited to provide diverse finance, accounting, payroll, and tax preparation functions for one of the largest international consulting firms.

- Responsible for preparation of financial statements: payroll, sales and property tax returns, and income tax returns.
- Streamlined accounting processes to reduce workpaper and document requirements.
- Worked closely with clients in structuring general ledgers and evaluating their software needs.

COMPUTER SKILLS

- Experienced with the following software for payroll preparation: QuickBooks/QuickBooks Pro, Peachtree, PenSoft Payroll
- Skilled in most accounting software programs including Impact Encore, Peachtree, Preform Plus, ProSystems and Quicken.
- Proficient in Excel, Word, Access and Lotus.

The cover letter

A cover letter must be professionally presented in format, grammar and spelling. It generally is one to two pages long, and should have a 'bottom line' organisation – i.e. it should go straight to the point. Your cover letter should have something that stands out.

There are three main kinds of cover letter:

- A letter written in response to a job advertisement
- A 'cold contact' letter, written unsolicited (without being requested in advance) to a senior member of a targeted company. This should not be more than one page, so as not to take the recipient's time. Always follow up a cold contact letter with a phone call after a week to ten days
- A referral letter, mentioning a contact within the company or a previous conversation held with a staff member. A referral letter may open with a

line such as, 'I am attaching my CV, as you requested during our recent conversation regarding the Human Resources counselling position opening up at your firm.'

The cover letter generally has four paragraphs, covering the following material:

Opening paragraph: indicate the purpose of writing.

Second paragraph: state relevant skills and experience.

Third paragraph: demonstrate your knowledge of the company or organisation.

Fourth paragraph: close with confidence and request an interview.

When sending a 'cold contact' letter, it is best to address it to the manager of the section you want to work in (rather than to the Human Resources Department). The advantages of this are that, even if you are not employed, the manager will at least know your name and may remember you if you apply for an advertised position within the company later. People who are eager and take initiative make a good impression professionally. Also, if the manager is dedicated to his/her area of specialty, chances are that he/she would be willing to help newcomers to join the industry. Therefore, he/she may refer you to someone, or give you some very useful advice, if you approach him/her directly. It is unlikely that the HR Officer would have the same commitment.

Cover letter tips

Here are some general tips for writing an effective cover letter:

- Always type your cover letter, unless the job advertisement specifically asks for a handwritten one. A CV should always be typed.
- Keep paragraphs short (2–4 sentences).
- Adapt the content to the particular organisation and job position for which you are applying. That is, show that you are an insider to the industry.
- Include contact details (name, address, phone number, fax, email), either in a letterhead or in the concluding paragraph.
- Do not point to any of your weaknesses. Instead, match your skills and experience to the requirements of the position.
- Do not refer to personal interests or hobbies unless they are directly relevant to the position or you share an interest with the recipient of the letter.

- Do not use sarcasm or irony.
- Do not criticise a former employer.

How bad can your writing get on your CV? We end the chapter with some real-life examples of CV 'howlers':

Bad Writing in CVs

Education: Curses in liberal arts, curses in computer science, curses in accounting.

I am a rabid thinker.

Proven ability to hunt down and correct erors.

My intensity is at supremely high levels, and my ability to meet deadlines is unspeakable.

Personal details: Married, 1992 Chevrolet.

Personal interests: Donating blood. 15 gallons so far.

Cover letter: Thank you for your consideration. Hope to hear from you shorty!

Source: Gordon, B. (2008) The Apprentice: When your CV contains no information to misconstrue. *The Telegraph*. http://www.families.com/blog/monday-morning-funnies-mistakes-to-avoid-on-your-resume

References and Bibliography

Aitchison, J. (1999). *Cutting edge advertising.* Sydney: Prentice-Hall.

Alred, G. J., Brusaw, C. T. and Oliu, W. E. (2000). *The business writer's handbook.* 6th ed. New York: St Martin's Press.

Asimov, I. (1991) Revisions. G. Dozois *et al.* (Eds.) *Writing science fiction and fantasy.* New York: St Martin's Press, pp. 221–225.

Ball, P. (2006). Walk this way. *New Scientist,* 4 February, pp. 40–3.

Ballenger, B. (2007). *The curious researcher: A guide to writing research papers,* 5th ed. New York: Longman.

Bargiela-Chiappini, F. and Nickerson, C. (eds.) (1999). *Writing business: Genres, media and discourses.* London: Longman.

Barker, T. T. (2003). *Writing software documentation: A task-oriented approach,* 2nd ed. New York: Allyn and Bacon.

Barnett, L. (1948). *The universe and Dr Einstein.* London: Dover.

Barry, P (2006). What's done is done… *New Scientist,* 30 September, pp. 36–9.

Bateman, J. (2011). *Multimodality and genre: A foundation for the systematic analysis of multimodal documents.* London: Palgrave.

Batty, C. and Cain, S. (2010). *Media writing: A practical introduction.* London: Palgrave.

Bazerman, C. and Paradis, J. (eds.) (1991). *Textual dynamics of the professions.* Maddison: University of Wisconsin Press.

Bazerman, C. and Prior, P. A. (eds.) (2004). *What writing does and how it does it: An introduction to analyzing texts and textual practices.* New Jersey: Lawrence Erlbaum.

Bell, A. H. and Smith, D. M. (2010). *Management communication.* New York: John Wiley.

Bhatia, V. (1993). *Analyzing genre: Language use in professional settings.* London: Longman.

Bhatia, V. (2004). *Worlds of written discourse: A genre based view.* London: Continuum.

Bivins, T. H. (1999). *Public relations writing,* 4th ed. Lincolnwood, IL: NTC/ Contemporary Publishing Group.

Bohm, D. (1998). *On creativity,* edited by L. Nichol. London: Routledge.

Booth, W., Colomb, G. and Williams, J. (1995). *The craft of research.* Chicago: The University of Chicago Press.

Branscum, D. (1991, March). Ethics, e-mail, and the law: When legal ain't necessarily right. *Macworld,* 63, 66–67, 70, 72, 83.

Branson, R. (2012). Richard Branson on why we need more women in the boardroom. *Entrepreneur,* September 24. Available at http://www.entrepreneur.com/article/224476.

Brown, F. A. (1954). Biological clocks and the fiddler crab. *Scientific American,* 190, pp. 34–7.

Brown, F. A. (1962). Response of the Planarian, Dugesia and the Protozoan to very weak horizontal magnetic fields. *Biological Bulletin* vol. 123 no. 2, pp. 264–81.

Bunnin, B. (1990, April). Copyrights and wrongs: How to keep your work on the right side of copyright law. *Publish,* pp. 76–82.

Burger, E. B. and Starbird, M. (2012). *The 5 elements of effective thinking.* Princeton, NJ: Princeton University Press.

Candlin, C. N. and Hyland, K. (1999). *Writing: Texts, processes and practices.* London: Longman.

Cockcroft, R. and Cockcroft, S. (2005) *Persuading people: An introduction to rhetoric,* 2nd ed. London: Palgrave.

Columbia Space Shuttle Accident Investigation Board Report (2003). Retrieved from http://caib.nasa.gov/

Cornelissen, J. (2010). *Corporate communication: A guide to theory and practice,* 3rd ed. London: Sage.

Cottrell, S. (2003). *Skills for success: The personal development planning handbook.* Basingstoke: Palgrave.

Cottrell, S. (2011). *Critical thinking skills: Developing effective analysis and argument,* 2nd ed. Basingstoke: Palgrave.

Csikszentmihalyi, M. (2003). *Good business: Leadership, flow and the making of meaning.* London: Hodder & Stoughton.

Cull, N. J. (2011). WikiLeaks, public diplomacy 2.0 and the state of digital public diplomacy. *Place Branding and Public Diplomacy* 7, pp. 1–8.

Davidson, C. (1998). Agents from Albia. *New Scientist,* 9 May.

Davis, A. (2004). *Mastering public relations.* Basingstoke: Palgrave.

DeWitt, S. L. (2001). *Writing inventions: Identities, technologies, pedagogies.* Albany, NY: State University of New York.

Dias, P. *et al.* (1999). *Worlds apart: Acting and writing in academic and workplace contexts.* Mahwah, NJ: Lawrence Erlbaum.

Dwyer, J. (1997). *The business communication handbook,* 4th ed. Sydney: Prentice-Hall.

Elbow, P. (1998). *Writing with power: Techniques for mastering the writing process,* 2nd ed. New York: Oxford University Press.

Eyrich, N., Padman, M. L. and Sweetser, K. D. (2008). PR practitioners' use of social media tools and communication technology. *Public Relations Review,* 34 (1), pp. 412–14.

Fahnestock, J. (1986). Accommodating science: The rhetorical life of scientific facts. *Written Communication,* 3, pp. 275–96.

Fahnestock, J. (2004). Preserving the figure: Consistency in the presentation of scientific arguments. *Written Communication* 21, 1, pp. 6–31.

Faigley, L. (2012). *The little Penguin handbook,* 2nd ed. Boston: Pearson.

Fielden, J. S. and Dulek, R. E. (1998). How to use bottom-line writing in corporate communications. In K. J. Harty (ed.) *Strategies for business and technical writing.* New York: Allyn and Bacon, pp. 179–88.

Finkelstein, L. Jr. (2000). *Pocket book of technical writing for engineers and scientists.* New York: McGraw Hill.

Fiske, J. (1990). *Introduction to communication studies,* 2nd ed. London: Routledge.

Flower, L. and Ackerman J. (1994). *Writers at work: Strategies for communicating in business and professional settings.* Fort Worth, TX: Harcourt Brace.

Fox, B. (2001). Raising the dead – can Russia bring its space shuttle back from the grave? *New Scientist,* 30 June.

Freund, J. E. and Simon, G. A. (1992). *Modern elementary statistics,* 8th ed. Englewood Cliffs, NJ: Prentice Hall.

Gardner, H. (2004). *Changing minds.* Boston: Harvard Business School.

Garrison, B. (2004). *Professional feature writing,* 4th ed. Mahwah, NJ: Lawrence Erlbaum.

Garzone, G. and Archibald, J. (2010). *Discourse, identities and roles in specialized communication.* Berne and New York: Peter Lang.

Greenbaum, S. and Quirk, R. (1990). *A student's grammar of the English language.* Harlow: Longman.

Gunnarsson, B.-L. (2009). *Professional discourse.* London and New York: Continuum.

Gurak, L. J. and Lannon, J. M. (2007). *A concise guide to technical communication,* 3rd ed. New York: Longman.

Hacker, D. (2007). *The Bedford handbook,* 7th ed. New York: Bedford St. Martins.

Hamer, M. (1998). Roadblocks ahead. *New Scientist,* 24 January.

Harper, G. (2012). *Inside creative writing: Interviews with contemporary writers.* London: Palgrave.

Harris, R. (2000). *Rethinking writing.* London: Continuum.

Harris, R. (2009). *Rationality and the literate mind.* London: Routledge.

Harty, K. J. (ed.) (1999). *Strategies for business and technical writing,* 4th ed. New York: Allyn and Bacon.

Hauser, G. (1986). *Introduction to rhetorical theory.* New York: Harper.

Hawkins, D. (1995). The future of fun. In F. Biocca and M. R. Levy (eds.), *Communication in the age of virtual reality.* Hillsdale, NJ: Lawrence Erlbaum Associates.

Hay, V. (1990). *The essential feature: Writing for magazines and newspapers.* New York: Columbia University Press.

Herndl, C. G., Fennell, B. A. and Miller, C. R. (1991). Understanding failures in organizational discourse. In C. Bazerman and J. Paradis (eds.), *Textual dynamics of the professions.* Maddison: University of Wisconsin Press.

Heskett, J. (2005). *A very short introduction to design.* Oxford: Oxford University Press.

Hill, S. (2001). Get tough! *New Scientist,* 30 June.

Hirschberg, S. (1996). *Essential strategies of argument.* New York, NY: Allyn and Bacon.

Holmes, J. and Stubbe, M. (2003). *Power and politeness in the workplace.* London and New York: Pearson.

Howard, T. (2003). Who 'owns' electronic texts? In T. Peeples (ed.), *Professional writing and rhetoric.* New York: Longman, pp. 250–63.

Huff, D. (1993). *How to lie with statistics,* 2nd ed. New York: Norton and Company.

Hyland, K. (2002). *Teaching and researching writing.* London: Longman.

Johnson-Sheenan, R. (2002). *Writing proposals: Rhetoric for managing change.* New York: Longman.

Jones, D. (1999). *The technical communicator's handbook.* New York: Allyn and Bacon.

Kaku, M. and Cohen, J. (2012) *The best American science writing 2012.* New York: Ecco Harper Collins.

Kane, T. (1984). *The new Oxford guide to writing.* Oxford: Oxford University Press.

Kawasaki, G. (2004). *The art of the start: The time-tested, battle-hardened guide for anyone starting anything.* London and New York: Penguin Portfolio.

Kawasaki, G. (2011). *Enchantment: The art of changing hearts, minds and actions.* London and New York: Penguin Portfolio.

Kent, M. L (2008). Critical analysis of blogging in public relations. *Public Relations Review* 34, pp. 32–40.

Kent, M. L. (2011). Public relations rhetoric: Criticism, dialogue and the long now. *Management Communication Quarterly,* 25(3), pp. 550–9.

King, S. (2000). *On writing.* London: Hodder and Stoughton.

Kirkman, J. (1992). *Good style: writing for science and technology.* London: Routledge.

Kolin, P. C. (1998). *Successful writing at work,* 5th ed. Boston: Houghton Mifflin.

Kostelnick, C. and Roberts, D. D. (1998). *Designing visual language: Strategies for professional communicators.* New York: Allyn and Bacon.

Landow, G. P. (2006). *Hypertext 3.0: Critical theory and new media in an era of globalization.* Baltimore: Johns Hopkins University Press.

Lannon, J. (2006). *Technical communication.* 10th ed. Boston, MA: Addison-Wesley.

Leval, P. (1990, March). Toward a fair use standard. *Harvard Law Review,* 1105–36.

Lewin, R. (1998). Family feuds. *New Scientist,* 24 January.

Littleford, D., Halstead, J. and Mulraine, C. (2004). *Career skills: Opening doors into the job market.* Basingstoke: Palgrave.

Long, K. (2003). *Writing in bullets: The new rules for maximum business communication.* Philadelphia: The Running Press.

Lott, J. R. Jr. (2005). The big lie of the assault weapons ban: The death of the law hasn't brought a rise in crime – just the opposite. *Los Angeles Times,* 28 June.

Mangold, W. G. and Faulds, D. J. (2009). Social media: the new hybrid element of the promotion mix. *Business Horizons* 52, pp. 357–65.

Manovich, L. (2001). *The language of new media.* Cambridge, MA: MIT Press.

Marsen, S. (2006). *Communication studies.* Basingstoke: Palgrave.

Marsen, S. (2011). Writing the "professional": A model for teaching project management in a writing course. In Martha Pennington and Pauline Burton (ed.) *The college writing toolkit: Tried and tested ideas for teaching college writing.* London: Equinox, pp. 239–254

Marsen, S. (2012). Detecting the creative in written discourse. *Writing and Pedagogy. Special Issue on Creativity in Writing,* Vol. 4 (2), Autumn 2012, pp. 209–31.

Matthews, R. (1998). Don't get even get mad. *New Scientist,* 10 October.

Maxwell, C. (2007). *Ultimate leadership.* New York: Thomas Nelson.

Morgan, G. and Banks, A. (1999). *Getting that job: How to establish and manage your career into the new millennium.* Sydney: Harper Collins.

Morris, T. and Goldsworthy, S. (2012). *PR Today: The authoritative guide to public relations*. Basingstoke: Palgrave.

Nesheim, J. L. (2000). *High tech start-up*. New York: The Free Press.

Newitz, A. (2006). The boss is watching your every click … *New Scientist*, 30 September, p. 31.

Nielsen, J. (2000). *Designing web usability: The practice of simplicity*. New York: New Riders Press.

Nielsen, J. and Tahir, M. (2001). *Homepage usability: 50 websites deconstructed*. New York: New Riders Press.

Northouse, P. G. (2012). *Leadership: Theory and practice,* 6th ed. New York: Sage.

O'Rourke, J. S. (2009). *Management communication: A case-analysis approach,* 4th ed. New York: Prentice Hall.

Osborn, A. F. (1963). *Applied imagination: Principles and procedures of creative problem solving,* 3rd ed. New York: Charles Scribner's Sons.

Pagels, H. R. (1983). *The cosmic code: quantum physics as the language of nature.* Harmondsworth: Penguin.

Paulos, J. A. (1996). *A mathematician reads the newspaper.* New York: Anchor.

Peeples, T. (2003). *Professional writing and rhetoric: Readings from the field.* New York: Longman.

Petelin, R. and Durham, M. (1992). *The professional writing guide: Writing well and knowing why.* London: Longman.

Qantas Twitter contest draws thousands of angry replies (2011). BBC News, 23 November 2011. Retrieved 10 January 2013 from http://www.bbc.co.uk/news/world-asia-15852965.

Rankin, I. (2001). *The falls.* London: Orion.

Rodman, L. (1996), *Technical communication,* 2nd ed. Toronto: Harcourt Brace.

Rosenblatt, R. (1999). The whole world is jumpable. *Time*, 19 July.

Roush, C. (2004). *Show me the money: Writing business and economics stories for mass communication.* Hillsdale, NJ: Lawrence Erlbaum.

Rude, C. (1998). *Technical editing,* 2nd ed. New York: Allyn and Bacon.

Sagan, C. (1995). *The demon-haunted world.* Chicago: Chicago University Press.

Samuel, E. (2001). Paint the town red. *New Scientist*, 30 June.

Schaub, B. (2006). My android twin. *New Scientist*, 14 October, pp. 42–6.

Sheldon, R. (1994). *First course in probability*. New York: Macmillan.

Shimp, T. (1997). *Advertising, promotion and supplemental aspects of integrated marketing communications.* Chicago: Dryden Press.

Sides, C. H. (1999). *How to write and present technical information,* 3rd ed. Phoenix, AZ: Oryx.

Srinivasan, M. and Ruina, A. (2006). Computer optimisation of a minimal biped model discovers walking and running. *Nature,* 439, 5, pp. 72–5.

Starkman, D., Hamilton, M., Chittum, R. and Salmon, F. (2012). *The best business writing 2012.* New York: Columbia University Press.

Steuer, J. (1995). Defining virtual reality: Dimensions determining telepresence. In F. Biocca and M. R. Levy (eds.), *Communication in the age of virtual reality*. Hillsdale, NJ: Lawrence Erlbaum.

Stewart, I. (1998). Rules of engagement. *New Scientist, 29* August.

Stott, R. and Avery, S. (2001). *Writing with style.* London: Longman.

Stott, R. and Chapman P. (2001). *Grammar and writing.* London: Longman.

Strunk, W. Jr. *et al.* (2000). *The elements of style,* 4th ed. New York: Allyn and Bacon.

Surma, A. (2005). *Public and professional writing: Ethics, imagination, rhetoric.* Basingstoke: Palgrave.

Swales, R. (1990). *Genre analysis.* Cambridge: Cambridge University Press.

Taylor, J. R. (1993). *Rethinking the theory of organizational communication: how to read an organization.* Norwood, NJ: Ablex.

Taylor, J. R. and Van Every, J. E. (2000). *The Emergent organization: Communication as site and surface.* Mahwah, NJ: Lawrence Erlbaum.

Taylor, M. (2011). Building social capital through rhetoric and public relations. *Management Communication Quarterly, 25*(3), pp. 436–54.

Taylor, N. (2009). *Brilliant business writing: How to inspire, engage and persuade through words.* Harlow: Pearson.

Theaker, A. (ed.) (2008). *The public relations handbook.* London: Routledge.

Thwaites, T. (2006). Hello solar. *New Scientist,* 14 October, pp. 52–5.

Toulmin. S. (2003). *The uses of argument,* updated edition. Cambridge: Cambridge University Press.

Twain, M. (1906). Chapters from my autobiography. *North American Review.* Project Gutenberg. Available at http://www.gutenberg.org/files/19987/19987.txt.

Van Alstyne, J. S. and Tritt, M. D. (2001). *Professional and technical writing strategies: Communicating in technology and science,* 5th ed. New York: Prentice-Hall.

Ward, M. (1998). There's an ant in my phone. *New Scientist,* 24 January.

Watts, R. (2003). *Politeness.* Cambridge: Cambridge University Press.

Windschuttle, K. and Elliott, E. (1999). *Writing, researching, communicating: Communication skills for the information age,* 3rd ed. Sydney: McGraw Hill.

Woolever, K., Trzyna, T. N. and Batschiet, M. (1999). *Writing for the technical professions.* Boston, MA: Addison-Wesley.

Index

accuracy   30, 32, 109, 144, 150, 159, 260

advertising   9, 10, 56, 71, 91, 98, 148, 150, 179, 184, 185, 206

agenda   9, 52–53, 152, 230, 232, 272

ambiguity   16, 33, 43, 48, 54, 78, 87, 91 256

appendix   8, 181, 182, 183, 185, 190, 197

audience (target)   5, 7, 23, 30, 46, 77, 78, 91, 99, 101, 107, 117, 122, 123, 135, 137, 176, 178, 188, 190

audience dynamics   5, 59, 63, 69, 116, 240

bad news message   7, 67–69, 155

blogs, blogging   89, 90, 153, 154, 155, 156, 270

boilerplate text   95

bottom line   51, 74, 157, 164, 211, 265, 280

bottom up writers   2
  see also top down writers

BP   155, 157–159

brainstorming   2, 15, 16, 18, 139, 177, 199, 227

brief   9, 10, 12, 23, 51, 186, 191, 197, 230, 262

brochure   55, 63, 95, 134, 145, 271

budget   9, 68, 166, 172, 174, 178, 193, 222, 224, 226, 279

bullet points   6, 51, 59, 64–67, 102, 151, 164, 187, 189, 249, 264, 275

business plan   70, 178, 180, 211, 233–234

careers   57, 99, 267–282

citizen journalism   153

clarity   4, 30–32, 43, 44, 47, 75, 145, 149, 164, 168, 170, 178, 198, 239, 262

clauses, and structure   39–41, 45, 235, 237, 241–249, 255, 256, 267

cohesion   42–46, 49, 75, 131, 149, 164, 169, 211, 222, 262

collaboration   89, 148, 218, 221–222, 232

complicity (writer–reader)   5, 41, 47, 155

conciseness   30, 38, 144, 164, 179, 239, 251

conflict   3, 67, 179, 219, 220, 224, 225, 226, 227, 228, 231, 232, 240

consistency   4, 32, 66, 67, 149, 196, 262, 262, 263, 264

copyright   91–97

corporate memory   82, 95

creative/creativity   2, 14, 15, 21, 70, 102, 104, 107, 114, 144, 147, 163, 236, 251, 261, 277

  creative industries   96

  creative style   25, 26, 29–30, 114

credibility   84, 88, 90, 116, 124, 150, 211, 234

crisis   10, 68, 82, 157

culture   130, 181, 182, 274

  company culture   56, 57, 173, 270, 272

  national culture   25, 146, 278

CV templates   276, 277

deadline   9, 11, 19, 22, 35, 161, 221, 224, 228, 237, 238, 241, 266, 282

demagogic style   27, 41, 213

demographic   6–8, 167, 175, 214

digital   22, 23, 67, 56, 63, 72, 89, 92, 122, 136, 137, 141, 143, 144, 147, 148, 157
discourse community   85, 176, 204
draft   2, 18–19, 22, 107, 221, 261, 265, 273

email   3, 4, 9, 12, 27, 29, 47, 49, 50, 51, 56, 57, 59–64, 78, 86, 95, 139, 143, 152, 154, 221, 266
essay   3, 86, 101, 163, 169, 170
ethics   79, 94, 204, 239
evidence   19, 20, 104, 116, 122, 127, 133, 165, 176, 204, 205, 206, 208, 209, 210, 211, 212, 213, 272
exaggeration   28, 88, 142, 213, 215
executive summary   168, 178, 180, 186, 187, 189, 190, 191, 192, 193, 266

Facebook   50, 84, 137, 153, 179
feature article   3, 23, 87, 100, 102, 104, 111–124, 134, 163, 174
feature creep 224–225
  see also scope creep
feedback   22, 59, 69, 75, 77, 78, 79, 89, 154, 162, 172, 177, 194, 196, 220, 2525, 228, 232
focus group   11, 77–79
fragment   22, 27, 30, 114, 236, 237
funding   9, 10, 11, 86, 96, 98, 166, 171, 172, 173, 176, 177, 180, 185, 226, 234, 260

generalization   5, 29, 86, 213, 214, 215, 216, 227

hard news   99
  see also soft news
house style   9, 23, 54, 57, 67, 163, 171, 196, 254, 261

IBM   15, 153, 154, 156
innovation   74, 101, 104, 114, 122, 139, 140, 156, 176, 211

internet   23, 60, 88–92, 93, 95, 108, 143–144, 146, 152, 153, 154, 192, 193, 195, 214
interview   11, 14, 66, 77–82, 86, 97, 100. 130, 154, 161–162, 176, 177, 190, 209, 232, 271, 272, 273, 281
inverted pyramid   100, 137–138, 145, 147, 262

leader(ship)   99, 129, 156, 202, 219, 222, 226, 228, 229, 231, 232, 241, 267, 271, 274, 278, 279
linker   42–43, 49, 119

manual   4, 13, 14, 25, 83, 96, 120, 196, 199, 263, 264
marketing   6, 7, 8, 27, 53, 63, 77, 135, 144, 176, 177, 179, 180, 183, 195, 265, 270
medium   3, 4, 23, 47, 56, 57, 63, 89, 93, 136, 137, 143, 144, 145, 152, 157, 163, 275
metaphor   28, 29, 30, 87, 104, 131, 139, 142, 177, 206
milestone   67, 222, 224, 230
mind map   16
money   35, 157, 179, 185, 206, 225, 226, 268
motivation   21, 157, 162, 219, 226, 230
multimedia   17, 143, 144, 145, 146, 151

NASA   11, 12, 130, 133, 142
newsletter   4, 25, 48, 50, 71, 83, 98, 136, 214, 247, 270, 271
newspaper   28, 47, 82, 83, 88, 216, 217, 269

objectivity   24, 52, 202, 216

parallel structure   44–46, 49, 66, 170, 193
participial phrases   237, 241–243, 246, 247, 248, 249
plagiarism   92–97

Plain English   30, 87, 209
policy   88, 135, 139, 159, 189, 195,
      202, 209, 225
popular science   27, 28, 87, 89, 109,
      110, 111
PowerPoint   4, 11, 72
press release   9, 50, 63, 67, 82, 84, 87,
      96, 97, 100, 135, 137–142
privacy   23, 83, 92, 95, 182, 183
promotion 55, 66, 225
   promotional material   95, 140–141,
      142, 150, 151, 157, 270
   promotional writing   27, 87,
      138–139, 142
pronoun   41, 43, 44, 45, 113, 114,
      116, 130, 235, 243, 244, 245
proofreading   47, 260, 261, 262
psychographic   6, 7, 8, 175
publicity   58, 97, 142
push–pull media   137, 162

qualitative research   166
quantitative information   26, 136, 137,
      140, 208–210
quantitative research   165

referent   41, 43, 114
research *see* qualitative research,
      quantitative research
revision   1, 61, 64, 85, 108, 221, 261,
      262, 263, 266
rhetoric   2, 3, 29, 50, 118, 155, 177,
      204, 205, 109, 211, 217
rhetorical questions   131

scope creep   224–225
   see also feature creep
sentence structure   4, 24, 31–37, 38,
      41, 75, 102, 104, 169, 211,
      235–238, 246, 265
shareholder   9, 26, 55, 157, 217, 254

social media   38, 44, 50, 84, 135, 136,
      137, 140, 153–156
soft news 99
   see also hard news
Space Shuttle   4, 11, 129
stakeholder   2, 10, 50, 65, 75, 136, 224
statistics   165, 208–120, 212, 213,
      214, 215, 217
storyboard   17, 18
subjectivity   24
subordinate clause   39, 40, 237, 239,
      242, 248, 252, 254
summary *see* executive summary
surveys   60, 66, 77–80, 144, 181, 182,
      183, 185, 192, 194, 273
synonym   43, 139

target audience *see* audience
templates   4, 9, 12, 57, 101, 163, 171,
      231, 233, 234, 274
   CV templates   276, 277
tone
   oral   160, 162, 177, 213
   written   4, 5, 24, 26, 27, 28, 36, 38,
      41, 46, 98, 104, 130, 155, 199,
      263
top heavy writing   51, 102
top-down writers   2, 17
transition   41, 46, 101, 114, 127, 131,
      169, 211, 212, 246, 262, 263
Twitter   15, 50, 84, 153, 155
typography   47, 145, 148–149, 152
typology of style   25–30
typology of sources   86–88

unique selling point   139, 156, 179,
      270

wiki   83, 89, 90, 147, 153, 193

YouTube   84, 136, 153, 157